THINGS I HAVE
SAW AND DID

Gleun & Brubar—
Hope this book brings some
joy and fond memories. Thanks
for the great treat of staying
in your Condo.
Bless. y.

Dan
Joh 3:16

THINGS I HAVE SAW AND DID

50 Years of Thinking Out Loud

DANNY ANDREWS

Library of Congress Control Number:		2014916879
ISBN:	Hardcover	978-1-4990-7387-4
	Softcover	978-1-4990-7388-1
	eBook	978-1-4990-7386-7

Rev. date: 09/29/2014

To order additional copies of this book, contact:
Xlibris LLC
1-888-795-4274
www.Xlibris.com
Orders@Xlibris.com
635885

CONTENTS

Dedication

This book is dedicated to my family, who sacrificed much as I was involved in my journalism career, and to the many folks who honored me by reading anything I ever wrote.

Things I Have Saw and Did
Fifty Years of Thinking Out Loud

For years friends have said, "Andrews, you need to write a book." So, in February 2014, I decided I'd get busy on the project.

God has blessed me with two great careers—working for 39 years as sports editor and then editor at *The Plainview Daily Herald* and, for the past eight years, as Director of Alumni Development at my alma mater, Wayland Baptist University.

Memorable experiences in both professions, and also as a sports broadcaster and basketball magazine publisher, as a former sports official, as a leader in numerous community activities, as a Christian layman, and as the proverbial person who "never meets a stranger," have been the genesis for almost 250 stories in this book.

I'm sure I've overlooked 250 more, but then, if I didn't find a stopping place, I couldn't have afforded to have this book printed and you couldn't have afforded to buy it.

The book contains more than 1,000 names. Maybe one is yours – or at least someone you know.

While some of the stories are "Andrews history," I hope those won't bore you too much and that you'll find something of interest in the various other topics.

I considered picking out maybe 100 favorite newspaper columns from all those years of writing two a week, but that would have been too time consuming and the words of a so-called friend kept coming back: "Andrews, I didn't like your stuff the first time I read it in *The Herald*. Why would I want to pay for it a second time?" But I did include a few columns.

While the stories are mine—and 99 percent are true—I hope most make you laugh and a few make you shed a tear or two. I also hope many will trigger some great memories from your own life experiences. Maybe they'll even inspire you to write your own book.

I owe the grammatically incorrect title of this book to my late great friend Jimmie Chennault.

Jimmie had many wonderful traits. Unfortunately, he and the King's English were not close friends.

Jimmie once told me, "I've *saw* some of the things he's *did*."

Two other dear friends, Tom Hall and Eddie Owens, insisted that if I ever wrote a book, "Things I Have Saw and Did" had to be the title.

The subtitle "Fifty Years of Thinking Out Loud" comes from the name of the column I wrote for 28 years at *The Herald* and also the title for my musings in *Footprints*, Wayland's alumni magazine.

Now you know the story behind the title.

FAMILY STORIES

Danny and Carolyn Andrews

Danny and Carolyn tie
the knot in 1969

The young Andrews clan in 1985

Brandon Andrews

Kayla and Craig Peltoma

Brad and Kayla K. Andrews

I'll keep the 50-year model, thank you

I first spied the shapely lass with the long brown hair in the fall of 1965, just shy of my 17th birthday, in "Dummies Geometry" class for the mathematically challenged at Plainview High School.

Carolyn Etta Fuson—late of Lamesa, Texas—had moved to Plainview with her parents, who wanted their only child to attend Wayland Baptist College.

I urged another classmate, Hope Ott, to introduce me. I wouldn't say it was love at first sight or even instant attraction. We had a date to an annual signing party the next spring but didn't begin dating steadily until the spring of my senior year.

Our first date was to the Granada Theater to see *Inside Daisy Clover* with Natalie Wood. She leaned over to me at 10:20 and whispered, "I have to be home by 10:30."

My first thought was, "Does this girl live in a convent?"

Anyway, the romance warmed considerably and I decided in the spring of 1968 that I ought to propose. Her parents gave a somewhat reluctant blessing, and we went to Zale's Caprock in Lubbock and picked out rings.

We got hitched on June 6, 1969, at College Heights Baptist Church by the pastor, Wayne Blankenship—I was four months shy of 21and she was five months from turning 20—and honeymooned in Colorado Springs. Several years ago, I found the bill for the Roadway Inn—$14.50 a night.

One evening we saw *Where Eagles Dare* with Clint Eastwood and Richard Burton. It was so good we stayed through it a second time. When I told a friend that, he smirked, "Doesn't say much for the honeymoon."

As I muddled through school, finishing 69th in a class of 70 students in 1972, Carolyn decided after three semesters that college wasn't her cup of tea.

While I worked on the Wayland newspaper, did sports information, and worked at *The Herald*, she was employed at the Hale County Tax Office. I drove a 1963 Plymouth Fury and with our meager income we were able to purchase for a mere $150 a 1953 Ford that smelled heavily of crankcase oil for Carolyn's transportation.

During that first year we lived in Collier Hall married-student apartments. Then we moved to the Marquis Apartments at Seventh and Fresno for a year, before a house at 1509 W. Ninth, catty-cornered from St. Paul Lutheran Church, became our home. While we lived there our oldest son, Brandon Wade, was born Jan. 15, 1973, at the Hale Center hospital.

Later that year, Carolyn and I purchased our first home for the scary (for us) price of $15,500. We changed its paint from gray to light green and replaced the dingy gray carpet with the green, gold, and pink colors popular at the time.

We sold that house three years later for the inflation-charged sum of $33,000 and moved to 3305 W. 16th near the Water Treatment Plant. Fourteen years and two kids later (Kayla Michelle on June 20, 1979, and Bradley Dean on March 26, 1982), we moved on Labor Day 1991 to 207 S.W. 10th, just a couple blocks west of where I grew up.

Exactly 19 years later, we moved to what I hope is my last earthly home, 1305 Itasca.

I worked at *The Herald* for 39 years before moving to Wayland as Director of Alumni Development in July 2006. During those years Carolyn was employed at First Baptist Church in several capacities. Then she worked a while for the Day, Owen, Lyle, Voss, and Owen law firm. For 15 years she served as children and pre-school minister at the church prior to becoming assistant to Dr. Paul Armes when he was named president of Wayland in 2001.

Carolyn is extremely loyal and very organized. She loves working for a man who "comes to work in the same good mood every day."

We have been blessed with talented and outgoing children who were involved in lots of school and church activities. Brandon played football three years for the Bulldogs and was in A Cappella Choir; Kayla was a basketballer through her sophomore year then decided debate and A Cappella Choir were more in line with her skills; and Brad played varsity golf for two years.

All of three of our children attended Wayland and have rewarding jobs—Brandon as manager of Western International Gas and Cylinder, an acetylene company in Berwick, Pennsylvania; Kayla as finance director for the Baptist Standard Publishing Co. in Dallas; and Brad as corporate clothing and footwear buyer for Gebo's Farm and Ranch Store in Plainview.

Kayla is married to Craig Peltoma, a special projects manager for AT&T, and has a stepson, Josh Peltoma, 12, and Brad's wife, Kayla K., is a great mom to their three children—Karsten Dean, 7; Brylee Kay, 4; and Kallie Mae, 8 months—and is a partner in Not Your Momma's Laundry, primarily serving college students.

Like all families, we have had our ups and downs with various challenges along the way, but our faith, friends, and church family have seen us through.

Carolyn is still a good counselor for our kids, telling them to "Cowboy up!" and "No blood, no foul" in tough situations, and she's a loving grandmother.

We live pretty simply. We eat out probably more than we should and sometimes fall asleep watching *NCIS* or *Blue Bloods* or the Texas Rangers. She frequently finds something on her I-Pad to show me, and she can use it to play Solitaire when she can't sleep.

We kid that we've never considered divorce—murder, yes, but never divorce. My mumbling gets worse by the year and her hearing's not so hot. That's a bad combination. But she has a lifetime job combing the back of my hair each morning and knowing how to switch the remote from TV to movie mode.

The long brown hair of her youth is now stylishly gray, and she still turns the head of a guy who is now 80 pounds heavier than the skinny kid with the Hitler haircut she married 45 years ago.

All told, we've been together nearly 50 years. I hope the Lord lets us stay together for a lot longer.

*   *   *

Andrews grandkids: Karsten Dean, Brylee Kay,
and Kallie Mae

Josh Peltoma

Grandkids say the darndest things

No truer words have been spoken than these: "If I had known how
much fun grandchildren are, I would have had them first."

What they say and how they say it just fascinates me. You wonder, "Where in the world did they hear that?" or "How did they come up with that?" Art Linkletter, and later Bill Cosby, hosted a show called *Kids Say the Darndest Things*. They sure do.

We're pretty sure our four are the handsomest, prettiest, and smartest you'll ever want to encounter. You probably think the same about yours. I'll leave you to your own delusions as I relate some of my favorite "grandchild moments."

By the way, Karsten, came up with our names "Maymee" and "Poppy." We had thought "Grammy" and "Gran-Dan" sounded good. We like his choices a lot better. Brylee followed suit and we're sure that Kallie will call us the same when she begins to talk. Our step-grandson, Josh Peltoma, 12, thinks Danny and Carolyn are appropriate. I'm sure he says many clever things, just not in our earshot.

Let me share some of the delights these neat grandkids have provided us.

Karsten Quips

* As he sat in the back seat with the car wash apparatus making a lot of noise, Karsten, about four at the time, declared, "I need a sandwich to calm my nerves."
* When he told me he had been put in jail, I asked him if he had been given bread and water. Unable to pronounce his l's," he said, "No, they yocked my yegs."
* He told his mother, "My mouth gets dry when I talk. Poppy's mouth must be dry a lot." He also determined that Brylee and I "should be brother and sister because they talk all the time."
* He liked to sit on the basement steps and play "catch." When I fired a soft rubber ball a little too hard and hit him in the head, he said, "I didn't see that one coming."
* Both kids got their nose out of joint while playing games with us. Karsten accused his grandmother of cheating at checkers and Brylee

crossed her arms and declared, "I'm mad," when I said she couldn't turn over three cards when trying to match various figures.

* When I suggested Merrill as the name for their new brother or sister, Karsten immediately replied, "That's hideous," and Brylee chimed in, "That's *heneous*."

* Karsten loves his grandmother's chocolate cake, even helping her with mixing the ingredients. He offered this praise: "Maymee, you're the *best* Maymee."

Brylee Banter

* When I took Karsten to Dairy Queen after the opening ceremonies for baseball season, I told him it might be pretty crowded. "That's OK, maybe they'll see I have my uniform on and know I'm a player." Brylee chimed in, "They knewed it."

* Brylee liked for me to toss her and Karsten on the pillows in the guest bedroom. In a slow drawl, she'd plead, "Poppy, frow me on the bay-ud."

* While adorned in pigtails and wearing a T-shirt that said, "I'm Busy Being Cute," she melted her granddad's heart when I urged, "Say 'Hello, Poppy.'" She repeated those words with a big grin in a way that I could never have coaxed in a million years.

* I told them I was tired of them picking at each other and Brylee assured me, "We're brother and sister and we can argue if we want to."

* When I pondered why she likes French fries and her brother doesn't, she said matter-of-factly, "Maybe that's the way God made him."

* One of my video treasures is Brylee reciting the Great Commission of Matthew's Gospel: "Go ye therefore and make disciples . . . "She combined it with cheerleader moves and declared it should be done "in the name of the Fah-thuh, the Son, and the Holy Spiwit."

Kallie's Coming

I can't wait to hear what Kallie has to say, if she can get in a word edgewise with her siblings in the room.

*   *   *

Dr. C.C. "Doc" Andrews   **American Legion commander in 1951**

My daddy was a proud man for many reasons
(I wrote this column, in 2003 after the passing of my father, Dr. C. C. Andrews, a chiropractor in Plainview from 1949–79.)

A week ago this past Thursday, I wrote a column for Sunday's paper about my dad finding a 1990 family reunion tape in his VCR that hadn't worked in several years.

I watched the tape and remarked in the column how it included now-deceased family members, including my father, telling stories I had heard Daddy relate for years.

I told Daddy I would get a VCR and bring it to his room at Fruit of the Spirit Private Care Home and we'd watch the tape.

Little did I know that when he called me last Friday afternoon, it would be the last time I would hear his voice.

Daddy, who had a wonderful 84th birthday celebration a month ago, said he wished he could die in his sleep like my mother's mother did. Or go quickly as Mother did with a heart attack 3 1/2 years ago.

Last Saturday night, while I was covering the Plainview-Andrews playoff game in Lubbock, Daddy got his wish. The old ticker played out about 9:30 p.m. He, of course, had been listening to the game, so mine was one of the last voices he heard.

He probably was lying in his bed, remembering his days as a quarterback at Childress High School in 1938. "Sammy Baugh (a star at TCU and later the Washington Redskins) had nothing on you," one coach told him.

Daddy, who had a steel-trap memory and was never known to exaggerate, says he threw six touchdown passes in a game to his buddy "Nubbin" Booth, who shared his first name (Clarence) and was so dubbed because he declared one day after practice that he was "worn down to a nubbin."

I could never verify that six-touchdown feat. I'll let it rest alongside the story of his cousin fooling the opponent by walking toward the line of scrimmage, glancing up and marveling aloud, "Look at all those ducks!" When the opponents took the bait, his cousin took the snap and headed off for a touchdown.

My daddy was a proud man.

Born Oct. 29, 1919, in Childress, Texas, he was proud of his roots and told hundreds of stories about his hometown and its people—and those within a 50-mile radius.

He was proud of his railroader father, homemaker mother, four brothers, and three sisters.

He was proud to have been a football and basketball standout for the Bobcats and later of helping start the Quarterback Club here, the forerunner of the Bulldog Booster Club.

Daddy was proud to have worked hard as a youth at a variety of jobs, to have had such a good work ethic that Foxworth-Galbraith Lumber Co. in Dalhart named him manager while he was in his early 20s, and to have worked at the carbon black plant at Cactus for a couple of years during "the war."

He was proud to have served in the United States Army in both the Pacific and European theaters at the end of World War II—though not in combat—but relished relating his "war stories" in detail.

At Daddy's 80th birthday party, his old friend Carroll Foster, who passed on in June at 86 and with whom he visited almost every day for more than 20 years, declared: "I've been through the Panama Canal 4,000 times." That got Daddy's goat but it was just too funny.

He was proud to have earned a degree from Texas Chiropractic College and of his 30 years in practice here. I suspect had it not been for a partially paralyzed hand, he would have worked into his 70s. If I had a nickel for everyone who has told me through the years how much good "Doc"—as he was known by many—did them, I'd be a wealthy man.

Daddy was proud to have served as commander of the American Legion in 1951, especially seeing off boys going to military service during the Korean War.

He was proud to be a faithful member of Ninth and Columbia Church of Christ where he taught youth Sunday school for many years.

We were always the first people to arrive at church—three times a week—and Daddy continued making coffee in the fellowship hall even after Mother died. I figured Daddy maybe missed church two or three times a year, if that often, in his 54 years as a member of that congregation.

He was proud of his photographic memory—something I think I've inherited and which can be both a blessing and a bane. I believe he remembered every conversation he ever had. I've heard some of his stories scores of times. Even when he'd launch into one I could tell almost as vividly as he could and would ask, "Have I told you this before?" I'd shake my head "no" and off he'd go.

One story he recounted many times was about being burned in 1956 as a spectator from what seemed like a safe distance when a huge tanker and several smaller ones exploded at the McKee Refinery at Sunray.

He had gone to the site with my uncle, a volunteer fireman from Dumas. Nineteen men were killed in the explosion—one of the worst industrial accidents in Texas history—and Daddy bore scars on his left arm and left ear the rest of his life as a result of the giant fireball.

He was proud to possess "ESP," telling many stories about thinking about a particular individual and then having them show up at his office soon thereafter.

He read the Lubbock and Plainview papers cover to cover and was a self-proclaimed "analyst of the news."

Daddy was proud that he never had a credit card in his life, despite the best efforts of JC Penney manager Bill Waddell, and owed money to no man.

When he could no longer drive, he rode Cap-Trans every day to the Senior Citizens Center for lunch and dominoes and to the YMCA three days a week for water aerobics. He knew the transportation and those activities were a godsend.

He was proud to have been able to live by himself for more than three years after Mother died, doing domestic chores he'd never done before. He lived frugally, he lived with pain, he lived alone, but he lived with determination until his old body just pretty much wore out right after the Fourth of July.

Daddy was proud to have been married to the same woman for almost 61 years. He took up with Claudia Mae Privitt when they were teenagers. Clyde and Claudie married on July 4, 1939, in Dalhart.

He was proud of his four children—with special appreciation for his firstborn daughter and my brother, who also served in the Army—10 grandchildren and five great-grandsons.

Daddy would have been proud of the three-man contingent from Fort Hood, where he did his basic training, that folded the flag at the graveside service and of the veterans from the Legion and VFW—some not far from his age—who fired off the 21-gun salute.

Yes, my daddy was a proud man.

And I'll always be proud to be called his son.

*   *   *

Claudia Andrews   "Claudie" in 1938 at Childress High School

My mother was an unpretentious woman

For those who didn't know her, I think you would have liked my mother.

Unless you were a scoundrel, she liked just about everybody, though she did call oft-married actress Elizabeth Taylor a five-letter word starting with W. But that's another story.

Claudia Mae Privitt was born April 5, 1919, in Childress, Texas, and seldom ventured far from home until she married my father on July 4, 1939, in Dalhart, where Daddy was working at Foxworth-Galbraith Lumber Co.

They were baptized together in the Dalhart Church of Christ by Guy Caskey, namesake for my brother and later a missionary to Africa and Jamaica.

In a Pathe newsreel promoting the XIT Rodeo, Daddy rode in on a horse and Mother played a pioneer woman.

Mother was a cute and lively woman. She won the Charleston contest at Childress High School where she met a handsome, dark-haired quarterback everyone called "Clyde." She had a little overbite that always made her self-conscious.

After my sister was born in Dalhart, they moved to Sunray when Daddy went to work for the carbon black plant at Cactus during World War II, and she and Donna stayed in Waco for part of the time Daddy served in the Army as part of the occupation forces in Europe and then Japan.

Daddy used the G.I. Bill to attend Texas Chiropractic College in San Antonio, where I was born. The small family moved to Plainview in July 1949.

Mother stayed at home to raise four children but worked at Evalene's Imports when Evalene McDonald opened that store in 1972.

Mother enjoyed having coffee with two dear neighbor friends, Fay Barns and Hazel Johnson, and she loved to "people watch."

I wouldn't say Mother was cheap, but she definitely was frugal. We never ate extravagantly—"goulash" (hamburger meat, noodles, tomatoes, and peppers), baloney sandwiches, fried chicken (I always got the pulley bone), and inexpensive steak, mashed potatoes, and gravy were staples.

One of her favorite sayings was "Save some for Darrell," meaning don't eat everything in case an unexpected visitor shows up.

Wednesday was always "Hamburger Night" before we went to church. I precipitated a brief skirmish between my dad and brother when Guy smarted off about my stupid pickiness after I frowned because Mother had put the meat on the top bun instead of the bottom.

For several years, Mother served Mexican Stack on Christmas Eve. My brother was none too happy when Mother bought a single package of tortillas. "They're 79 cents a package and she buys just one," Guy fumed.

Later in life, Mother found it easier to give a $20 bill and a package of Big Red gum on special occasions rather than buying presents.

Mother, who occasionally made taffy and "snow ice cream" when I was a kid, made excellent chocolate and coconut cream pies. When I remarked that the chocolate pie of Pat Mann, who cooked for the public, was in Mother's league, it was not taken as a compliment.

She and Daddy volunteered at Care Inn nursing home for several years, and Mother would take a couple of pies for the residents to enjoy.

We often had homemade banana ice cream in the summer, usually cranked a hundred miles an hour by my dad as one of us kids sat on the freezer. That was Daddy's favorite flavor so our choice was banana or banana.

One of her grandchildren's best memories was of Grandma "pumping" them around the neighborhood on her bicycle, usually wearing pedal-pushers.

One of my most precious memories is seeing Mother sitting in the kitchen floor shining all of our shoes on Saturday afternoon so we'd look presentable in church on Sunday. She was not above threatening us with the use of a Brillo pad if our elbows were "rusty."

Long before she had a dyer, Mother hung our clothes on a clothes line in the backyard.

She was pretty tolerant of our mischief, but none too happy when I dived onto her folding table while playing a "shoot 'em up" scene with neighbors in the garage.

Although no Bible scholar, Mother helped Agnes Billington in the fourth-grade Sunday School class for several years. We always sat down close to the front at Ninth and Columbia Church of Christ, where she was a faithful member for 51 years.

After she died in April of 2000, a week after her 81st birthday, a young Hispanic woman told me, "Your mother always made me and my husband feel welcome at church."

I know my mother was proud of me because she told me often or a friend would relate, "Danny, your mother is sure proud of you."

The last time I talked to her was on a Friday before she passed away the next Wednesday.

I called her to tell her that Wayne Horton, a former minister at Ninth and Columbia, was riding his bike through town for a fundraising effort. I could tell she was distracted, and when I looked at my watch, I knew why. It was 12:55 and *Days of Our Lives* was just winding up. Bad timing.

I wish I could tell her one more time, "I love you."

With better timing, of course.

*   *   *

Donna Blair   Guy Andrews   Marihelen Johnson

Small pre-war but large post-war family

My daddy always said he had a small pre-war family and a large post-war family.

Donna Gayle, born in Dalhart, already was 8½ when I came along in San Antonio in 1948. Guy Dale was born in 1950 and Marihelen in 1952, both in Plainview.

Donna Blair served in the U.S. Army, including time as a records clerk at Walter Reed Medical Center in Washington in the early 1960s. She was an Okie for many years and now lives in Roswell, New Mexico, where she is a former substitute school teacher and remains a hospital volunteer. She has four children, five grandsons, and three great-grandchildren.

Guy was a stenographer for the FBI, then served in the Army, including time in Thailand. He was with Bell Telephone and AT&T for many years, including some time in the St. Louis area, before he became Director of Community Development for the City of Conroe and then Director of Economic Development for the Odessa Chamber of Commerce.

He recently was named Executive Director for Communications and Organizational Development for Saulsbury Industries, Odessa's largest employer, which specializes in heavy industrial contracting.

He and wife Valerie have four children and five grandchildren.

Marihelen Johnson is Office Supervisor/Staffing Manager for Adecco, a human resources consulting company. She and her husband Jim, a project engineer for Indiana Packers, live in West Lafayette, Indiana. They have a son and two grandsons.

We don't see each other all that often, but we're proud of our Plainview heritage, including all being graduates of Plainview High School.

*   *   *

O.E. Fuson

An awkward start to a long relationship

I'll never forget the first time I laid eyes on my future father-in-law. I stepped on his foot as I nervously went to shake hands when I arrived to pick up his daughter Carolyn on our first date.

If O. E. Fuson remembered that inauspicious start to our 36-year relationship, he never mentioned it. In fact, he never said an unkind word to me in all those years, although the fact that I didn't know a screwdriver from a hacksaw probably caused him some consternation.

He occasionally referred to me as his "favorite son-in-law." He, for sure, was my favorite father-in-law for the almost 33 years I was married to his only child before his passing.

I went from calling him Mr. Fuson to O.E. (short for Ople Eugene) to "Pappaw," which is what our three children called him.

O.E.—who was born in Yell County, Arkansas, and came to Lamesa in a covered wagon with his family as a boy—was one of the most energetic men I've ever seen. He had a nervous habit of constantly moving his legs while seated, as if he were about to jump and run to the nearest job.

He and my mother-in-law Anna—or "Mimmaw" as the kids call her (and just "Maw" now by her great-grandchildren)—lived on some acreage west of Lubbock for several years. They turned a trailer into a house, built a barn and water tank, raised a big garden, tended a few head of cattle and some goats, had a couple of horses, and raised alfalfa for sale.

I have never been as relieved as I was the day O.E. decided he would no longer grow alfalfa. That meant my rather fragile body would cease to be endangered by "hauling hay"—easily the hardest work I've ever done.

I also wasn't too sad when he sold the horses. One ran to the barn with me aboard. Not knowing if he planned to stop, I bailed off and sustained a sizable "strawberry" on my shoulder. I'm lucky the horse didn't kick me in the head.

O.E. was a hard-working farmer in the Lamesa area (including a place called Punkin Center) for the first eight years of married life.

One afternoon, thanks to the conviction he felt in his heart at a funeral for an uncle whose spiritual condition was in doubt, the subsequent witness of a couple of preachers, and some fervently praying friends, O.E. got down off the tractor in a field he was plowing and gave his life to Christ.

I can still hear him telling me how he was down on his hands and knees in the dirt "holding on for dear life" as he dealt with the Holy Spirit working in his heart. He "got up with the burden lifted." That night, he made his decision public in a church revival.

Soon after, he felt the call to preach. Although he never graduated from high school, over the next few years, he attended Hardin-Simmons, Wayland, and Hobbs Junior College as he also worked part-time and preached on the weekends.

He laughed when he recalled he made 17 on his first test at Hardin-Simmons but a professor assured him he would do better.

He eventually pastored churches in Vealmoor, Sparenburg, Patricia, and Andrews and started a mission work in Tucson, Arizona. A heart attack in 1962 led to his reluctantly leaving the pastoral ministry, but he continued witnessing to people and telling what the Lord had done for him as he worked for Universal Life and later Lincoln Income Life Insurance.

O.E. always was disappointed he couldn't fulfill his call to the pastoral ministry, but I've heard him tell many stories about inquiring of others where they stood with the Lord.

My father-in-law loved God, his wife, his daughter, his grandchildren, me, the Dallas Cowboys (most years), and John Wayne movies, in that order. Come to think of it, I might have finished behind John Wayne.

He and Anna were married almost 59 years, and I've never seen a couple more devoted to each other. Usually when you saw one, you saw the other.

O.E. had a lot of health problems, but I seldom heard him complain. He was just a steady, dependable Christian man, husband, father, grandfather, and neighbor.

Two heart attacks in nine days took too much of a toll on his 84-year-old body.

In February of 2002 at Covenant Hospital in Lubbock, our beloved "Pappaw" went home to be with the Lord.

I sat up with him a week before he passed away, and he was feeling well enough to talk a little. I was pleased when I gave him a drink and he said, "Thank you, fella." It had been a long time since he had called me "fella."

When the end came, he was gripping Anna's hand and my hand, and he seemed to be gently tugging on the reins of a horse-drawn plow. "Just like 'Pappaw,'" I thought, "working right to the end."

A few minutes later, he relaxed and breathed easily. Shortly, his eyes became fixed. "He's looking up to Jesus," Anna said with tear-filled eyes. "The author and finisher of our faith," I responded, recalling a verse from Hebrews.

After a beautiful service here at which a brief invitation to trust Christ was offered—just as O.E. requested—an old friend I think the Lord put in my path at the hospital, Rev. Clifton Igo, gave the parting words at the graveside in Lamesa.

O.E.'s earthly body was still witnessing at the end—his right finger pointing to an open Bible and John 14:6: "Jesus said, 'I am the way, the truth and the life; no man cometh unto the Father but by me.'"

Because we share a common faith, I'm going to see that wonderful man again someday.

I don't even think O.E. would care if I stepped on his foot at the Pearly Gates.

*   *   *

Anna Fuson

Anna Fuson: An old-timey Southern Baptist

My mother-in law never liked her middle name of Bell.

Anna Fuson's middle name probably should have been "Hardwork." That's about all that feisty little woman knew for most of her life before she passed away at age 89 in September of 2014.

Her mother died when she was 13, and she helped raise her brother, Dean Bradley (namesake for our youngest son, Bradley Dean) who was killed in a 1954 accident in Germany where he was serving in the military.

Born in Antlers, Oklahoma, Anna Bell Bradley married Ople Eugene Fuson (Few-son) in Carlsbad, New Mexico, when she was not quite 18 and he was 25.

She was a farm wife for about the first eight years of married life—barely tall enough to drive a tractor or pickup and surviving a rattlesnake bite—before O. E. was saved and "surrendered to preach." She worked at Hendricks Hospital in Abilene while he was attending Hardin-Simmons.

As he pastored churches in several small communities, Anna did her best to make spare parsonages livable. She was thankful for the "poundings" of church members but discretely discarded things donated that "weren't worth Effie's soap," a family expression that likely needs little explanation.

After a heart condition forced O. E. to leave the ministry, the Fusons moved to Plainview in 1965, and she was a checker at Bryan's College Food just east of the Wayland campus while O. E. sold life insurance.

They later were houseparents for Buckner's Children's Home in Vernon for a short time, and Anna worked for Buckner's in Lubbock for 11 years before they moved back to Plainview in 1988.

I guess I was scared enough of my future mother-in-law that I hunkered down in the floorboard of a friend's car when she took Carolyn home, hoping Anna wouldn't see me.

When Carolyn and I started going steady, I didn't like okra, squash, canteloupe, tomatoes, cauliflower, and broccoli. But I learned pretty fast that if Anna was going to keep serving that fare, I'd better learn to like it.

Even though there were only four of us at the table on most occasions until our kids came along, Anna still fixed meals like we were hoe hands about to go out for a day in the fields.

Christmas morning was always special because she served fried pork chops, eggs, biscuits and gravy, and fresh orange juice. Her squash dressing has been a family favorite for years.

She brooked little nonsense and allowed that rowdy children—including her own three grandkids from time to time—"need some of 'Henry Taylor's candy.'" I'm sure you get the idea.

Her assessment of her lone son-in-law, who has few useful skills, was measured, but appreciated: "Danny does a good job at his work and witnesses for the Lord."

She was a witness herself, seldom meeting anyone without eventually inquiring about their church membership and standing with the Lord.

Though not a proud woman, one of Anna's favorite words substituted for happy. "I'm sure proud you got to go to New York." "I'm sure proud you had a good time at your birthday party."

She was a member of First Baptist Church and, after O. E. died, she formed a great bond with her Sunday School teacher, Leota Hardgrove, whose late husband also had been a pastor. Her Bible and Sunday School quarterly were always near her favorite chair in the living room.

She also enjoyed working in the Covenant Hospital Auxiliary's gift shop as a Pink Lady.

Although she had little formal education and O.E. never got a college degree, Anna wanted to help ministerial students at Wayland with their expenses, so she established the O.E. and Anna Fuson Endowed Scholarship. She also loved and supported Wayland mission efforts.

Never one for flowery sermons and certainly not enamored with the "praise music" of recent years, Anna told me, "I'm just an old-timey Southern Baptist."

That may not need much explanation either.

*　*　*

Maternal grandparents: Al and Vi Privitt

My mother's parents were Alfred Marion and Viola Eglantine Culpepper Privitt of Childress, Texas. I think Grandma's mother found that middle name in a book. I doubt there's another Eglantine in history—we should all hope.

We loved it when Grandma and Grandpa came to Plainview in their 1951 cream-over-red Plymouth, especially my brother and I because we knew we'd get a quarter if we shined Grandpa's shoes.

A native of Childress, Grandpa worked his way up from sweeping up the shops at the Fort Worth & Denver Railroad for 11 cents an hour to a supervisory role. Grandma was born in Greer County, Oklahoma.

My daddy had a lot of respect for his in-laws and never called them by their first names. It was always Mr. and Mrs. Privitt.

Grandma, a stout woman of somewhat stern countenance, was what you'd call a stay-at-home mom, though she frequently was out and about in the neighborhood after getting seven kids—A.M., Jr., Helen, Ethel Ruth, Claudia Mae (my mother), Peggy, Sammy, and Mary (another girl, Lorena, died in infancy)—off to school.

She enjoyed drinking coffee, catching up on the latest gossip, and probably spreading some of it herself.

She made great sage dressing for Thanksgiving and cake with a dash of Mogen David Wine she kept in the kitchen cabinet.

A plain-spoken woman, Grandma, clad only in her underpants, walked into the lone bathroom in the house just as I was crawling out of the bathtub at about age 10. She announced, "My God, it looks like a naked parade in here."

It was amusing to hear Grandma, sitting in the front bedroom of our house, watching TV but hollering out the answer to questions posed by Grandpa, Mother and Daddy as the visited in the living room. That's what they now call "multi-tasking."

A nominal Presbyterian, Grandma was rather fascinated when she attended Ninth and Columbia Church of Christ with us and witnessed an immersion baptism "in that bathing pond."

When Grandpa gave her a ring for their 50th wedding anniversary, I happened to be in the room. Grandma took one look at the ring, another at her husband of a half century and said, "You old fart."

Grandpa, who liked to snack on sardines and crackers, wore sleeveless undershirts, and declared as he surveyed his sagging arms, "My muscles are dee-tore-e-ated."

The story is still legend in our family about the night Uncle Buster Ratican crawled into bed with Grandma, not realizing that the homeowners were no longer sleeping in the middle bedroom.

When Grandpa decided to retire a little later, he threw on the bedroom light and exclaimed, "My God, what are you doin' in the bed with the Old Lady?" Buster loved to tease but his goat was severely gotten.

Grandma died in her sleep in May of 1963 at age 65, and Grandpa, who later married a woman we adjudged to not be always playing with a full deck, passed away in 1974 at age 82.

*   *   *

Pass those big ol' biscuits, Grandma

My dad's mother was Cordia Free Andrews, a native of Water Valley, Mississippi, whose family migrated to Childress, Texas, in the early part of the century.

She met Luther Benson Andrews, a native of Anniston, Alabama, at a party when they were teenagers. His mother emphatically ruled there would be no dancing, but as soon as the music started, Grandpa Luke danced across the floor by himself.

I never knew my paternal grandfather. He died of cancer at age 58 in June 1949, eight months after I was born. A railroader, he lost a leg in a work-related accident and bought a farm southwest of town with his settlement from the Fort Worth & Denver.

Luke and Cordie raised eight children—five boys and three girls: Irene, Myrl, Ross, Howard, Clyde (Daddy, whom Grandpa called "Brownie"), twins Ardeen "Beanie" and Kathleen "Kat," and Ernestine, who was nicknamed "Pil" by Uncle Beanie.

Grandma, who lived to be 95, resided in a white frame house in the southwest part of town. She was a modest woman who often kept the nursery at the Church of Christ not far up the road. Aunt Kat, who had epilepsy, never married, and lived with Grandma.

My most vivid memories of Grandma (oddly enough, all her other 10 grandchildren called her "Mammaw," but we four Andrewses called her "Grandma") were of her big ol' biscuits topped with brown gravy, and sleeping under quilts on the screened-in back porch.

Her mother, Nancy Free, lived to be 89. I vaguely remember her. She may have been the first person I ever saw in a casket. Daddy says she dipped snuff, as women were wont to do in earlier times, and one Christmas he took her a tin of Levi Garrett and a little bottle of perfume.

"Grandma," he said, "I brought you something to make you smell bad and something to make you smell good."

A grandchild was asking her to describe Heaven. When she finished, another granddaughter reminded her, "When you go to Heaven, don't forget your snuff, Grandma," knowing she wouldn't be happy walking the streets of gold without a dip.

Not long before Grandma Andrews died in 1985, I went by to see her in the nursing home at Childress, taking my three kids.

She uttered a parting comment I'll never forget: "I hope you'll come back soon. I love you and pray for you every day."

The Andrews clan weren't "the kissin' kind" like Ma Joad told son Tommy in *The Grapes of Wrath*. My dad shook hands with his sisters.

But I'd love to hug Grandma's neck one more time and tell her, "I love you, too."

*　　*　　*

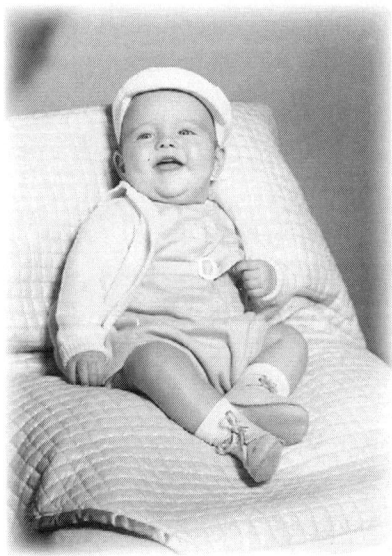

Danny: Happy guy in '49

Middle name is now a badge of honor

When the subject of "How did you get your name?" comes up, I always have to tell folks who don't know me well, "Bet you can't guess my middle name."

To help them, I add: "The first name is Daniel and the second— well, you have one in your kitchen and two in your bathroom."

About half finally come up with a puzzled look and then answer incredulously: "Drain?"

The story is this: My dad went to Texas Chiropractic College after World War II. He had a buddy named Edwin Pool from Albany, Georgia. His wife and my mother were both pregnant, and they got to discussing what they were going to name their sons, if they had male offspring.

Pool said he was naming his son Daniel David after Daniel David Palmer who was the founder of chiropractic. His theory was that the misalignment of the bones in the body was the basic underlying cause of all "dis-ease," and the majority of these misalignments were in the spinal column.

Daddy said he was going to name his son Daniel Drain after Dr. Palmer and Dr. J.R. Drain, president of Texas Chiropractic College.

When my Uncle Myrl Andrews in Fort Worth got the word about his new nephew's name, he said, "My gosh, that can't be right. Who'd name a kid Drain?"

I have a good number of friends who call me "Danno," maybe after Steve McGarrett's partner on "Hawaii Five-O," but I also have friends who call me Drain and Drainer.

Of course, I hated the name when I was a kid, especially if my mother hollered both names when it was time to come in for supper.

Now, it's a badge of honor.

*   *   *

You look Mickey the Monkey to me

They say everyone has a twin or a look-alike somewhere.

I always thought I looked like Mickey Dolenz of The Monkees, a hot musical group in the 1960s and 1970s.

When I told a friend that, he said, "You look like a monkey to me."

I was in CVS Pharmacy a few months ago and a young man asked, "Are you Ron Roberts?" apparently thinking I look like the veteran Lubbock TV weatherman.

Christa Smith, who tried unsuccessfully to teach me how to speak French when I was at Wayland, told me I look like Ted Kennedy, probably due to the white hair that my barber Mark Cano has been cutting for about 35 years.

On that subject, in pre-hair spray days, Herald Editor Jim Servatius once observed, "Danny, you're hair just hangs there and looks like Hell."

Now I'm second only to Fox analyst and former Dallas Cowboys coach Jimmy Johnson in the amount of hair spray used.

Anyway, when I mentioned Christa Smith's observation in an email to Wayland external campus executive directors, and added that "if I don't lose some weight, I'm going to start waddling like Ted Kennedy," one of them—no doubt a Democrat—took umbrage, apparently feeling I was disparaging the Senator from Massachusetts.

One day I was at United Supermarket and ran into Mary True and her daughter Kaitlyn, who was about five at the time. "I said, 'Hi, Miss True.'"

A little while later as they were checking out, Kaitlyn said, "Look, Mom, there's that man."

"What man?" Mary asked.

"That man that called me 'Miss True,'" Kaitlyn explained.

Looking around, Mary couldn't find me. "Where is he?" she asked her daughter.

"There," said Kaitlyn, pointing to *Newsweek* magazine's cover that featured then-Speaker of the House Newt Gingrich.

Yeah, white haired and fat. Not sure if he waddles.

*   *   *

Our house at 114 S.E. 10th

You can run but you can't hide

When I was a kid, we lived in four different houses: 705 W. Seventh (now Bublis Enterprises), 507 Milwaukee (future home of James Thomas, my future boss at *The Herald*), 303 S.E. Sixth, and 114 S.E. 10th, a small three-bedroom abode moved in from a farm several years before.

One Saturday afternoon when Mother was away, my younger brother Guy and younger sister Marihelen and I decided to chase each other through the house.

Figuring that Guy was going to beat on me if he caught me, I ran to the front bedroom and held the door as tight as I could while Guy tugged mightily to gain entrance. My strategy was to let go and then bolt to the bathroom maybe 50 feet down the hall and lock myself in.

As Guy yanked on the bedroom door and I turned loose, I had a sinking feeling that this wasn't a good idea. Sure enough, Guy crashed into the wall, creating a sizable crack.

Mother's assessment was the same as mine when she came home to find us all sitting quiet as church mice: "Your daddy is going to kill you."

That night we held our collective breaths as Daddy walked down the darkened hall several times on his way to watch TV in the bedroom Guy and I occupied.

I told you it was a small house.

We were still figuratively "running scared" the next day as Daddy fiddled with the thermostat before he sat down to eat.

"Claudie, what is this?" he asked, spying the crack.

Fortunately, Marihelen had brought a friend home from church, probably saving three miscreants from a severe thrashing.

Mother, bless her heart, put up a perforated board on which she could hang pictures, hiding the cracked wall, which was not repaired for many years.

It just proved the old saying, "You can run, but you can't hide."

*   *   *

Daddy finds his boys employment opportunities

When I was in the seventh grade, my dad bought a lawnmower and told me and my brother, "You boys get out and make you some money."

So we went door to door seeking jobs. The first to hire us—God rest her soul—was local English teacher Wanda Weaks, who lived on Crestway.

We probably made less than $5 mowing her yard. Of course, that was when minimum wage was $1.15 and gas was 30 cents a gallon.

My biggest "take" ever was $11 for mowing and raking the very large yard of Mr. and Mrs. Roy Lippert, owners of Lippert's Court Reporting School. Sometimes my brother and I would work on the yard together and Winia Lippert would reward us with homemade peanut butter cookies and Cokes in nice glasses served on a silver tray with thick Scott napkins. All that for a couple of dirty urchins.

Owing that it's a capitalistic society, my other business partner, Mike Wadzeck, and I bailed out on the $2 gig at Effie Mae Kerr's house, since she kept adding jobs each week for no more pay. We headed across the street to help Leland White reduce his grass from jungle status to something a bit more manageable.

He was offering us $5 each. The decision, in retrospect, was quite easy. However, Mrs. Kerr was none too happy and called Mike's mother to express her displeasure. I'm sure Mary Wadzeck handled it diplomatically.

A little less so, apparently, than my brother, who alleged that he knocked a neighborhood man—reportedly "gay" in the days when that term was not used—on his keister when he made a pass at Guy as he was mowing his yard.

Always on the lookout to keep his boys employed, Daddy found me a job helping the late Joe Crockett, the custodian at JC Penney, for a couple of two-week stints after my sophomore year in high school. We mostly tagged garments and took out the trash.

I hated it when we had to wash windows because I wasn't very good with the squeegee and only exasperated Joe.

My brother and I also cleaned up Smitty's Barbershop, owned by Hoye Smith, next to my dad's office every Sunday afternoon to earn our haircuts.

Part of my senior year I worked as a stocker at the then-new Gibson Discount Center in the Village Shopping Center.

After I graduated, Daddy located more employment for me selling shoes at Anthony's downtown, and in the Gabriel-Wayland Shopping Center, and then a better-paying job at Baker Castor Oil, headed up at the time by future Plainview mayor John Anderson.

We worked in the nursery "bagging plants," and I'm not sure I had the first clue about what I was doing. Hope I didn't have any direct impact on Baker Castor Oil's ultimate demise.

But I will be eternally grateful to John Anderson for letting me go to work when a job opened at *The Herald* several weeks before the end of our scheduled departure from the fields.

When I compared working outdoors with working indoors, I always knew the Lord was calling me to an air-conditioned office.

*   *   *

Wonderful memories of summer vacations

Aside from a couple of trips to Nampa, Idaho, to see Mother's sister, our family vacations consisted of several days at Aunt Helen and Uncle Buster Ratican's place on Lake Travis west of Austin, and a couple of days in San Antonio where Daddy did continuing chiropractic education.

A clanging bell on the gate signaled our arrival at the Ratican's two-story Austin stone residence. Mother's oldest sister, heavily perspiring from working in her flower beds or mowing her St. Augustine grass, would come to greet us, accompanied for several years by her only "children," Cocker Spaniels Blackie and Blondie.

After supper, which might include some venison grilled by Uncle Buster, an employee of the Lower Colorado River Authority, we'd sit out on the patio, shaded by a huge oak tree.

Around 9 p.m. Aunt Helen would ask a question she already knew the answer to: "Anybody ready for ice cream?" She'd serve up the real stuff as opposed to the cheap Mellorine we frequently ate at our house.

Our favorite spot was the swimming pool at Lake Travis Lodges, owned at one time by State Treasurer Jesse James, who lived next door to Helen and Buster.

Jesse got a little too much hooch one night and told Buster, ol' buddy, ol' pal, that he could swim in his pool anytime he wanted. Although he was an award-winning fisherman and consumer of Pearl and Lone Star beer, I'm not sure Buster ever went swimming as an adult.

My sister ignored Mrs. James, a rather crabby woman, when she told her she couldn't go swimming since she wasn't an invited guest.

I nearly drowned in that pool at about age seven. My dad jumped out of the innertube he was lounging in and rescued me. As a teenager, I stole a kiss under the diving board from a Houston gal whose family was staying at the lodges. Years later Carolyn and I turned red as lobsters from lounging too long in the water.

We always stayed at the Granada Hotel on the river in San Antonio and loved to ride up and down on the elevators operated by young Hispanic women.

One summer several of us sons of chiropractors made our way outside on the top floor and one or two decided it would be fun to hurl pennies at a woman sunbather at a pool about 50 yards away.

I emerged from the stairwell into the lobby just in time to be confronted by the bellman who angrily asked if I had been on the roof throwing pennies. I could honestly say, "No, sir," only seconds before the bellman walked off and the culprits came spilling out into the lobby.

Well, Helen and Buster are gone, and the old house on Webb Lane has been torn down to make away for a far more luxurious dwelling.

But they can never demolish my wonderful vacation memories.

*   *   *

A special father-son excursion to Baltimore/D.C.

After she graduated from Plainview High School in 1997, my daughter Kayla and her mom took one of those all-inclusive trips to Zihuatanego, Mexico (to which Andy Dufresne escaped in *The Shawshank Redemption*).

So I decided to take Brad on a trip to Baltimore to see the Orioles play and then down to Washington on Amtrak to see the sights.

Shopping around for a reasonably priced hotel, I told a woman at Days Inn that I was "just a poor newspaper editor trying to take my son on a once-in-a-lifetime trip" and could she suggest any place less expensive.

"Just a minute," she said, leaving the phone. When she returned, she said, "I have a room for you at the Holiday Inn, 100 steps from Camden Yards (where the Orioles play). It will be $69 a night, and your son will be having his final checkup at the University of Maryland Medical Center. You need to ask for Cynthia when you check in."

When we arrived at the hotel, I told Brad to look as sick as possible.

The clerk said the cost would be $125 a night. When I told him I was instructed to ask for Cynthia, he said, "Oh, in that case it will be $69."

I don't know who Cynthia was, but I still like her to this day.

We also got VIP treatment when Chuck Lewis, head of the Hearst Washington Bureau, used his pull for us to bypass the long lines for a White House tour. Sometimes you just gotta know the right people.

Congressman Mac Thornberry arranged for us to take an Interior Department tour that included Ford's Theater, the Lincoln Memorial, Washington Monument, all the military memorials, Arlington National Cemetery, and Congress.

By the strangest coincidence, when I called *The Herald* from Mac Thornberry's office, he was sitting in my office.

And probably not having nearly as much fun as we were.

*   *   *

Driver's education and brushes with the law

I have been lucky to have received only one or two tickets from law enforcement in my 50 years of driving automobiles, though I certainly was deserving of others.

Like many other students in the 1950s–1980s, I took driver's ed from Harrell Weatherred, learning in a 1963 Ford Fairlane during the spring of 1964 as a freshman at Coronado Junior High.

This was in the days when 14-year-olds could drive a car legally up to 70 mph. What *was* the State of Texas thinking?

I regret not being able to drive a standard automobile because I learned on an automatic. Jim Wood, our preacher's son, let me try driving his shift model, but he soon feared I would damage his sporty red vehicle since my hand-foot coordination was pretty poor.

Harrell had a brake to slow the vehicle if a student was driving too fast. One afternoon soon after lunch—probably just about the time Harrell was about to nod off—I made a left hand turn off Columbia onto 16th while doing about 30 mph. "Boy, the name of the game is to slow down," Harrell grumped.

My brother is alleged to have thrown Harrell's books in the floor intentionally by hitting the power brakes too hard. That didn't make him any too happy.

One time I lost my temporary permit and lived in fear Harrell would find out before I located the piece of paper.

Driver's ed was always an adventure. I usually got to practice with two or three girls. One afternoon, one of the young ladies misjudged a turn, hitting a curb and causing one of the other girls to emit a discernible noise. We all got tickled, including Harrell.

I flunked the driving test for my official license the first time I took it in the fall of my sophomore year. Having my blinker on and intent on making a left hand turn out of the right hand lane onto Columbia and failing to executive a decent parallel park didn't help any.

I think my first ticket was for doing 75 on my way to cover the Floydada-Lockney football game in Floydada in the fall of 1967.

Highway Patrolman Bud Rainey flagged me down and asked if I had an emergency.

"I'm just trying to get to the football game," I explained.

"They'll wait on you," he said matter-of-factly as he wrote out the ticket.

They didn't.

The next week, I went to the courthouse, thinking of pleading my case. But when I saw that the judge looked to be older than Moses, I decided to just pay the fine.

One spring afternoon, I was hurrying to finish the Wayland newspaper in Floydada, where it was printed—thanks to the patient *Hesperian* owner Wendell Tooley who tolerated my frequent tardiness—and to get back to Plainview to umpire a junior varsity baseball game for the princely sum of $10.

That 1963 Plymouth Fury I bought from Maggard-Nall for $850 ran like a top at 115 mph between Floydada and Muncy. It dawned on me that wasn't a very good decision, so I slowed down to about 85. That car was overheating when I got home and never did run right again.

I got a ticket coming through White Deer in1993 and had to take defensive driving from Lee Dent down at Hale Center, the last time I had to accomplish that thrilling task. Lee was dismayed when "Comedy Defensive Driving" was introduced, wondering how anyone could make a serious subject funny.

Through the years, I've been stopped several times while on business for my employer but haven't been financially pained either because of courtesy (a patrolman outside Vernon gladly accepted my gift of a 39-cent Wayland pen), sympathy, or maybe the highway patrolmen were Baptists.

My favorite story, though, is about getting stopped by a city cop in Chicago about 20 years ago.

When I saw the lights behind me, I pulled over in a park area, got out and said, "No license plate, huh?" since the rental vehicle had no plate and only a small piece of paper taped in the back left windshield.

"No," said the cop, wearing that goofy-looking checkered cap sported by Windy City policemen, "you were in a left-hand-turn lane back there, and you didn't turn."

I flashed a puzzled look and then said, "You know, we don't have those in Texas."

He just rolled his eyes and walked back to his car.

And I drove on without a ticket.

*   *   *

A real "growing up" experience in New Mexico

I had a real "growing up" experience in the summer of 1965, after my sophomore year in high school.

Thurman Thomas owned a ranch near Encino, New Mexico—located between Vaughn and the Providence of God—with his brother, J.C. "Boog" Thomas. They had installed water pipe on a significant portion of the ranch and, after several years, it was leaking at the couplets.

Thurman enlisted the services of George Meriwether (he was married to George's mom Doris at the time), brothers Mike and Pat Buchanan, my neighbor pal Mike Wadzeck, and me while Boog picked up a couple of hitchhikers on his way over from Albuquerque.

The pay was $1 an hour (slightly below the prevailing minimum wage of $1.25) and all we could eat at a local café.

I packed some jeans, including an old pair of white ones, some T-shirts, and a pair of white high-top tennis shoes I bought at Star Discount for $1.

When I vaulted out of Thurman's white pickup in my all-white attire, Boog Thomas snorted, "Hell, looks like you came to work."

Mike Wadzeck says he never saw anyone jump so high as when Mike Buchanan stepped on a rattlesnake. This is the same Mike

Buchanan who swallowed half his mouth guard when he bit it in half after being tackled in the Plainview-Tascosa game in the fall of 1963.

George Meriwether sat on the hood of Thurman's Mercury, guiding a wheel that was supposed to gauge the distance between couplets. Sometimes we dug right down to one about three feet below the surface and sometimes we dug a trench about 30 feet long.

The first night in camp—actually an old motel—Boog consumed a little too much firewater. He commenced to drawing a map on the leg of his khakis, cut it off with a pocketknife, and tacked it to the wall.

Later, he took a couple of us out in his Ford station wagon, equipped with a .45 in a holster on the steering column, and fired off several rounds at jackrabbits . . . or maybe ghosts. It was a bit unsettling to a kid unaccustomed to gunfire.

The hitchhikers resembled the two goofy robbers in the *Home Alone* movies. The short, pudgy one had a big battleship on his chest, and the tall skinny one got all goosey when a little rattlesnake crawled up on a mound of dirt beside him.

Well, we survived some hard work in the hot sun and Boog Thomas' escapades and had some great stories to tell when school resumed that fall.

*   *   *

I'd pay double to do it all over again

Entertainment opportunities of my youthful days were not quite as abundant as they are now.

We spent some fun times at the Plainview Roller Rink and occasionally at the bowling alley that went by several names through the years.

The American Legion Swimming Pool, with a heavy smell of chlorine, was the place where I learned to swim, and I was instructed at about age 12 to shoot at .22 rifle at the National Guard Armory in the YMCA program. Since I'm not a hunter, that may have been the last time I fired live ammo.

Of course, a quarter would get you a feature movie at the Granada Theater and you might even be able to see a B double feature at The Fair a little farther south on Broadway for 15 cents. I think I went to The State on the north side of the square once and maybe a single time as well to The Texas at Seventh and Broadway.

Owing to the fact that our hormones were kicking in, Mike Wadzeck and I told his mom we were going to a movie at The Granada but, when she was out of sight, hightailed it to The Fair to see the racy (for that time) *Irma La Douce* starring Shirley MacLain.

Let me tell you, she looked a whole lot better then than she does now. But, then, so did I.

Easily the big deal when I was a teenager was cruising West Fifth and circling the Arrowhead Drive-In at Fifth and Vernon or the Trio Rebel at Fifth and Travis. This was a few years after "the place to be" was Eddie's Drive-In at Fifth and Joliet.

Cruising Fifth or "Dragging Broadway" was especially fun if you were in the company of a good-looking gal (as I was from time to time) and in a sporty car (which I wasn't, since I was driving the family Plymouth).

The radio was tuned to KOMA in Oklahoma City for all the top hits, or perhaps to a high-powered Mexican border station like XERF with gravelly-voiced deejay "Wolfman Jack."

Those drive-ins probably sold more Cokes than food, but another great place was the Burger Train, not far from Fifth and Joliet. The Sweetheart Burger ("Half for Her, Half for Him") with a frosty mug of A&W Root Beer was especially tasty if you were on a tight budget.

I was not amused that one of my girlfriends working the ticket booth at The Granada actually made me fork over 75 cents to get in.

If I could relive those days, I'd gladly pay double.

*   *   *

When I discovered I must be poor

Funny how you come to the knowledge you must be poor.

My dad had a Dr. in front of his name, but chiropractors didn't make near the money medical doctors did. I know Daddy charged $4 for an adjustment for a long time and only $10 when he retired in 1979.

Like a lot of other folks, my parents shopped at Furr's Supermarket on Wednesday—Double Stamp Day—so we could eventually redeem our stamp books for various items.

Daddy would push the cart about 50 mph as mother grabbed items on her list. Then Daddy would irritate the checkers by adding faster in his head than they could calculate on the register. And, woe be those who overcharged.

Speaking of push, Daddy used an old unmotorized lawn mower for years, even though he was welcome to use the gasoline-powered number he bought for me and my brother to make money in the neighborhood.

One day I asked if I could get a copy of *Sport* magazine, then only 25 cents. Just like *Mad Magazine*—"25 cents cheap. 35 cents in Canada, not so cheap."

Daddy said things had been pretty slow—meaning he hadn't seen many patients—so the purchase was nixed.

I guess I could presume we were poor since we were on a "party line." What was particularly poor was my brother's behavior when he burped in across-the-alley neighbor Lisa Arnold's ear when she didn't get off the line as quickly as he thought she should.

In my seventh-grade yearbook, the late Lloyd "Buster" Reese and I are the only players wearing *black* high-top tennis shoes. Everybody else has on white Chuck Taylor Converse All-Stars.

My mother was never one for "putting on airs," and when a neighbor woman inquired as to what the Andrews boys were going to wear to school (like Levi brand jeans), Mother said bluntly, "Probably whatever they can drag up."

I didn't own a pair of real Levis until I was an adult.

And, though I would not classify myself as anywhere near poor, I think my wife on more than one occasion has taken a look at my wardrobe and asked, "Where did you drag that up?"

*   *   *

The stressful and inopportune "Call of Nature"

I guess there's nothing as stressful as the "Call of Nature" when it comes upon you in an urgent way.

In 1962, our family took a trip to Idaho with a stopover in Denver to tour the U.S. Mint. My mother got in a bad way and desperately sent us scurrying from floor to floor trying to find an open restroom.

Almost 25 years later, I took my own family on a trip to St. Louis and Chicago that included a visit to the famed Arch spanning the Mississippi River in downtown St. Louis.

We rode up in a conveyance that looked like a clothes dryer and was about as small. Unfortunately, the Arch had no restrooms but Nature doesn't seem to care.

Fortunately, in both situations restrooms were accessed just in the nick of time.

I probably would have gotten the pee knocked out of me when I inadvertently wandered into a women's restroom after a professional hockey game in Tampa, Florida, 10 years ago.

However, I was wearing a souvenir Christmas cap the home team distributed, and that kept the occupants from immediately noticing a male was in their midst before I had time to escape.

*   *   *

A good alternative to being dead

Prior to a very cold Saturday morning in March 1975, I had only been in a couple of "fender benders" in my life. And, other than a few athletic physicals, had been to a doctor only a time or two.

Heck, having a chiropractor father who was suspicious of the medical community, my brother, sister and I didn't even see a doctor when we had whooping cough in the summer of 1959.

Actually, one auto accident I was in was a bit more than a "fender bender" when teammate Tommy Simmons broadsided a female driver at 10th and El Paso while ferrying several of us football players to the Hilton Hotel for a Lions Club meeting at which the Bulldogs were guests. Fortunately, the driver wasn't hurt but both cars sustained some damage.

Jimmie Chennault's pickup was not so lucky as he and I were headed to Hale Center to referee in a Little Dribblers tournament.

About five miles out of town, we hit some "black ice" and the pickup spun backwards and started to skid sideways toward the ditch.

Funny what you'll do under duress. I reached out and grabbed Jimmie by the hair and hollered, "Hang on . . . hang on!"

The pickup turned over—with me crashing into Jimmie—but it landed upright in a field. The impact blew out the windshields and I found myself in the floorboard, my left leg tucked under my right and my head on the glass-covered seat.

Gasping for breath, I first thought, "Man, this is a lousy way to die."

"You OK, Bub?" I wheezed, referring to Jimmie by the nickname we called each other after meeting D.M. "Bub" Holt at an Olton baseball tournament a couple of years before.

"I think so, Bub," Jimmie said, obviously in some pain.

Before long, an ambulance showed up, thanks to a farmer who saw the wreck and used his C.B. unit to alert authorities. The ambulance attendants had to haul me on a backboard through the rear window.

I didn't feel all that bad until Dr. Coe Branch used a pair of scissors to cut off my black official's pants . . . and they were brand new. I had changed into them after we left Plainview when Jimmie picked me up at *The Herald*. Thank goodness, I wasn't caught with just my underwear on.

I started to cry, maybe a combination of realizing I very well could have died and relief that I didn't.

As it turned out, I spent a week in the hospital and, because *The Herald* didn't offer compensation for accidents back then, the only money I made that week was from listening to Tut Tawwater do Bulldog baseball games on the radio so I could keep a scorebook and dictate the stories to *The Herald*'s Gal Friday, Betty Hingst.

I suffered a compression fracture of two vertebras and wore a very uncomfortable brace for about six weeks.

Compared with being hospitalized . . . or dead . . . it wasn't a bad alternative.

* * *

I guarantee you, I won't do *that* again!

Not long after Carolyn and I married in June of 1969 and moved into the palatial Collier married-student apartments, we were invited to a neighboring couple's place to play some board game—Yahtzee, I think.

Things were going along swimmingly until I managed to gain considerable advantage on Carolyn and exacerbated the situation by gloating loudly.

Whereupon she dumped her glass of iced tea in my lap.

If that won't get your attention, nothing will.

After an awkward moment of silence, I think we all broke up laughing.

I'm not sure she ever apologized.

Nevertheless, I can guarantee you, I never did *that* again!

* * *

Why I don't buy jewelry for my wife

Carolyn and I have this tacit understanding: I don't buy jewelry for her.

Well, I did buy her a very nice Marquis diamond ring at a Wayland Gala several years ago. It was from the estate of former Wayland Registrar Audrey Boles.

When my colleague Mike Melcher went to a jeweler to have the ring appraised, the owner walked away suddenly after peering through his magnifying glass.

When he returned, he apologized: "I haven't seen a diamond that pure in a long time and wanted to make sure it was real."

I had a maximum amount I thought I could pay for the ring in the Gala auction but got nervous as the price climbed higher, thanks to an unknown bidder seated a few tables in front of me.

As it turned out, it was Mike Melcher's son. Suddenly, his mother, Deb, knowing I was planning to buy the ring, if possible, demanded of her son: "You quit bidding right now . . . that's Danny's ring!"

Let me just say it's worth quite a bit more than the $300 we paid for Carolyn's wedding ring 45 years ago at Zale's in Lubbock.

By the way, I had no cash and certainly no credit to buy that first ring, naive as I was. I had to call my dad to vouch for me, and I guess the manager, fellow by the name of Naaman Lipinsky, must have agreed to let me pay it out.

In 1980, on my first-ever trip to New York, I looked at just about every booth at an arts and crafts show in Central Park, trying to find something special for my wife.

About to give up, I came upon a woman from Portugal who was doing scrimshaw—carvings on bone or ivory—for which she was creating necklaces. I spied one with a beautiful long-stemmed red rose and asked if she could paint a "C" on it for Carolyn. She did and it was lovely.

Carolyn seemed glad to receive it but only wore it a time or two. When I inquired as to why she hadn't worn the necklace, she explained—rather lamely I thought—"It doesn't match my eyes."

I think I blinked in disbelief and responded, "Good grief, woman, the only people with red eyes are albinos!"

Right then and there I swore off buying jewelry—the ring being the exception.

*   *   *

Oh, last of the big spenders, huh?

One of the real treats in my life was taking a cruise to Alaska with Carolyn and our friends Bill and Sue Coward of Granbury on our 35th anniversaries in 2004.

Starting and ending the trip in Seattle, we enjoyed a whale watch and salmon dinner out of Juneau; a train excursion out of Skagway into the mountains; watching the glaciers "calve," and a horse-drawn wagon ride in Ketchikan.

The nightly shows on board were fantastic and the food was delicious. At dinner each evening, we enjoyed getting to know the friendly wait staff from various countries. I didn't mind wearing a suit, but might have drawn the line at sporting a kilt, as a fellow at an adjoining table did.

One evening I asked a tall, slender waiter from Croatia, "If I order a bottle of wine and we don't drink it all, can you put the cork back in it so we can have the rest tomorrow night?"

He pulled himself up to his full height, cocked his head, and said in playful disdain: "Last of the big spenders, huh?"

That line was worth the trip.

*   *   *

That poor dog just ran out of gas

We never had pets when I was growing up.

Well, my older sister had a couple of white mice for a science experiment but a neighbor kid picked them up and when they got to squirming he squeezed them to death.

When we moved to 3505 W. 16th in 1977, previous owner Jim Fitzgerald said he'd let us have a pool table in the basement and a blonde Cocker Spaniel named Buffy if we wanted them.

I told several friends that we really liked that dog, except for the fact that she pooped in the yard a lot.

"One spring, I decided to scalp the grass and decided to pour the gas and oil out of the lawnmower into an aluminum pie pan and put in new gas and oil," I explained more than once.

"When I went into the house for a second, that crazy dog lapped up quite a bit of gas and oil out of that pie pan and then took off like a shot. She ran around the yard about three times and just keeled over," I continued.

Several times someone would respond with a sorrowful look: "Did she die?"

"No, she just ran out of gas."

I must have told that story so well that my friend Vicki James bought it twice.

My youngest son, Brad, brought home a female lab one day. I had fun chasing that little gal around the neighborhood. But, as she got older, we knew our porous backyard fence would not contain her. So, we gave her away.

About a year later, the new owners came by with a dog that now resembled a small horse.

One thing about that pool table. It never got any bigger.

*   *   *

Out of the mouth of babes comes the truth

Nearly 20 years ago, I intercepted Kace and Keeton Hatch, sons of Kyle and Kenna Hatch, as they were headed to some meeting at church.

I asked if they were playing baseball and swimming and otherwise enjoying their summer. I continued pumping them for more information.

Finally tiring of the inquisition, Keeton, about five at the time, looked up and said flatly, "You have to quit talking now. We need to go."

I thought, "I've got a lot of friends who would like to say that to me if they just had the nerve."

But I have given explicit instructions when it's time to go on to my Great Reward that all I ask of the undertaker is that my mouth will be open so people can walk by the casket and say, "Don't he look natural?"

*　　*　　*

Family expression means something to us

I guess every family has an expression that means nothing to someone else but needs no explanation when we hear it.

David Roberson, a burr-haired neighbor kid, would frequently come to our screen door at dinner time (that would be what we now call "lunch," not to be confused with the last meal of the day we called "supper") and say, "You don't want me to eat with you, do you?" Mother would frequently invite him in.

One Christmas, David's maternal grandmother gave him one of those globes that "snow" when you turn it upside down.

When we requested a closer look, David asked, "Are you jealous of Granny Dorsett?"

From that day forward, anyone who showed the slightest inclination to want what someone else had got the requisite response: "Aw, you're just jealous of Granny Dorsett."

*　　*　　*

The Dancin' Deacon tag not exactly correct

I have never been very good at dancing, the relatively few times I've tried it.

I grew up in the Church of Christ, and we weren't supposed to engage in that kind of activity, and I guess it is widely assumed Baptist deacons don't do that either.

But my mother, bless her heart, told me not long before she died that "We never did forbid you kids from dancing."

Although I used to watch Arthur Murray's dance program on TV, for some reason I never did learn how and didn't date girls who either did or cared to press the issue.

But, when my daughter Kayla got into the Debutantes program in the mid-1990s, one of the requirements at the Debs Ball was that each young lady waltz with her daddy.

By this time, Kayla—also a graduate of the Cotillion program—was quite adept at the two-step and other "foot functions," despite having received a negative report while attending First Presbyterian Pre-School: "Kayla has a difficult time skipping." I attributed this to a hereditary deficiency from myself and her mother, a non-dancing Baptist.

Local dance instructor Pat Stoner gave us fathers a few tips, and I was able to muddle through the Debs waltz without stepping on Kayla's dress more than once or twice.

Since that time, another dad—Joe Reed of Kress—a dancing Methodist, has called me "The Dancin' Deacon" every time I see him.

I really shook him up a few months after he stuck me with that moniker by giving a bear hug to my good friend Leroy Henry when I saw him at Leal's.

Joe happened to be there and witnessed the embrace with some sense of mock dismay.

"You're not only dancin', now you're also huggin' men in public," Joe fumed.

Somebody warned me once: "There's no telling what dancing will lead to."

Now, I know.

*   *   *

An 'honorary Negro' and proud of it

I know my complexion doesn't attest to it, but I'm proud to be an "honorary Negro."

I was afforded that title by several black friends years ago because I covered about the first 20 Black History and Martin Luther King Celebrations in the Austin Heights Community.

The events for youth, senior adults, and a community gathering were held in various churches, although one year's celebration was at the Ollie Liner Center.

Some of the most precious friends I have happen to have darker skin than mine, and many of them have called me "Mister Andrew" through the years, dropping the "s" from my last name.

With apologies to all for not being able to mention everyone, here are a few who have been very special to me (others are mentioned in stories elsewhere):

*   **Essie Givens:** Now heading toward 100, "Sister" Givens can preach, sing, and play the piano and guitar. She and her husband, the Rev. E.N. Givens, founded Emmanuel Church

of God in Christ, and she has pastored Good Samaritan Outreach Pentecostal Church of God for many years. She always looks elegant in her hats when she "gets her church on." Best of all, she always smiles when she sees me and calls me "Precious."

* **Alfred and Rubye Henderson:** Retired educators in the Plainview system, Rubye, a co-founder of the Martin Luther King and Black Awareness Celebration, is a remarkable Christian woman who has courageously battled cancer for several years, and Al is in my Sunday School class. We enjoy talking about *Sanford and Son* episodes and music on *The Gospel Greats.*

* **Louise Ray:** Coach of the Hawks girls' softball team for years, "Miz Ray" was the grandmother of two of the most outstanding athletes in Plainview High School history—basketball guards Katrisa O'Neal, who starred at Texas Tech, and Dibi Ray, a top-notch player at Missouri and later a teacher and coach here. There were so many people at her funeral at United Baptist Church that I stood outside and visited with a score of former PHS athletes to which she was a "second momma."

* **Joe Crockett:** A longtime employee of The Hamby Co., he was pillar at Ash and Carver Church of Christ. I can hear Joe leading an old hymn: "There to my heart was the blood A-plied . . . glory to His Name."

* **Ed and Marilyn Jennings:** Ed, a former school board member, works for Xcel Energy and pastors New Fellowship Missionary Baptist Church. Marilyn is a veteran Plainview teacher and church pianist. Ed played accused murderer, Marine Cpl. Harold Dawson, and I played Lt. Sam Weinberg, an attorney, in a local production of *A Few Good Men* in 2003.

* **Joe Berry:** Music teacher at Lakeside fifth grade for more than 20 years, he now is a recruiter for the Wayland School of Music. He's still the most famous man to ever come out of Lovelady, Texas.

* **Sandra and Kenneth Tolson:** Two of the sweetest people on God's earth, Sandra blessed a lot of folks with a great voice and we always joked that we were going to find a venue to sing "Highway to Heaven" together. Sadly, she passed away last August. Kenneth makes a wonderful sweet potato pie.

* **Leanna McCutcheon:** The mother of such stalwart athletes as Lawrence, Larry, and Roland McCutcheon; John Sneed Jr., Charlie Sneed, Robert Sneed, and Bill Carter, she was a spindly woman who always reminded me of the great actress Cecily Tyson.

* **Kathleen Jackson and Ruby Riggins:** Former athletes at Booker T. Washington and daughters of Roland, Sr. and Leanna McCutcheon, they have been like sisters to me. Kathleen has worked at First Methodist Church's Calico Caboose pre-school for years, and Ruby, who is retired, has been an LVN at the Plainview-Hale County Health Department. Emmanuel Church of God in Christ—where Kathleen's late husband Walter Jackson was pastor—seldom opens the door without them.

* **Lester Fennell:** A former standout running back at PHS, he also is an umpire in the Summer Baseball Program and an all-around good guy.

* **Fred and Emma Herring:** Fred's a soft-spoken guy who has kept a lot of yards looking nice, and Emma worked at City National, First National, Norwest, and Wells Fargo banks. Emma, a feisty, tell-it-like-it-is gal, looked down her nose at me when I tried to imitate the swaying walk of women at the Black Community Service. "You haven't got it," she said pointedly.

* **Doris and Ernest "Honey Bear" Washington:** My dad claims he was Doris's first customer when she went to work for Hale County State Bank in 1970. Daddy would have been very happy to have Doris bring out his savings in a wheelbarrow when I took him to the bank in his later years. "Bear" was a

supervisor at Cargill Meat Packers for many years and a pretty fair golfer.

* **Jerry "Moe" Wall:** Another former supervisor at Cargill, Jerry has become a dear friend in the last few years as we have worked Emmaus "walks" together. Of course, his biggest claim to fame is being the father of one of the most talented PHS athletes of all time, Jamar Wall.

I don't know if I have any "black blood" in me, but all I know is when we sang "Lift Every Voice and Sing" (the so-called Negro National Anthem) at the Black Awareness celebration, something got up inside of me.

Here are the first two verses:

> *Lift every voice and sing,*
> *till earth and heaven ring,*
> *Ring with the harmonies of liberty;*
> *Let our rejoicing rise*
> *High as the listening skies,*
> *Let it resound loud as the rolling sea.*

> *Sing a song full of the faith*
> *that the dark past has taught us,*
> *Sing a song full of the hope*
> *that the present has brought us;*
> *facing the rising sun of our new day begun,*
> *let us march on till victory is won.*

Honorary Negro? Yes, sir, and proud of it.

CHURCH AND FAITH STORIES

Some highlights of my spiritual journey

Since I have been in church almost literally all my life and a Christian since age 12, I would be remiss if I didn't mention a few spiritual highlights not otherwise related in these pages. All glory is solely due to God the Father, Jesus the Son, and the Holy Spirit.

* I was baptized in March of 1961 at Ninth and Columbia Church of Christ during a "gospel meeting" conducted by Truman Spring of Houston. His subject was "The Hardest Thing for Man to Do." The hardest thing for me to do was to wait for him to stop preaching so I could "walk the aisle" and make my profession of faith. Bob Hawkins, the local minister, baptized me as the congregation sang "O, Happy Day." It certainly was.

* Six years after Carolyn and I were married, I was baptized at First Baptist Church by the pastor, Carlos McLeod, in the summer of 1975 after a message by Baylor's Grant Teaff. The night before, he had directed one of the teams in the Coaches All-America Football Game played at Texas Tech for several years.

* Carolyn and I are happy that all three of our children are Christians, never leaving it up to Sunday school teachers or even preachers to explain to them how to have eternal life. I

was thrilled to help my grandson Karsten come to the Lord earlier this year.

* I have taught Sunday school for adults for most of the past 40 years. I substituted in the 8th grade boys' class one time and decided that if God wanted me to teach junior high boys, he'd have to hit me over the head and we'd have one major rule: "When I talk, you shut up."

* I was ordained as a deacon at First Baptist in April of 1984 when Dr. Fred Meeks was pastor. I actually got some votes when I wasn't even a member of the church, still officially a "visitor."

* A great experience was going on a Walk to Emmaus—a wonderful weekend of worship, discipleship and fellowship with other men—in 1998 in Slaton. I have been privileged to work five "Walks," including serving as lay director in 2010. I enjoy a weekly gathering of men, led by Dr. Coe Branch, for fellowship and prayer. Regulars include Barry Miller, Ricky Kelm, Don Eversole, Tom Ray, Ron Roberts, Ted Wilson, Darwin Cox, Melvin Vanlandingham, Fred Willis, Kim Seago, Steve Mason, and Ralph Langley.

* I served as general chairman of the Go Tell Crusade with evangelist Rick Gage in 2011 at Bulldog Stadium and Hutcherson Center. A total of 1,100 decisions for Christ were registered, including 550 professions of faith.

* For several years, I assisted Tommy McMillan as a facilitator for the Coaches Outreach Bible Study at Plainview High and for the past five years have led the study each semester at Wayland. Our area director is John Dudley, head baseball coach at Lubbock Coronado for 30 years.

* One of the great blessings of my life has been visiting the community's assisted living centers and nursing homes weekly and giving devotionals there from time to time. I have made some precious friends through the years and have said goodbye to far too many.

* About 2000, Robert Black let me join the choir at First Baptist and I thank Alan Schantz, Dan Turner, Dave Purkey, Gary Manning and Greg Hall for letting me hang around. I don't read music and I don't know if I'm a tenor or a bass or some hybrid, but I sure love being part of a group that helps our church worship the Lord in song, ably assisted by two super-talented individuals, pianist Sally Bass and keyboardist Martin Duckett, and other musicians. For Easter and Christmas presentations I'm usually seated between bass Randy Kaufman and tenor Rick Shaw to try and help them. Poor guys can't sing a lick.

* I love the Lord's reassuring words to his disciples in John 14: 1-6: "Let not your hearts be troubled..." but my favorite single verse is Philippians 1:6: "He who began a good work in you will continue to do it until Jesus Christ returns."

*　　*　　*

Memorable mission experiences in Brazil, Ukraine

I was privileged to go on two unforgettable mission trips to Recife, Brazil, in 1981 and Sevastopol, Ukraine, in 1993.

The first trip was part of Texas Baptists' Mission to Brazil effort through International Crusades directed by Ben Meith of Glen Rose, who recently endowed a missions chair at Wayland. The second was with a group from various parts of the country led by Taylor and Eva Henley of San Angelo.

The Brazil trip was an adventure in that we rode orange Volkswagen taxis at high rates of speed over sometimes bumpy roads. In fact, we went down one street, and it looked like bombs had hit it. By the way, they say there are two kinds of pedestrians in Brazil—the quick and the dead.

We stayed in a hotel guarded by military personnel. The electrical power was not always reliable and the toilet paper tended to be religious—you know, hole-ly.

We had dinner one night at a baker's home. I told him, "If you come to Texas, we'll put on the dog." I had to hasten to explain that idiom. Every time he saw me after that, the host pastor said, "Danny, put on the dog."

Dr. David Jester, new president at Wayland at the time, led our group. When he had to return to the States early to speak at Southwestern Seminary in Fort Worth, I preached the final service in a nice church.

Five thousand miles from home, a West Texan who mumbles was trying to convey a message through a Portuguese interpreter that while we sing a song called "Just As I Am," many people are reluctant to come to Christ because they don't think they are "worthy" until they quit whatever sins they feel are holding them back. I said the Lord will accept you just as you are and help you change your lifestyle.

When the invitation was offered, a young man came from the very back pew and said through the interpreter, "You're telling me that Jesus will accept me just like I am?"

I thought that could only be explained as the power of the Holy Spirit.

As in Brazil, in Ukraine we found loving and accepting people, although a bit more cautious since they had lived under oppressive rule for so long. This was just four years after the Cold War had begun to thaw considerably.

I thought the Moscow Airport would be a showplace to demonstrate Russian progressivism to arriving passengers. Instead, we found a couple of indifferent security personnel, only a couple of scanners to pass through, and a dingy lobby that appeared to be illuminated by 40-watt bulbs. We visited Red Square, but it was too late to see Lenin's tomb and I briefly—and without permission—directed a Russian band playing Dixieland music on the street.

One woman asked if I could interpret a dream for her; another cried because of the poor condition of the former Communist meeting house she managed and in which we held a meeting; and a young man in a mental hospital gave me a book in which he had drawn the Statue of Liberty "because I love Americans."

We were told the KGB was probably keeping an eye on us, but we moved about freely, even around the submarine base, since Sevastopol is headquarters for the Russian fleet.

I gave a testimony at a soccer field and told an inquisitive young man who asked which was better, democracy or communism, that man-made institutions are all flawed and that we should follow "Jesus Christ, the same yesterday, today, and forever."

At the end of a long Sunday service, I encouraged our group to sing one more song, "There's Room at the Cross for You." It ends, "Though millions have come, there's still room for one. Yes, there's room at the cross for you."

An old babushka in black dress and black scarf came running down the aisle waving her hand and asking in Russian, "Is there room for one more?"

I hope to see her and that young man from Brazil when we all get to Heaven.

What a day of rejoicing that will be.

*   *   *

Mission offering named for an actress?

Southern Baptists have three major offerings they take every year to assist mission efforts.

They are the Lottie Moon Christmas Offering for foreign missions; the Annie Armstrong Easter Offering for home (U.S.) missions, and the Mary Hill Davis Offering for state efforts.

One Sunday after a deacons' meeting, several of us trekked to the Family Life Center to catch the last few minutes of a Dallas Cowboys game before the evening service started.

Blaine Smith was leader of the Royal Ambassadors mission group for boys and was quizzing the youngsters on the name of the current offering being taken.

Lottie and Annie got a couple of votes before Blaine coaxed, "It has three names." His own son, Patrick, excitedly blurted, "Mary Tyler Moore!"

Speaking of Lottie Moon—a little woman who gave her life to missions in China from 1873-1912—Dale Durham, a former Minister of Education at First Baptist, told a great "payback" story involving Lottie.

Seems a banker went to a conference in Florida and was able to pass a counter check in a liquor store, signing the name of a teetotaling member of First Baptist in Levelland.

The banker couldn't wait for the gossip to get around that Deacon Smith was off in Florida buying booze.

Not very happy about this shenanigan, Deacon Smith asked Dale, "Want to see the Lottie Moon Christmas Offering grow?"

He wrote a $2,000 counter check and signed the banker's name.

It went through and the banker never said a word.

*   *   *

Carlos McLeod

Carlos McLeod was definitely one of a kind

If ever there was a one-of-a-kind person, it was Carlos McLeod, pastor of First Baptist Church-Plainview from 1968–81 and then Director of Evangelism for the Baptist General Convention of Texas until his death in 1992.

Never far from his country roots, what Carlos may have lacked in polish, he made up for in enthusiasm. In fact, someone said of Carlos: "He'll go to Heaven if he doesn't go past it."

I think my favorite Carlos line described him to a T: "An ol' boy jumped into a taxi and the driver said, 'Where do you wanna go?' The passenger said brightly, 'Don't make any difference, I got business all over town.'"

Carlos was one of those guys like Lyndon Johnson. When he talked to you he was right up in your lapels.

He was not amused when I quoted scripture that said the Kingdom of God will not be brought in by much speaking.

Raised in Farmersville, Texas, Carlos Ray McLeod was "called to preach" while attending Howard Payne College at Brownwood and eventually wound up pastoring the First Baptist Church of Halfway (and don't dare call it Halfway Baptist Church). That congregation gained Rural Church of the Year honors under his leadership.

Carlos said he came to Wayland one day in March of 1958 and found many people looking sad or even in tears. He assumed someone important must have died.

Well, some*thing* important had died: The Flying Queens' 131-game winning streak as they lost to archrival Nashville Business College in the semifinals of the national tournament at St. Joseph, Missouri. It's still a record for men or women.

Carlos pastored First Baptist-Silverton and then San Jacinto in Amarillo before being called to the Plainview church, which enjoyed great growth during his ministry.

He did tend to preach long and loud. The late Marshall Formby, a colorful lawyer-newspaperman-politician, said he never saw the kickoff of a Dallas Cowboy game at noon because Carlos was still preaching.

Marshall would throw his right arm in the air, then take a long look at his watch. He threatened to put up a calendar on the front of the balcony.

Carlos probably never saw him as he tended to preach over the congregation and off said balcony. That's why his wife, Bonnie, had no chance of catching his eye one morning when he preached on "Blind Barabbas" rather than "Blind Bartimaeus." At least he stuck with the rabble-rouser all the way.

By the way, a cat vaulted off the balcony one Sunday morning, raced to the front of the church, circled behind Jeannine Greene at the piano, past the choir loft, and out the west door . . . all while Minister of Education Shelby Baucum was praying.

One Sunday, Carolyn and I happened to be sitting in the front row of the balcony with our eldest son, Brandon, then about five. Carlos, no doubt, was hammering away at sin.

Brandon rubbed his forehead and moaned, "Brother Carlos makes my head hurt."

Paul Lyle, who loved to give his preacher a hard time, said he was driving back home from Dallas one Sunday and around Post could hear Carlos preaching. "Then I turned on the radio and could really hear him better," Paul quipped.

Despite a broken leg, it would not do for Carlos to forego baptizing a man, figuring he could protect his cast by encasing it in a plastic bag. What he forgot was that when plastic gets wet, it also gets slippery. Carlos almost drowned the man as he danced around the baptistry, trying to stay upright.

During a Christmas program, Carlos decided it would be impressive if, after Merle Wittner, wife of Minister of Music Ed Wittner, sang and played "Sweet Little Jesus Boy" on the autoharp, the spotlight shone on him behind the Lord's Supper table.

So, as Merle was nearing the end of her song, Carlos tiptoed down the steps. Suddenly, his feet went out from under him and he bounced unceremoniously part way under the table.

Deacon Maurice Hanna, manager of the Higginbotham-Bartlett Lumber Co., was seated next to the table. He turned toward the commotion and asked rather matter-of-factly, "Carlos, what are you doing under the table?"

"Trying to get up before the lights come on," the pastor whispered as he dragged himself to his feet.

Norman Wright, longtime banker-insurance man, said Carlos would occasionally call him and say, "Norman, come go with me to the hospital in Lubbock. We need to visit some folks."

"Where are you?" Norman would inquire.

"In your driveway," Carlos would say. That's because he had a car phone well ahead of the time most people owned one.

R. L. Kirk, minister of First Methodist Church about the same time, said he found an old dial phone and put it in his car and would pick up the receiver when he was at a red light because he wanted to "look as important as Carlos."

As much as he liked to preach, Carlos enjoyed finding ways to draw a bigger crowd to 205 W. Eighth or to the annual "Church in the Park" with such celebrities as Dallas Cowboys Coach Tom Landry and kicker Rafael Septien; Pittsburgh Steelers rookie quarterback Terry Bradshaw; Texas Tech football coach Jim Carlen; astronaut Jim Irwin; talented musicians; actor Tom Lester, who played Ebb on *Green Acres*; Bob Harrington, the Chaplain of Bourbon Street; and venerable Baptist preachers such as R. G. Lee, Vance Havner, Baker James Cauthen, Ramsey Pollard, and his hero, W. A. Criswell, pastor of First Baptist Church in Dallas for more than 50 years.

Several of Carlos's mannerisms mimicked Criswell, and he liked to say in answer to the question, "What would you be if you weren't a Baptist?": "I'd be ashamed."

I went with Carlos to an evangelism conference in Greenville one night, and he had the audience eating out of his hand with stories I had heard often enough I could have told them better than he did.

James Pleitz, pastor of the very upscale Park Cities Baptist Church in Dallas, told me after Carlos was elected president of the Baptist General Convention of Texas: "You know, Carlos can appeal to the educated man and to the common man."

That was because he loved everybody and wanted badly for them to personally know the Jesus he served almost all his life.

Carlos might have been ashamed if he wasn't a Baptist but he was, like the Apostle Paul, never ashamed of the gospel of Jesus Christ.

*   *   *

Robert Black

New music man: He's full growed, ain't he?

One of my favorite people is Robert Black, minister of music at First Baptist Church from 1984–2000 and then Director of Church Music at Wayland for 10 years.

Robert weighed about 300 pounds when he came to Plainview from Temple where he was a music minister, taught at Temple Junior College, and also was an editor for Word Music in Waco.

He was just what you call a 'big ol' boy."

Not realizing he was sitting by Robert's wife Martha Jo, a former teacher at Edgemere Elementary, an older man, wondered aloud to a fellow church member, "Wonder what that new song leader looks like?"

When Robert arrived at the podium with other ministers, the man declared, "Well, he's full growed, ain't he?"

Robert played Santa Claus one year when my youngest son was at Edgemere. When he strode into the room with a loud greeting of "Ho, Ho, Ho!," Brad looked up from his desk and said matter-of-factly, "Hi, Robert." Then he went back to coloring.

Like other music ministers, Robert was called on to sing for funerals across the street from the church at Lemons Funeral Home. One time the request was both unusual and out of Robert's baritone range: "Whoop-ee-ti-yi-o get along little doggies." The family had intended for him to sing "Happy Trails to You."

A kind and compassionate soul, Robert introduced me to some songs I had never heard. One of my favorites is "Wonderful, Wonderful Jesus." The last stanza and chorus go like this:

> There is never a guilty sinner,
> There is never a wandering one,
> But that God can in mercy pardon
> Through Jesus Christ, His Son.
>
> Wonderful, wonderful Jesus,
> In the heart He implanteth a song:
> A song of deliverance, of courage, of strength,
> In the heart He implanteth a song.

Robert and I attended the Baptist General Convention of Texas' annual meeting in El Paso in 1986 and between us we knew just about everybody there. Almost everyone who greeted him called him "Robbie."

I never did. Sounded like a small boy's name to me and, after all, he was "full growed."

*　　*　　*

Having the cake and some ice cream, too

One of my all-time favorite recollections I call "The Suit Story."

In the late 1980s, I became acquainted with Moreland McManigal of Happy, a retired farmer and father of Janie Hart, Plainview teacher and counselor and wife of Travis Hart, pastor of First Baptist Church.

Janie, who grew up in Happy, and I started Wayland in the fall of 1967, but she and Travis got married the next summer and moved off to Fort Worth so he could attend Southwestern Baptist Theological Seminary.

I stopped by Happy a couple of times on my way to or from Amarillo to see Moreland and Kate McManigal. This included a visit while he was terminally ill with cancer.

Moreland died in the fall of 1991, just about the time I was getting ready to go to a Hearst meeting in Washington, D.C., that included a visit to the White House.

I thought it would be appropriate to wear a dark suit to meet President George H.W. Bush, but didn't have one and, because we had just moved, money was tight.

So I began to pray about the Lord providing a dark suit for me. I thought he might even let me win one in some contest. You know, he does work in mysterious ways.

One morning, Travis called me for the first time in several months and asked if I could meet him for coffee at Le Patio, the little cafe next door to the Warrick Inn at Eighth and Broadway.

Travis wasn't much for chit-chat and, I promise you, the first thing out of his mouth was this: "I brought a dark suit home from Moreland's. You interested in it?"

I nearly fell out of my chair and tears welled up in my eyes.

Looking shocked, Travis said, "What did I say?"

"You can't believe what I've been praying for," I told him.

When I got to church on Wednesday night, Travis said, "I've got a sport coat over at the office. You want it?"

Not only did God provide the "cake," he threw in a little "ice cream" as well.

I had lost some weight and after I had the length of the pants let out, that suit looked very nice. I have a picture of me shaking hands with George Bush the Elder in the Oval Office. Kate McManigal was proud to see it.

Speaking of Kate, she delivered two priceless lines after she was diagnosed with dementia and moved out to Santa Fe House. Janie and I have laughed about them often.

The first time I visited her, I said, "Kate, I'm Danny Andrews. I'm a good friend of Travis and Janie."

"Yes," she responded, "you look very fertile," obviously meaning to say "familiar."

I thought, "Well, at one time I was."

The next time I saw her, I went through the same introduction and she decided with a smile, "Yes, you look like you did when you didn't."

I chuckled to myself: "Well, I hope I look like I do when I don't."

*   *   *

Call me the Bottom-of-the-Barrel Preacher

I have had the privilege of preaching in some 40 area churches—Baptist, Methodist, Christian, Presbyterian, and nondenominational—in more than 30 communities.

Several of my relatives figured I'd grow up to be a preacher since I'd stand on a stool at my grandparents' home and "preach away." The subject matter totally escapes me.

I've always called myself the "Bottom-of-the-Barrel Preacher," you know, the guy churches call when they run out of options for a "real preacher."

Usually I have only had one sermon I think is pretty good—"Don't Fear Death," in recent years—so I've had to tell churches, "I can only come on Sunday morning."

I've made this offer to many preacher friends: "If you wake up some Sunday sick as a dog, call me and I can usually get there in 30 minutes to an hour."

Well, one Sunday my pastor, Travis Hart, called about 7:30.

"Danny, when's the last time you preached?"

"Three weeks ago for Les Griffin in Crosbyton."

"Well, you better drag it out. I'm sick as a dog," Travis said, as though his raspy voice didn't give him away.

When I went to the pulpit at First Baptist to preach for the first time, I said, "I know about 90 percent of y'all, and I love about 50 percent of you, and I'm not afraid of any of you, but I'm a little nervous."

Travis called on me to preach on Father's Day several years ago and gave me a $150 gift certificate to Dillard's. The next week, I was asked to preach at First Baptist in Halfway and received $75.

I couldn't resist telling Travis, "You know, we must have had about 600 in worship when I preached at our church and I got $150 but there were only 10 at Halfway and I got $75. I can't make the math work out."

"I'll try to do better next time," Travis said sheepishly.

"Hey, don't worry," I exhorted him, "that sermon at Halfway wasn't worth $75," much less double that amount in my home church.

But the Bottom-of-the-Barrel Preacher appreciated it anyway.

*   *   *

Marrying, burying, baptizing, and life saving

Although I am not an ordained or even licensed minister, I have had the privilege of presiding at two marriages, conducting five funerals, and assisting with a baptism.

Two of my former reporters at *The Herald*—Kristy Spicer Martinkewiz of Hobbs and Mary Vuong Beck of Houston—were kind enough to ask me to direct their wedding vows.

For Kristy's wedding in 1990, I borrowed a dark suit from Wayland band director Jim Hansford and an outline from religion professor Gary Manning.

Today, Kristy, who directs the Lea County United Way in Hobbs, and her husband Keith have two grown children. Her son recently married.

For Mary's wedding on Easter weekend of 2010, I worked closely with her and Sean on their vows and borrowed a black robe and white clerical stole from my pastor, Travis Hart, for the outdoor ceremony.

Mary, who worked at the *The Herald* for six months as a Hearst Fellow and now is a freelance writer and editor after several years at the *Houston Chronicle*, has a two-year-old daughter.

I have been honored to conduct the funerals of longtime Plainview car dealer Don Johnston, former Plainviewans Wilson and Jean McEachern, and two of my former Sunday School class members, Woody Harper and James Bentley.

Because I had encouraged former Wayland basketball player Johnny Terra to make his public profession of faith, Travis Hart asked if wanted to baptize him.

Sure, I thought, except that Johnny is 6-8. I might be able to get him down in the water. Getting him up seemed a daunting task.

It was, even for his coach, Robert Davenport (now the athletic director at Oklahoma Baptist) who is 6-4. I stood in the baptistry, ready to help as needed—which turned out to be a fairly futile effort.

When Robert was called on to baptize another 6-8 Brazilian basketballer, Rigo Silva, who was probably 20 pounds heavier than Johnny, the coach went solo.

As he struggled to get Rigo upright, Robert groaned, "I baptize you in the name of the Father, the Son and the HO . . . leee Spirit."

It was a moment that drew joyous laughter from the congregation.

I suspect the Lord might have been chuckling too.

Oh, yeah, I probably saved a life in 2007 in Wayland's Harral Auditorium.

Terra Watson, daughter of Rodney and the late Lana Watson, had just been crowned Miss Wayland when Terra's proud 90-year-old grandmother, Reva Lou Grisham, got a bit off-balance and started to pitch headlong into the orchestra pit.

I grabbed Reva Lou, staring into the 7-foot deep pit, by the neck of her dress and held on until help could arrive, keeping her from falling into the abyss. Fortunately, she suffered no serious injuries.

I suspect the Lord might have been holding his breath on that one. I know I was.

*   *   *

Sharon Wright

Some folks can take the air right out of you

Ever notice how some folks can take the air right of you, no matter how enthusiastic you are about something?

My friend Sharon Wright—I still call her "Sharn Jean" after listening to Tulsa radio antagonist Roy D. Mercer tapes and spewing ice cream all over the table at her house the first time I heard one—loves to recall such an occasion.

For three years, several Plainview families conducted Vacation Bible School for the Glorieta Baptist Church just down the road from the Glorieta Baptist Conference Center near Santa Fe.

Carolyn was Children and Pre-School Minister at First Baptist Church at the time and we would take the materials she ordered for VBS and re-use them at Glorieta.

In addition to driving a van to pick up children in the area, I also taught the adult class each evening.

One night I came back to the Plainview cabin—coincidentally the first church cabin built at Glorieta when it opened in the early 1950s—all excited about one of the attendees giving her life to Christ.

Sharon and I were in the kitchen and she looked up from making a sandwich and asked flatly, "Did you have that booger hanging out of your nose when you were talking to that woman?"

I think Sharon, longtime principal at LaMesa Elementary, former president of a state elementary principals' group, and now an administrator for the school district, is still ticked because of a picture I ran of her when she was Meet Your Neighbor on the front page of *The Herald*. About all you could see of fair-skinned Sharon was bright red lipstick.

I have to admit it wasn't very flattering.

In fact, it was a real booger.

*   *   *

Carr's Chapel: Recommended by Ted

Every once in a while, life brings you an unexpected blessing. I got one back in 2002, when I finally found where I was intending to go.

My friend and fellow PHS Class of '67 graduate Ted Wilson was pastor of First United Methodist Church in Petersburg at the time and took me up on a recent offer I had made when I ran into him at Covenant Hospital in Lubbock.

He and his wife Jodi were getting ready to go to Norway to help with the Emmaus discipleship work, and I kiddingly told Ted I had one good sermon if he ever woke up sick some Sunday and needed someone to fill in.

So, Ted called me a couple of weeks later and asked if I could speak at FUMC in Petersburg as well as his "charge" at Carr's Chapel, a little church over in Floyd County that was founded in 1914.

Ted gave me good instructions on how to get to the church, which met at 9 a.m., two hours ahead of the Petersburg congregation.

Unfortunately, going down FM 789 about 8:40, I figured I had passed FM 37—where I was supposed to turn left—and decided to follow a car I spotted making a turn to go east. "That car may even be going to Carr's Chapel," I reasoned.

Wrong—it was headed to the community of Barwise. This made for a future sermon illustration: Just because somebody looks like they're going the right way, they may not be.

I turned around and hauled it back the way I came as the clock ticked mercilessly toward 9 a.m.

Headed south again, I soon spotted FM 37. "Go past the Harmony Community meeting house," the instructions said, and turn south. Well, I passed the turn and was headed toward Lockney.

Exasperated and about to be late, I called a Mr. Charles Carr in the Harmony Community on my cellphone, reasoning if his last name was Carr, surely he knew where Carr's Chapel was.

Indeed, he said he did. Unfortunately, he thought I was coming from the opposite direction and told me to turn right—a suggestion that eventually led down a dirt road and into a field.

I called him back and he instructed me to go on a bit farther west and turn again. Same scenario—more dirt road. Then it hit me—now I know where that church is. The instructions said *south*.

I'm going *north*.

About 9:10, I pulled up to the church where three cars sat. I tugged on my suit coat and opened the screen door. "I hope that's our speaker," a voice said.

Fortunately, they didn't apply the "10-minute rule" in effect at some Sunday Schools and churches: "If the speaker or teacher doesn't show up in 10 minutes, we're outta here."

I was greeted by four smiling women.

Maye Williams, whose folks helped start Carr's Chapel, showed me a picture of the white clapboard church with two nearby outhouses—they had one for men and one for women—and a turnstile between barbed-wire fences to allow the parishioners in and keep the cattle out.

Carolyn Davis said she came to these parts from Iowa and won over skeptical in-laws.

Zilla Smith said her name can be found in the Bible, but everybody knows her as "Sis."

Her daughter, Judy Hollums, a woman about my age, said she grew up at Carr's Chapel and prefers a small church. With only 13 members then on the roll but determined to keep going, this church fit the bill.

Mrs. Williams, who said she likes to tease, asked a prospective woman minister if she played the piano, or led the singing or could preach and swat wasps at the same time.

The woman, a bit bewildered, answered "no" to each inquiry.

"Well," Mrs. Williams decided with a straight face, "I don't think you'll make it out here."

After a bit of getting acquainted, Mrs. Williams decided we ought to sing, so she hobbled up to the low stage and sat down at the piano. The five of us sang all verses of three songs out of the beloved little *Cokesbury Worship Hymnal* "which has been prepared to serve the Methodists who like to sing in church."

Not bad for Church of Christ-turned-Baptists, either.

We sang "This Is My Father's World," "In the Garden," and one I'd never heard—but a good 'un—"Till I Become Like Thee."

> *O Jesus, Saviour and my Lord.*
> *Who livest now in me*
> *Have Thou Thy way in all my life*
> *Till I become like Thee*
>
> *Like Thee . . . like Thee*
> *Till I become like Thee*
> *Have Thou Thy way in all my life*
> *Till I become like Thee*

Then it was time to pray and Mrs. Williams gave me permission to close. Those women quietly and earnestly "prayed up a storm," being careful to ask the Lord's favor on the "sick and afflicted."

One thing that doesn't change, regardless of the size of the church: There is always a group of folks who are sick and afflicted (like me, with no sense of direction).

I couldn't help but smile when Maye Williams said, "Lord, we don't know this man personally, but if Ted has invited him, he's OK with us."

What a ringing endorsement: Recommended by Ted.

I talked to them about Colossians 1:27: "Christ in you, the hope of glory," but turning that around to say that "Christ in you is glory's only hope" since God has called Christians to the ministry of reaching others.

They all stayed awake and were sweet in their praise. Best of all, they said I could come back sometime.

With Ted Wilson's endorsement, I could hardly wait.

* * *

Fred Meeks   Tim Marrow

The interesting hunt for a new preacher

It's been my honor to be on the last three pastor search committees for First Baptist Church. All have been interesting experiences to say the least.

Longtime banker-insurance man Norman Wright, who has been on the last five committees, attorneys Gene Owen, Paul Lyle, and

Lanny Voss and I were elected by the congregation to find a successor to Carlos McLeod in 1981.

About a year later, we all went to Oakwood Baptist Church in Lubbock to hear Dr. Fred Meeks. We couldn't have picked a better Sunday, as he baptized, gave the children's sermon, directed the Lord's Supper, preached an excellent message, and welcomed new members.

It's rare for a committee to see a candidate in so many roles in one visit.

Fred led our church for just over three years before joining the religion faculty at Wayland, serving there for more than 20 years.

We same five found Wayland graduate, Dr. Travis Hart, in Olton about four months later. He pastored the church for 25 years.

In 2011, Claude Lusk, Monty Bowen, Tim Hardage, Steve Olson, Debbie Meriwether, Norman, and I served on the committee that recommended Dr. Tim Morrow of First Baptist Church-West Albuquerque.

One thing about pastor search committees: They stick out like a sore thumb, even when they try to split up and look inconspicuous.

Norman, alternate Charles Bassett, and I went to Gambrell Street Baptist Church, across from Southwestern Seminary in Fort Worth, to hear Joel Gregory, who years later became pastor of the huge First Baptist Church in Dallas.

During the welcome time, an elderly woman turned and said, "We're glad to have you men today, but don't be taking our pastor." She didn't smile when she said it either.

Several weeks later, the committee went back to Gambrell Street to hear John Hatch of Tacoma, Washington, later pastor of First Baptist Church in Lake Jackson, Texas, for more than 20 years.

When we left that morning, John couldn't recall my name and said, "Good to see you again, uh, Brother Editor." I related that story to my friend Jimmy Neff, himself a Baptist minister, and ever since he has called me "Brother Editor."

That committee also made a trip to hear a young man suggested by a venerable minister from this area who cautioned, "I hear good things about him but I've never heard him preach."

Let me assure you he didn't miss a thing. The poor guy had a strained look on his face like he needed a laxative.

Furthermore, the church had died about 20 years before and nobody had told them.

Of course, hiding out in Olton was impossible, so we all sat rather uncomfortably on the back row to hear Travis Hart, who vividly recalls coming to Plainview "in view of a call." to Plainview.

The church was still doing the Living Christmas Tree, and rather large choir member Jeff Petillo accidently stepped on Travis's foot, causing him pain as he preached.

Monty, Claude, Norman, and I all went to Albuquerque on the same Sunday and spread out across the sanctuary. But Tim Marrow later told our church, "Danny was passing out bulletins for the second service."

Sometimes we had to fudge a bit when a church member might be a little too inquisitive, possibly suspecting us of being "preacher stealers."

I still chuckle about Norman's assessment of the chicken takeout I brought to a "secret" meeting of a candidate who didn't want his congregation to know he was looking at other opportunities.

"That food wasn't up to our usual high standards," Norman decided.

"Well, his wife went back for seconds so I guess it wasn't that bad," I said in self-defense.

Norman, who I have long said I'd choose as my "second daddy," and I still laugh about our committee's interview with Tim Marrow.

Each member was assigned to ask a series of questions. By the time we finished, we'd asked about everything except what size underwear Tim wears.

Norman endured about an hour or so of questions before it was his turn, and I thought his first query of Tim needed a follow-up, so I jumped in and asked another question.

Norman looked at me rather sternly and said, "Danny, do you want to do this?"

He was immediately embarrassed, but we all laughed and I said, "That's OK, Norman, my daddy talked to me like that all the time."

*   *   *

Let the "oughtness" of it motivate you

Like a lot of other folks, I had good intentions to read through the Bible, but every time I tried I got bogged down in the rules and regulations in Leviticus and the begats in Numbers in the Old Testament.

I did discover early in my college career that it is difficult to read through the entire New Testament in one morning.

On the honor system, beloved religion professor Dr. Ivyloy Bishop gave extra credit for each book read but I had procrastinated and had read only a couple of books. I think I made it through Philippians by test time.

In the early 1980s, an English preacher by the name of Dr. John Blanchard held a revival at First Baptist.

After a noon service, I confided my frustration to the minister, expecting he might pull out a bottle of magic potion, sprinkle it on me and—Praise Jehosophat!—I would zip right through the Good Book.

Instead, Dr. Blanchard said in a distinctly British voice: "Perhaps you should let the *oughtness* of it motivate you."

Or, like the Nike slogan says: "Just do it."

Many years later, I participated in a wonderful discipleship renewal weekend called "Walk to Emmaus." Several friends gave me a One-Year Bible with passages in the Old Testament, New Testament, Psalms, and Proverbs that allow you to read through the Scriptures in one year.

I thank Dr. Blanchard for his admonition and my friends for a transformational gift.

*   *   *

Mistaken identity: Good morning, Father

On Memorial Day Weekend 2002, Carolyn and I went to New York for the retirement of Frank Bennack, Jr., chief executive officer of the Hearst Corp.

It was a big shindig at Lincoln Center, including a performance by the New York Philharmonic Orchestra, a five-course dinner and a knock-'em-in-the-floor gig by the great country duo, Brooks & Dunn.

On Sunday, Carolyn and I decided to go to church. The Manhattan phone directory only listed two Southern Baptist congregations, one being Metro Baptist Church.

When I called and inquired as to the time of service and appropriate attire, a young intern from Wake Forest University in Winston-Salem, North Carolina, said the church was quite informal. Nevertheless, I wore a black pin-stripe suit with a black pullover.

The small congregation met in a former Polish-Catholic Church on West 40th in the Hell's Kitchen section of Manhattan. It was a big staging area for relief efforts following 9-11.

After the service, we were walking back to a main street where the cab let us off. A small older woman approached me and, apparently mistaking my outfit for clerical garb, said respectfully, "Good morning, Father."

I was tempted to make the sign of the cross and say, "Bless you, my child," but I just smiled and walked on.

*   *   *

Dressed like a Presbyterian

"Robed up" and looking like a Presbyterian

Drew Travis asked me to fill the pulpit for him at First Presbyterian Church several years ago.

Since Drew stood about 6-6 and weighed way better than 300 pounds, "filling the pulpit" took on a whole new meaning.

I wanted to look like a Presbyterian minister, but I knew one of Drew's robes would engulf me like the whale that swallowed Jonah. So I went to my pastor, Travis Hart, and asked if he might loan me one of the robes he wore on occasion for weddings. He even threw in a white stole.

When it was my time to preach, I started to climb the three or four steps into the pulpit but couldn't move. Second try, same results. Eerie feeling. Maybe the Lord's not happy with me trying to preach to these Presbyterians, I reasoned.

Then it dawned on me. I was standing on the "hem of the garment." I hiked my skirt and proceeded without further incident. The next time Drew invited me, I let a suit suffice.

I had one of those "small world" moments involving Drew Travis some time before that.

At a Hearst editors and publishers meeting in San Antonio, I sat on a bus with Rex Smith, editor of *The Albany Times-Union* in New York's capital city. He told me his father was a Presbyterian minister in South Dakota, and I remarked that we had a fine Presbyterian minister in Plainview.

We talked on and I said, "Drew's a great guy."

Rex turned in his seat and asked, "Are you talking about Drew Travis? I went to school with his brother at Trinity (University in San Antonio). I've been to their house in Tulia (where Drew's father, Murray, had been pastor) several times."

Drew's grandfather, Frank Travis, was pastor of First Prez (as some parishioners like to call it), in the 1950s at Eighth and Baltimore, where the Hale County Appraisal District is now located.

My dad lived at the fire station most of his senior year in Childress in the late 1930s when Frank Travis was pastor there and the church was next door. Daddy and Frank Travis played pool together at the fire station.

When Drew came to Plainview from Clovis, New Mexico, the church had been hoping to revitalize its youth program. It killed two birds with one stone since Drew and Rhonda brought along six kids.

And speaking of Presbyterians, I love the story about Ara Parseghian, sitting across the desk from Theodore Hesburgh, the president of Notre Dame, when Ara came from Northwestern to coach the Irish in 1964.

Hesburgh had a frown on his face as he perused the new coach's resumé.

"Having trouble with Par-see-ghun?" asked Ara.

"No," said Hesburgh, "Presbyterian."

*   *   *

Methodist women have a distinctive look?

My wife has often said she wants to be a Methodist before she goes on to her Great Reward "because Methodist women are so pretty."

Maybe they also have a certain "look."

Several years ago I was at Kimbrough Stadium in Canyon for a PHS playoff game, and Childress had just finished its game with Spearman.

Wondering about the health of a cousin who grew up in Childress, I intercepted an elderly woman and asked, "Ma'am, would you happen to be a Methodist?"

"Why, yes," she said, taken back a bit, "why do you ask?"

"Do you know Louise Andrews?"

"Why, yes, she's in my Sunday School class. But how did you know I was a Methodist?"

"Oh, I don't know. You just look like a Methodist to me. Do you know how my cousin Gene is doing?"

She gave me a report and went off chuckling, probably still puzzling over whether Methodist women have a distinctive look.

Speaking of Methodist women, I fondly remember regular visits on Saturday to the Knoohuizen Building at Ninth and Broadway where my dad had his chiropractic office for several years.

Mother would take me, my brother Guy, and sister Marihelen to see Berta Bitler, whose husband, Harry, was the bookkeeper for W.T. Cain Motor Co. Sometimes we'd get a special treat of going to Blasingame's restaurant on Broadway for a piece of pie.

Mrs. Bitler, a slender, gray-haired, genteel woman from Georgia, would sit at her upright piano and play and sing hymns for us.

One I will never forget. It's variously titled, "I Am a Stranger Here," and "The King's Business." I discovered years later while reviving the Royal Ambassadors missions program for boys for First Baptist Church that it was the organization's theme song.

> I am a stranger here, within a foreign land;
> My home is far away, upon a golden strand;
> Ambassador to be of realms beyond the sea,
> I'm here on business for my King.

This is the message that I bring,
A message angels fain would sing:
"Oh, be ye reconciled,"
Thus saith my Lord and King,
"Oh, be ye reconciled to God."

Mother tried every way she could to ascertain Mrs. Bitler's age—a very closely-guarded secret among many Southern women—even sneaking a peek in her Bible . . . but no luck.

Let's just say she was a youthful-looking Methodist.

                        *   *   *

Sliding safely into "home" at church

When I was a kid, our family went to quarterly "zone meetings" at church—a potluck dinner and maybe some words of admonition and encouragement from an elder like Herbert Godfrey or Dee Martin or Kelly Newman, who often preached when we were between ministers.

While the adults were upstairs, several of us kids would head downstairs to the auditorium, illuminated only by the light beaming through the "cry room" windows.

Auditorium is what some high-falutin' church folks call the "sanctuary." We also called that place where everyone gathers to talk the "vestibule" rather than the "foyer." And, no, we had no earthly idea what a narthex was.

Ninth and Columbia had nice, tight-weave carpet. It was extra good for practicing sliding for us wannabe baseball stars. And, because the aisles were long, you could get a good running start before curling your left leg under your right and scooting several feet onto a make-believe base—a hymnal perhaps.

Some folks may have thought we were not being respectful of the Lord's House. But I always felt He might be smiling since someone was putting the facility to good use on some day other than Sunday or Wednesday.

I always felt safe in church . . . and safe at "home."

* * *

And please bless Tex Ritter while you're at it

I've always maintained that most people grow up praying prayers they've heard other people pray . . . sometimes using arcane language in the process.

Folks my age are known to mix Elizabethan terms and modern language: "Lord, thank Thee for Thy goodness and we pray Your blessings on all of Your people," abandoning *Thy* in the latter part of the petition.

When I was a kid at Ninth and Columbia Church of Christ, W. C. Boyd, the local Conoco jobber, would pray, "Would'st Thou bless us," and old Brother Paul Roach, a Watkins products dealer, finished his prayers with a curious request, "Own us and crown us the morning of the resurrection."

I can assure you I never prayed like that.

Raymond Akin, a farmer-auctioneer who was emcee of just about every program in the area for years—including the long-standing Edmonson Farm Dinner—took the biblical admonition to "come boldly before the throne of grace" literally. Kind of like "Lord, this is Raymond speaking. Are you listening?"

Raymond liked to gig his non-Church of Christ friends: "I was a Presbyterian 'til I learned to read."

Frequently, the Lord was implored to "take us safely to our respective places of abode."

For some reason, Baptists pray what I call "Just Prayers": "Lord, just bless us today and just keep our families safe and just heal the sick and just let us serve you each day." He is a just God, after all.

Here's a classic reminder that you should know who doesn't feel comfortable praying in public: Not long after Fred Meeks became pastor of First Baptist Church in the early 1980s, he had a men's prayer breakfast at the Holiday Inn and called on farmer Woody Harper to pray.

I think Woody got "Dear Lord" out and then stammered and stuttered a few seconds before declaring aloud, "Lord, you know I'm not any good at this."

Coincidentally, at a Wednesday night prayer meeting several months ago, Fred Meeks started a prayer for the sick and bereaved, "Dear Father, you know my memory's not what it used to be . . ." realizing he couldn't remember everyone's name that had been mentioned.

I never think of prayers, though, without recalling the time Tex Williams of the Sunset School of Preaching in Lubbock, came to preach at Ninth and Columbia.

An old brother concluded the service and asked the Lord to "Please bless Tex Ritter."

You could hear people all over the auditorium stifling a laugh due to the inadvertent reference to a cowboy actor and singer.

Oh, well, God bless him, too.

*   *   *

Familiar prayer: Lord, lead, guide, and direct us

One of my favorite stories about prayer involves my good friend Mike Parker.

Mike was called on in Optimist Club to invoke the blessing and finished by saying words I have heard hundreds of times in church: "Lead, guide, and direct us" or even "Guard, guide, and direct us."

I told Mike rather sternly (though tongue-in-cheek), "You don't need to say all three words—they all mean the same thing. Just pick one."

I had Mike so flustered, he started the pledge to the flag: "Our precious Heavenly Fath . . ."

I wrote a column about it and it also was published in *The Baptist Standard* newspaper for which I was serving as a director.

A good brother in Dripping Springs wrote to say, "Mr. Andrews, I enjoyed your piece on prayer, but let me point out that God does, indeed, lead, guide, and direct us."

He furnished numerous scriptures on how God does all three.

And aren't we glad he does?

*　　*　　*

Enjoying the great songs of the church

Having grown up in the Church of Christ and now being a Baptist for 40 years, I have been exposed to a lot of great hymns and what are known as "praise songs."

Sometimes an old hymn we sang when I was a kid (and probably dropped when a new hymnal came out) will come to mind.

Herbert Godfrey, a longtime barber at the Hilton Hotel; Riley Armstrong, an oil and butane jobber who was a regular in the Lions' Minstrel Shows; and Lloyd Stone, a fertilizer salesman, were the main "song leaders" at Ninth and Columbia Church of Christ.

Herbert's favorite song seemed to be "Trust and Obey"; Riley liked "One Day"; and Lloyd, who never raised his hand to "beat time," frequently led "Faith is the Victory."

My Daddy couldn't sing a lick but he loved a song called "Lead Me Gently Home Father."

> *Lead me gently home, Father,*
> *Lead me gently home,*
> *When life's toils are ended*
> *And parting days have come;*
> *Sin no more shall tempt me*
> *Ne'er from Thee I'll roam,*
> *If Thou'lt only lead me, Father,*
> *Lead me gently home.*

I suppose "How Great Thou Art," "Amazing Grace," "In the Garden" and "Because He Lives" are still favorites of older folks since you hear them at a lot of funerals.

I have several "favorites" but it seems to me that anytime and wherever this song is sung, it is "lifted" with a great deal of conviction.

> *When peace, like a river, attendeth my way,*
> *When sorrows like sea billows roll;*
> *Whatever my lot, Thou hast taught me to say,*
> *It is well, it is well with my soul.*
>
> *Refrain:*
> *It is well (it is well), with my soul (with my soul),*
> *It is well, it is well with my soul.*
>
> *Though Satan should buffet, though trials should come,*
> *Let this blest assurance control,*
> *That Christ hath regarded my helpless estate,*
> *And hath shed His own blood for my soul.*

My sin—oh, the bliss of this glorious thought!—
My sin, not in part but the whole,
Is nailed to the cross, and I bear it no more,
Praise the Lord, praise the Lord, O my soul!

And Lord, haste the day when the faith shall be sight,
The clouds be rolled back as a scroll;
The trump shall resound, and the Lord shall descend,
Even so, it is well with my soul.

*　　*　　*

Every church has its characters: We sure did

I guess every church, regardless of size, has a character or two.

We did at Ninth and Columbia Church of Christ when I was a kid. Sadly, Louella Dennis's elevator didn't go all the way to the top.

My good friend June Wells, the unofficial church historian, recalls that Mrs. Dennis had the disconcerting habit of pinching people of all ages as the spirit moved her, which it often did.

Each Sunday, just as communion was about to be observed, Mrs. Dennis, a thin, redhaired woman, would rattle her keys, jump up, and head for the exit.

The old building had "saloon doors" (forgive me, Lord) which the ushers would open wide when they saw her coming.

One morning, when my mother was home recuperating after giving birth to my sister, Daddy was seated near the aisle with my brother and me beside him.

Mrs. Dennis stopped abruptly at our pew and told my father rather forcefully, "Those aren't your kids."

She didn't wait for a response, but my quick-witted dad likely would have told her, "Oh, yes, they are. Nobody else would claim them."

We also had a tall, rawboned fellow who seemed to walk the aisle every Sunday asking for prayer. I'm sure everyone wondered, "What's wrong with Joe? (not his real name)"

I've thought about that a lot through the years and wondered if Joe never got hold of God's grace in his life or maybe he was more sensitive to his own shortcomings than the rest of us.

*   *   *

Sabbath sermon: He be good to me, I be good to Him

In the late 1970s, I went a couple of times with the Wayland track team to the Border Olympics in Laredo, one of the premiere meets in the state.

On one trip, the legendary/infamous "Blue Goose" mini-bus broke down in Junction and the school had to send new transportation to get us on to the border community.

Vernon Hilliard, namesake for the "Wayland Bowl" on campus, was serving as athletic adviser at the time and insisted I attend a luncheon for coaches at Laredo Junior College.

A prodigious storyteller, the former Plainview High football coach of the late 1930s was not spinning a yarn when he said the steaks were the biggest I would ever see. They looked like a roast.

My good friend and Wayland colleague Danny Murphree joined me for a walk downtown, even taking my picture with a big sombrero on.

We wandered into an electronics shop and I struck up a conversation with the owner who had migrated from Brooklyn, New York, about 20 years before.

He mentioned that he was Jewish so I asked if he was Hasidic, knowing from his absence of facial hair and long locks he was not.

"No," he said, apparently about to allude to his lack of strong adherence to his faith, "He be good to me, I be good to Him. He be bad to me, I be bad to Him."

I thought, "Sounds like most of us, regardless of our faith. We think if God is being good to us, we'll go to church, act right, give our money. But, if our judgment is that God's not being "good to me," the slightest issue gets us down, a sniffle keeps us out of church, and the pocketbook—if ever it was much open—closes tighter than a drum."

That fellow preached a sermon on a Sabbath eve afternoon and didn't even know it.

* * *

"Pastor, I sure was glad you didn't go fishin.'"

Some of the funniest stories I've ever heard were told by preachers about their pastoral experiences.

Travis Hart, pastor of First Baptist Church for 25 years, says when served the small congregation at Jermyn, between Olney and Seymour, while a student at Southwestern Seminary in Fort Worth, the first thing he asked, "Is there anything I need to know?"

"Yes," said a member of the pulpit committee. "Don't call on Brother So-And-So to pray because he prays forever."

When I heard that, I immediately thought of Fred Wiginton, one of our deacons when I was a kid. Fred worked for Pioneer Natural Gas. I wouldn't be so unkind as to say he was full of hot air, but, man, he seemed to take the biblical admonition "pray without ceasing" literally.

I think Joe Don Martin, who was rich enough to have his own wristwatch, once timed him at 15 minutes, and that seemed like the proverbial eternity.

Anyway, the first time Travis was going to preside over the Lord's Supper, his wife Janie had pressed and starched the table cloth, and the bread and juice were in their shiny containers.

Just as Travis lifted the lid covering the communion "crackers," he said, "I know the air sucked right out of my lungs." In the tray was a generous array of rat pills.

"All I could think of was, 'Brother So-and-So (the aforementioned long-winded congregant) would you lead us in prayer?'"

As the man launched into his oration, Travis gingerly picked the pills out of the tray.

R.L. Kirk, former minister of First United Methodist Church, said while pastoring a small church that he took the top off the bread tray and discovered it was empty. He whispered to a staff member, "Pray until I get back," then hurried next door to the parsonage to fetch some crackers.

Jack Bauer, former minister of St. Paul Lutheran Church, told me he pastored a small congregation of black Lutherans in Houston.

One morning, as he administered communion, the wafer slid off his finger and down the blouse of a well-endowed parishioner.

After the service, she told him with a wink, "Pastor, I sure was glad you didn't go fishin' today."

*   *   *

Travis Hart

Pastor, you're not as hot as you think you are

I need to relate two other stories Travis Hart told about his time in Jermyn.

He said about 20 people would show up on a good Sunday at the little white wooden church where ceiling fans bestirred the thick summer heat.

One morning, Travis asked a rather buxom member who drove a green Chevy Biscayne that had been sideswiped, forcing her to enter and exit by the passenger door, "Mrs. Smith, could you open one of those windows back there? I'm pretty hot."

"Pastor," she responded with arms crossed, "you're not near as hot as you think you are."

After church, Travis said to her, "I'm not sure how I should take what you said this morning."

To which she replied, "Pastor, you take it any way you want."

Travis and his wife Janie frequently rode into nearby Jacksboro for Sunday lunch with Spurgeon and Lorena Cooper.

One Sunday, in a bit of irritation that several church members had nodded off during his sermon, Travis briefly scolded them, without calling names, at the end of the service.

As they drove to Jacksboro, Mr. Cooper said, "Travis, I understand what you said this morning about people sleeping. It's rude. But some of those people have worked very hard this week and they're worn out. I don't think you should ever do that again."

And Travis said, "I never did that again."

*   *   *

Gene Louder, The Reluctant Baptizer

Joe Weldon, a semi-retired Baptist preacher, has some great stories.

Joe, who has pastored the church at South Plains northeast of Lockney for several years, left the staff of Parkview Baptist Church here in the early 1960s to go to Kelton, near Shamrock in the Panhandle, for his first pastorate.

About the same time, Gene Louder, now retired and living in Kress where he pastored First United Methodist Church, was assigned to his denomination's ministry there.

Joe says the Baptists in that burg that included the school, a store, the two churches, and a few homes would have a revival every year and some of the Methodists would "caravan" the block or so up the street.

"Every year someone from the Methodist church would get saved and I'd tell them they needed to go tell their pastor they needed to be biblically baptized by immersion," Joe related. "So, several of them would come to our church about 2:30 on Sunday afternoon for the baptism. Gene hated to baptize but I told him we had to go by the Bible."

One summer during Vacation Bible School, twin girls from the Methodist side made professions of faith and dutifully followed Joe's instructions to tell their preacher.

Knowing Louder's disdain for dunking rather than pouring, Joe saved up all the ice cubes he could on Saturday. When he looked down the road and saw the Methodists about to head to his church, he left the parsonage next door and dumped all the ice cubes into the baptistry.

Gene Louder, a good sport, began to sputter with laughter when he stepped into the baptistry in Joe's borrowed waders. When he reached to help one of the twins into the water, she spied the ice cubes and balked. They pulled back and forth as Joe exited his back row seat, stifling laughter but unsure how his prank would end.

Whatever, he figured he would be in "hot water" with his minister buddy.

*   *   *

A great prayer: "Let us win some by joy"

One of the best things I ever heard anyone pray was a request by Browning Ware, then pastor of First Baptist Church of Austin, probably 30 years ago.

Browning, whose brother Broadman at one time was minister of music at College Heights Baptist Church, across the street from Wayland, was a rather practical man who never seemed too "preachery," even around a lot of other preachers.

He and I served together on the board of the *Baptist Standard*, a state denominational newspaper, for several years. I had the honor of serving on that board for 18 years with gifted editors Presnall Wood, Toby Druin, and Marv Knox.

One day, Browning prayed: "Lord, let us live our lives in such a way that we may win some by joy."

He didn't mean if he go around with a smile on our face, or laugh a lot that people will automatically become Christians if they do the same thing.

But he felt we have a lot better chance of drawing others to faith if our lives reflect happiness rather than the down-in-the-mouth countenance far too many Christians manifest.

That reminds me of that wonderful old gospel song.

> Give the world a smile each day
> Helping someone on life's way
> From the paths of sin
> Bring the wanderer in
> To the Master's fold today.

Like the Bible says, "A merry heart doeth good like a medicine."

*   *   *

This is a *North* Dallas church

Some folks get pretty territorial about their church and their place in it.

For 17 years, James Pleitz was pastor of Park Cities Baptist Church in a very upscale area of Dallas.

He told me that an older woman came to him and said, "Pastor, there's something happening in this church I don't like. People are joining from all over Dallas. This is a *North* Dallas church."

The stories are plentiful about visitors coming into a church and finding a seat, only to be informed in no uncertain terms by a member of the congregation: "You're sitting in my pew," or "I always sit here" (and I plan to sit here today if you'll move your carcass).

Of course, it was common in churches back East for families to purchase a pew and woe to anyone encroaching thereupon.

I was making announcements at Ninth and Columbia Church of Christ one morning in the early 1970s and remarked: "The elders have asked everyone to move a little closer to the front and the middle so the fellowship and the singing will be better."

I should have left well enough alone, but couldn't resist adding, "If you don't think you can move, we'll get Brother Vanderpoel (local jeweler Charles Vanderpoel) to engrave a plaque to put on your pew."

There was only a tittering of laughter. I had quit preaching and gone to meddling.

*   *   *

We haven't taken out a membership yet

Different churches have different ways of accepting new members.

Methodists take newcomers on "transfer of membership." Baptist "move their letter" from their previous place of worship. Church of Christ folks "place membership." Lutherans transfer their letter. Some "walk the aisle" to do so; others meet with the minister or maybe a committee or church leadership and that decision is then made public.

My late father-in-law, O. E. Fuson, a former Baptist minister, said he visited a man and asked if he was a member of a local church. The man said no, and when O. E. asked how long he had lived in the community, the man said 40 years.

"Why don't you move your letter and join the church here?" O. E. inquired.

"Oh, I couldn't move my letter and hurt that little ol' church," the man responded.

Terminology for the salvation experience also varies: Got saved, trusted Christ, obeyed the gospel, gave his life to the Lord, made the Good Confession, saw the Light, found religion.

I'll never forget "knocking doors" with Kelly Carl Newman, our "summer youth minister" (a post later held by future missionary Kenny Sinclair) in the early 1960s. When one of the ladies of the house found out we were from the Church of Christ, she politely said we wouldn't have much response there: "We're dyed-in-the-wool Baptists, born of preachers and deacons."

A fellow who lived across the street from 10ᵗʰ and Utica Church of Christ, showed us a lot of books and claimed to be an expert on the cosmos.

I was visiting for First Baptist Church with my second-grade teacher, Hazel O'Bannon. We knocked on a door out in Hillcrest and a lady told us she and her husband had moved several years earlier from Dimmitt.

"Have you joined a church here yet?" Mrs. O'Bannon inquired.

"No," the woman explained, "we haven't taken out a membership yet," as if the prospects of that included payment up front.

Years ago, when my brother lived in San Antonio, he joined Trinity Baptist Church on "statement"—his profession that he was a Christian but not a Baptist.

I always said when they asked him what his statement was, Guy looked around the sanctuary and told the minister, "Man, this is a *nice* church."

*   *   *

Children's church: A risky thing to do

Stories are rife (and some unrepeatable) about responses kids make to ministers during "children's sermon" time in church.

I always cringe when someone asks innocent children a question that has the potential to unravel the congregation. Something like, "What kind of noises do your brother or sister make that bother you?"

I'll let your imagination take over here.

On the tamer end, a pastor of a very traditional church asked the youngsters, "What comes after the Gospel reading?" hoping someone would respond, "The sermon."

Instead, one little boy shouted, "Donuts!"

While he was pastor of First Baptist Church-Plainview, Travis Hart did a great job with the children's sermon. Some folks would admit they liked some of them better than the "real sermon."

Travis usually brought a "visual" to illustrate his point, including a huge ladder he climbed up on to tell the story about doing some repair on his office-workshop out by the airport.

One day he was working on the roof when the ladder he propped against the building fell, leaving him stranded. He waved at several cars passing by and the drivers, thinking Travis was being friendly, just waved and drove on. Finally, someone came along and helped him get down.

I have never heard a congregation explode in laughter as ours did one morning when Travis asked the youngsters gathered on the platform, "If you could change one thing about yourself, what would it be?"

"I'd like to change my eyes," a boy decided.

"I'd like to change my hair," a little girl announced.

After a brief pause, Timothy Eaves, a precocious but slow-talking fellow, drawled: "I'd like to change my mind."

It took a while for order to be restored.

* * *

A visit with the Deity . . . well sort of
(I wrote this column in 2006.)

I was sad to learn of the passing of George Plagenz, whose religion column, "Saints and Sinners," has appeared weekly in *The Herald* for more than 20 years.

Mr. Plagenz, 82, was an ordained minister in the Episcopal Church but told me in a conversation that he leaned more to the Unitarian Church.

He called me from his home in Columbus, Ohio, about 10 years ago, thanking me for a letter I had sent him in 1985. He called two or three months ago to say that he had just come across the letter again and wanted to know if he had written me.

I assured him he had.

My letter had complimented one of his columns. He had called but missed me, so he dropped me the note with this admonition: "Write again whenever the Spirit giveth utterance."

I decided to call him and we had nice visit, reminiscing about our only other phone conversation in 1982, when I did a piece about talking with the Son of God.

I hasten to explain.

I had called Plagenz to see if he knew a Eugene Changey (pronounced Chain-gee) who had been writing lengthy letters and sending books to me (and others in the media) for several years. The letters always started: "As Almighty God, I greet you."

If that doesn't get your attention, nothing will.

His letters usually were about peace and the nuclear arms race and ended something like: "I bid you a fond anon. This letter is signed by my Son, Eugene."

When I got a letter saying, "As the waning days slip silently by, My Son and I look forward to early retirement—near the end of this year, 1982," I began to worry. If *they* were retiring, what impact would that have on the rest of us?

Mr. Changey, a turret lathe operator in a Cleveland suburb, was seeking financial help to publish another book (he wrote nine) and admitted "the meager assistance from Social Security, a small bank account of $4,000 and a paltry pension is not enough to carry on Our Works in years to come."

Plagenz, based in Cleveland at the time, said he, too, had been receiving the same items for years and that Changey lived in nearby Maple Heights, Ohio.

I reached Mr. Changey by phone one afternoon and we had a pleasant—not to mention fascinating—visit. He was quick to point out that only he (not God) was retiring.

Answering my questions, which I posed respectfully—somewhat like the ministers quizzing George Burns in the movie *Oh, God*—Mr. Changey revealed in a grandfatherly voice with a distinct Eastern European accent:

"God wandered through time after Jesus died until we met (40 years earlier) in the corridors of a mental hospital in Cleveland. I began to hear voices and actually it was God talking. It's all explained in the book." He said God told him who he was and "I take his word for it." Or as George Burns said on the witness stand: "So help Me Me."

He said God didn't have another name like he did: "No man knoweth who the Father is and vice-versa."

He hadn't gone to church in years because he was "too busy with my mailing list (which included about 2,500 names). I have to work every day but Saturday and Sunday, you know."

He was not married: "If I was married, my father would disown me," he said emphatically. Given his age at the time (62), I'm pretty sure he meant God.

He said he thought TV preachers were "like magicians."

He didn't read the Bible much because he was too busy with that mailing list.

He admitted the men at the plant were a little uncomfortable working next to the Deity, "but everybody at the shop knows me. I've been giving them my letters for a long time."

He said God spoke to him in an audible voice: "I just let my mind become a total blank and he speaks to me." (If that's the criteria, I should be hearing from him constantly.)

He said God's main message to man was, "Bring peace on earth and cut out these fearsome nuclear endeavors" (we were still hotly involved in the Cold War with the Soviet Union back then).

I also asked him when he thought the world would end.

"The world is on a decline, but I have no indication. If things get any worse, it will come to an end."

They have; it hasn't—so far.

I sent Mr. Changey a copy of my column and he wrote back to thank me, adding, "However, I detected a note of skepticism."

I tried to find him again in Maple Heights a decade ago, but the operator said there was no listing for a Eugene Changey. I found out later he died at age 74 in 1994.

Perhaps he has gone on down the corridors of time.

I bid him a fond anon and hope his soul is at peace.

And George Plagenz, too.

*   *   *

Say, brother, is that in the Bible?

Rob Winkler, former associate pastor of Trinity Fellowship Church in Plainview, told a great story about an old minister preaching away one night at Trinity Church in Lubbock.

He drew his text from the Old Testament book of Numbers when the donkey a man by the name of Balaam was riding veered off into a field, crushed his foot against a wall, and lay down in the middle of the road because he spied an angel with sword in hand.

Three times Balaam struck the donkey, who was given power by God to rebuke his master for not doing God's will.

"Brethren," the old preacher said forcefully, "if God can speak out of Balaam's ass, he can speak out of yours!"

It was a good thing no one was drinking Coke or milk at that moment.

That reminds me of the story told about W. A. Criswell, pastor of First Baptist Church in Dallas for more than 50 years.

"Oh, I went moose hunting in Alaska recently," he said at service. "And we shot the biggest moose you've ever seen. The first night we had moose steak, and the second night we had moose stew, and the third night we had spaghetti and moose balls."

The audience broke up laughing and the somewhat naïve Dr. Criswell asked seriously, "Did I say something funny?"

* * *

Time to get your 'church' on, sister

My daughter, Kayla Michelle Peltoma, was a college housemate of Kayla Michelle Waters of Brownfield. They later owned a house together in Dallas.

When my youngest son, Brad, married Kayla Prather of Levelland, we designated them as Big Kayla (Waters), Little Kayla (Andrews), and Tiny Kayla (Prather).

Not long ago, while visiting in Dallas, we went to pick up Kayla Waters for morning worship. She lives in a gated community, and my son-in-law, Craig Peltoma, told the black female guard we were there to pick up Kayla Waters and "please tell her to get her 'church' on."

The guard doubled up laughing. When I kiddingly told her we were going to sing a favorite among black churches, "Wade in the Water," she said with a grin, "Gonna have a baptizin', huh?"

Then she added, "Say a prayer for me."

We did, 'cause we had our "church" on.

* * *

Thanks for letting us wake up in our right minds

Arvadie Thompson, a wonderful black man who lived into his 90s, helped start the Lone Star Baptist Church at Hale Center.

"The house we met in, you could see the ground through the cracks in the floor," he related.

Arvadie was one of the deacons who led the devotional at the start of the annual Black Awareness and Martin Luther King Celebration held in Plainview for more than 20 years.

I'll never forget Arvadie's word of praise: "Lord, thank you for lettin' us wake up in our right minds this mornin' and that our bed wadn't our coolin' board."

*   *   *

Did you mean Lodebar or Gotebo?

Several years ago, my dear friend Ron Brunson, who I call "the most Jesus man I know" due to his gentle spirit and love for and application of God's Word, asked if I would speak to his senior adults at New Covenant Church.

I told the story from 2 Samuel of Mephibosheth, the son of David's dear friend Jonathan and grandson of his nemesis, King Saul, being brought from a place of outcasts called Lodebar to live in the palace when David became king.

The next week, I ran into Ron and he asked a rather strange question: "Danny, are you open to rebuke?"

I said, "I guess so," and Ron continued, "Did you know you said Mephibosheth lived at Gotebo?"

That's a wide spot in the road in western Oklahoma that the late Plainview school superintendent Lamont Veatch always claimed he was from.

"Naw, not really," I protested.

"Yes, sir, you sure did," the preacher said with a big laugh.

I didn't argue with Ron and followed the admonition of an old hymn: "just to take him at his word."

*   *   *

What is a Deist? Let me tell you

Some people claim a number of the Founding Fathers were Deists who believed that God created the world but leaves humans to their own devices.

Lee Strobel, a former legal writer for the Chicago *Tribune*, was an atheist who came to Christ a number of years ago and is now one of the leading defenders of the faith.

He has served on the staff of Bill Hybels' Willow Creek Church in suburban Chicago and at the even larger Saddleback Church in California pastored by Rick Warren. He now is on staff at Houston Baptist University.

Several years ago, he and another apologist, Mark Mittelberg, were speaking at a conference in Atlanta and went to eat at a Cracker Barrel restaurant.

Just as they passed a young couple sitting in rocking chairs, Strobel thought the young lady asked her companion, "What is a Deist?"

Well, Strobel turned on his heels because they had just been contending that God is personally involved in our lives. He went on for several minutes and then asked, "Young lady, do you have any questions?"

Mittelberg leaned over to him and whispered, "I think she said, '*Buenos dias*.'"

*   *   *

Preaching icon Billy Graham: "Amen, brother!"

One of the great "modern" heroes of the Christian faith has been evangelist Billy Graham.

I attended the Billy Graham Crusade at Texas Tech's football stadium in 1975 and remember all the excitement about him coming to Lubbock. He was only 57 then and in the prime of his ministry.

The night I attended he spoke on the subject of "Jaws," drawing on the title of the blockbuster shark movie that had just come out, alluding to the destructive power of sin.

Also, that night, Baylor football coach Grant Teaff, whose team had won the Southwest Conference the previous season for the first time in 50 years, gave an excellent testimony.

I've always had special appreciation for Grant Teaff because he preached the morning I joined First Baptist. He had coached the night before in the Coaches All-America Game played in Lubbock for several years.

Grant and his wife, the former Donnell Phillips, a PHS and Texas Tech cheerleader and the second Plainview High School Queen in 1952, cut a radio promo for me when I was United Way chairman in the early 1990s.

Baylor played Penn State in the Cotton Bowl the previous January, and Billy Graham was in attendance, sitting much closer to the field than I did. He had just begun wearing his hair long as had become popular at the time.

I also heard Dr. Graham speak at the Baptist General Convention of Texas in the old Heart O' Texas Coliseum in Waco in 1981. A man in the upper balcony stood up and shouted something as Dr. Graham was preaching. He drew a laugh from the audience when he replied, "Amen, brother!"

The late Myrtie Mills, a dear friend of mine, grew up in Crowell, and H.A. Hamblen, the father of singer-entertainer Stuart Hamblen, who wrote "It Is No Secret What God Can Do," "This Old House," and "Until Then," was her pastor in the 1920s. Stuart Hamblen came to Christ during Dr. Graham's legendary tent revival in Los Angeles in 1949 and encouraged folks through his radio program to attend the crusade.

Also, William Randolph Hearst, head of the media empire that owns the Plainview paper, was so impressed with the young evangelist that he sent a message to all of his editors urging them to "Puff Graham"—give him plenty of good publicity.

I've enjoyed watching the "Billy Graham Classics" on the Trinity Broadcasting Network and reading several of his books.

The late James Thomas, who was publisher of *The Plainview Daily Herald* from 1979–89, and his wife Polly were excited to meet Billy and Ruth Graham as they all waited for a ferry to the Statue of Liberty for a celebration at which Dr. Graham was speaking in the early 1980s. Their grandsons went to school together in Boone, North Carolina.

James said a Methodist pastor in Boone wasn't too unhappy to see a big snowstorm hit the area one Saturday since he had had a busy week and hadn't had much time to prepare a sermon. He anticipated a small crowd but was a bit unnerved to see the evangelist and his grandson come in and sit on the back row.

I suspect that Billy Graham graciously uttered, "Amen, brother!"— verbally or otherwise—a time or two during that message.

*   *   *

Combining my natural with God's supernatural

It was my privilege in 2010 to go with a group of about 65 members of the First Baptist Church Worship Choir and spouses on a mission trip to New York.

We worked with Metro World Child (formerly Metro Ministries) in the tough Bushwick neighborhood of Brooklyn. Metro was founded about 35 years ago by Bill Wilson, who was abandoned by his mother on the streets of Pinellas Park, Florida, at age 11.

A stranger took him in and out of the pain of that experience Wilson started a ministry that does "Saturday Sunday School" for about 20,000 kids a week in the five New York boroughs.

He's been shot, stabbed, and robbed in doing his ministry that has branched out to major cities in the United States and around the world.

Wilson spends about 50 weeks a year on the road raising money and has been featured on several major network programs. He was in town when we were there and even drove one of the 47 buses—26 owned by Metro—the ministry uses to pick up kids in a 3-mile radius of their buildings.

The ministry is operated by a staff of about 150, supplemented by young people who come from all over the world to learn how to do such work in their cities, and by volunteers like us.

After getting a rare opportunity to hear the famed Brooklyn Tabernacle Choir in rehearsal on Wednesday night (we attended church there on Sunday and also sang at the cavernous St. John the Divine Church in the afternoon), we set out the next morning by subway for Metro's location.

We split up into groups to clean a parking lot, mow tall grass, prepare backpacks for youngsters when they start school, and other duties.

A huge task was to move a great deal of furniture donated by major companies up several flights of stairs in an old hospital the ministry had acquired. Staffers said we saved them three weeks of work. An impromptu collection among our group resulted in about $500 to purchase weedeaters and other needed equipment.

After a free day on Friday that allowed me to take a tour of the Hearst Building, ride the subway to Coney Island to enjoy a famous Nathan's Hot Dog, and see the Yankees play the Mets in Yankee Stadium, our group journeyed back to Metro on Saturday.

We served as chaperones on the buses and sat with the generally well-behaved youngsters as they attended a lively Sunday School program of music and a Bible lesson before getting a hot dog lunch to take home. This scenario was repeated three or four times that day.

I asked a Metro staffer named Bob—proudly wearing the Tilley hat given to him by Dr. Gary Manning, former Wayland religion professor—if the ministry to so many children wasn't physically and emotionally exhausting.

He made as profound a statement as I have ever heard: "Yes, but I'm able to do it when I combine my natural with God's supernatural."

I think we folks from Plainview did the same thing.

* * *

The last we'll see of this Jesus fellow

(I wrote this column for Easter Sunday, 2003.)

By JOHN THE JOURNALIST
Jerusalem Post Staff Writer

JERUSALEM—A 33-year-old itinerant preacher, who claimed to be the Messiah and "King of the Jews," was executed here Friday afternoon.

Jesus of Nazareth, a carpenter until his public preaching and teaching ministry began a little over three years ago, died about 3 p.m.

He was crucified outside the city on a hill known as Golgotha—Place of the Skull—where many have met a similar fate. Two men charged with several thefts were crucified with him.

"I've seen several of these crucifixions, but the image of that man Jesus, a good and innocent fellow, hanging there between those two no-goods, was something I'll never forget," one elderly man said with a tinge of sadness in his voice as he stroked his white beard.

Eyewitnesses reported that Jesus spoke several times during the agonizing ordeal and finally shouted, "It is finished!" just before he died.

Coincidentally, the entire region was blanketed in darkness and an earthquake rumbled through the region, just after he spoke those words.

Longtime weather observers and seismologists said neither event had been forecast.

Officials at the temple reported no great damage from the earthquake other than a mysterious tear from top to bottom of the curtain in a special area known as the "Holy of Holies."

A signboard, placed over Jesus' cross on orders from Pontius Pilate, Roman governor of this region, said "The King of the Jews."

A number of priests, elders, and other representatives of the local Jewish leadership objected to the sign, but Pilate's response was terse and typical of the plain-spoken politician: "What I have written, I have written."

A source close to the palace said Pilate was miffed with the Jewish leaders for demanding the death of a man he thought to be innocent.

"They brought this man, Jesus, to Pilate early Friday morning, saying he was blaspheming God, stirring up insurrection against the government, stuff like that," said the source, commenting on condition that he not be identified.

"Pilate did his best to pacify them and get them to take some other action, but he finally gave in to their demands to crucify the Galilean. Sometimes you just get boxed into a corner.

"Pilate knew it was customary at the Passover to let a prisoner go free, and he even offered to give them Barabbas, you know, that guy who really has been stirring up trouble against the government. He had to be happy, not to mention shocked, when they cut him loose and took Jesus instead," the source said.

The Nazarene began his public ministry more than three years ago near the Jordan River, apparently succeeding his cousin, another "roving evangelist" by the name of John the Baptist. A *Post* regional correspondent reported at the time that John the Baptist introduced Jesus to his audiences with a loud cry of "Behold, the Lamb of God who takes away the sin of the world!" and even baptized Jesus in the Jordan.

Numerous miracles have been attributed to Jesus, including turning water into wine, walking on water, healing blind, lame and leprous people, and reportedly raising several from the dead. In fact, a number of witnesses have sworn to the veracity of the story that he brought back to life a good friend, Lazarus, a few days ago in the community of Bethany.

Jewish leaders made no secret of their contempt for the charismatic, yet humble young man. While he taught in the temple—often preaching love instead of tradition—they tried to trick him with a number of questions. But he deftly answered each one or left them speechless with his responses.

However, his claims to be the Son of God and the Messiah and his assertion that he had the power to forgive sin particularly infuriated the Jewish high court, the Sanhedrin, which was involved yesterday in the court proceeding.

(*Post* legal columnist Artimaeus the Attorney has a special report on page 7A detailing the proceedings against Jesus. He contends a number of civil and religious protocols were violated before Pilate acquiesced to demands to crucify the accused.)

After a late evening dinner with about a dozen of his followers in the upper room of a local residence, Jesus was arrested by authorities Thursday night in the Garden of Gethsemane where he had gone to pray. One of his own men, Judas Iscariot—apparently the treasurer for the group--identified Jesus to the authorities by kissing him on the cheek.

The *Post* was unable to reach Iscariot for comment.

After the Nazarene was publicly scourged and taunted by the palace guards, he was forced to carry his own cross through the streets.

Typical of crucifixions—the most brutal of all deaths meted out by the government here—there was considerable taunting of Jesus and the two thieves by onlookers.

One man shouted, "He saved others, let him save himself!" Another yelled, "If you're the son of God, come down from the cross!"

That brought a chorus of laughter and jeers from the crowd, mixed with the sobs of his mother and several of his followers.

Some guards threw dice for his robe, and one gave him a drink of vinegar on a sponge.

During what some have termed the "slow death," Jesus was seen talking with the thieves. The two men on either side of him appeared to be arguing, and a guard reported that one of them, apparently delusional from the pain, asked Jesus: "Remember me when you come into your kingdom."

Jesus reportedly responded: "Today, you will be with me in Paradise"

"I have no idea what all of that meant," the guard related. "Jesus said several things that didn't make much sense to me. He yelled out, 'My God, my God, why have you forsaken me?' but later he said, almost quietly, 'Into your hands I give my spirit.' He also said, 'Father, forgive them; they don't know what they're doing.' I don't get it."

But the leader of the guard unit, who also overheard the conversation, had another observation.

With tears in his eyes, the man shook his head and said simply: "Truly, this was the Son of God."

Because the Jewish Sabbath was approaching Friday evening, the body was quickly taken down and buried in a nearby tomb by several unidentified followers.

One of the Jewish leaders was heard to say confidently to a colleague as they left the hill: "Well, that's the last we'll hear of this Jesus of Nazareth."

*   *   *

Graphic movie causes me to tremble
(I wrote this column in 2004.)

As have many of you who have seen Mel Gibson's movie, *The Passion of the Christ*, I have been sorting through my own thoughts and emotions the past several days.

First, I highly recommend the movie—perhaps the most talked-about in the history of film making.

Christians who "know the story" have had a rather "sanitized" view of the sacrifice Jesus made for the sins of the world.

The movie's graphic portrayal of the scourging, journey to Calvary, and crucifixion will drastically change that.

The hearts of agnostics, the non-professing, the "seekers"—however they presently see themselves—surely will be touched and caused to more seriously consider this Jesus they have so far not embraced.

I think my friend Fred Meeks, head of the Religion department at Wayland, said it well: "It's not a movie, it's an experience."

A few questions I asked myself . . . and my own answers:

* Why would some people be so opposed to this movie? Because Satan (ingeniously portrayed as both appealing and appalling) is at work and because people who do not have the Spirit of God in their lives cannot discern spiritual matters.

* Was the violence done to Jesus that bad? How bad did it need to be?

* Could people be that cruel? Just look around today.

* How could he have endured that shame and suffering? Because his will and his Father's were the same—to redeem fallen mankind. (For me, the most poignant words in the movie were when Jesus looked to Heaven before his horrific scourging and said, "Father, my heart is ready." I pray to the same Father that my heart will be ready if I'm called on to suffer for his cause.)

* Could he really have loved me that much? What does reflecting over the blessings of 55 years of living say?

* Can I ever look at the cross, at communion, at his teachings again, and be the same? How could I?

A beloved old spiritual asks the haunting question: "Were you there when they crucified my Lord?"

Thanks to *The Passion of the Christ*, I believe I was.

And it "causes me to tremble, tremble, tremble . . ."

PEOPLE STORIES

Tom Hall in a favorite hat

Wayland Dean Tom Hall

Tom Hall: Friendship doesn't get any better than this

I'm pretty sure I first encountered a man I consider to be my best friend when we were mutually bored at our sisters' piano recitals at the home of Myra Hayes, our next-door neighbor on Southeast Sixth in the mid-1950s.

But Tom Hall, born Oct. 9, 1948—10 days before me —went to Highland and I went to Hillcrest. He played in the American Little League and I was in the National. He went to Estacado Junior High and I attended Coronado. He was at First Baptist; I was at Ninth and Columbia Church of Christ. He played in the band and I was involved in athletics.

Thus, our paths didn't cross much again until we played American Legion baseball together before our senior year at Plainview High when I convinced him to try out for the team.

New coach Jim Sears about worked Tom to death getting him in playing shape. It was pretty obvious he not only was going to only help us as a first baseman, but he also swung a pretty good stick.

Now, along about this same time, Tom and I fancied ourselves as future broadcasting stars. We'd take a tape recorder to basketball games and do the play-by-play and color. We even bought matching sports coats that Gabriel's had on sale for $10. Even if they didn't fit, I told Tom they would improve the looks of our closets.

As it turned out, Tom was, indeed, one of the best hitters on our otherwise rather mediocre team. However, he did take a called third strike with runners on in a 7-6 loss to Lubbock Coronado, and someone threw a brick through the windshield of his green 1955 Ford.

After graduation, I went to Wayland and Tom went to West Texas State. But he'd come home during basketball season and help me do Wayland games for the campus radio station. We had a pair of earphones—kind of like a doctor's stethoscope—that weren't functioning properly. Tom sent them off for repair and the company wrote back and said they worked fine when they cleaned the ear wax out of them.

As my focus took a turn toward print journalism, Tom got on at KVOP as he finished up his education in Canyon.

Tom served as a groomsman when Carolyn and I married in June of 1969, and I was an usher when he wed Linda Liles of Vernon, whom he had met at college, in September. We all lived at the Marquis Apartments at Seventh and Fresno for a time and still laugh when we recall sharing the same room at the Kona Kai Motel in Dumas after covering a Babe Ruth tournament game. Linda covered some area football games when I became sports editor at *The Herald* in 1970.

Tom went to Vernon's radio station for a year or so but came back to run the Central Plains MH-MR's sheltered workshop, then was assistant manager of the Chamber of Commerce for six years.

During that time, he helped organize and was for many years director of the Plainview Queens Classic basketball tournament for high school girls and college women that was one of the premiere events of its kind in the nation. Early on, it drew teams from many major schools.

Tom and former Chamber Manager Jim Ferrell saw some of every one of more than 600 games played in the 29-year history of the tournament. On Thanksgiving Day, Tom would leave to have lunch with his family at the start of a game and return at the end of the next game.

One year, his brother Bobby (now Wayland's Executive Vice President and Provost) had to run a red light to get Tom to the gym in time to see the last second of a game, otherwise his streak would have been broken.

Tom read my mind when I bought my first house and agonized over painting it. "Got any boards that need to be replaced?" He still shakes his head when he recalls my tentative response when he asked me the first thing I'd do if I had a flat: "Take the lid off?"

A master of hyperbole, Tom loves to embellish a story about the time we drove to Canadian to see the fall foliage. He claims I introduced myself to a disinterested "towel head" as if I was somebody the man was supposed to know and then was not satisfied for a short walk across a scenic bridge but insisted on forcing him to walk two miles in his new boots.

Tom, of course, succeeded Tut Tawwater as the Voice of the Bulldogs in the early 1990s and combined with his brother for the best combo to ever broadcast PHS football.

Tom worked in various capacities at Wayland for 17 years, then did a 12-year stint as sportscaster and co-host of the "Wake Up Kickin'" morning show on KKYN before returning to Wayland in 2009 as Executive Director of Student Services and Dean of Students.

During his time at KKYN, he was behind the mike for Plainview's run of three straight state girls' championships and a shot at the fourth. For the past 18 years, he has coached a lot of the varsity players on the Lady Air team during the summer.

An iron man, Tom would get up at 4:30 to start his day at the radio station and, even when we'd go to San Angelo to do a football game that night, would drive both ways, thus putting in a 21-to-22-hour day.

When Mark Finkner got more involved broadcasting Texas Tech football in 2000, Tom asked me to do color and stats. That job lasted through 2011, including three trips to the state quarterfinals. He and I are in our third season of doing Wayland football with dairyman Reed Mulliken and retired DPS sergeant Gordon Miller helping us as sideline reporter and spotter, respectively.

Sometimes it's been a bit scary how we may be thinking the same thing. He chides me on-air about making up statistics, and I get after him for his opinionated comments about officiating.

My two favorite games with Tom were Plainview's 46-42 victory over Andrews in 2001 when Taber Minner, now on the Bulldog coaching staff, returned a kickoff 102 yards with 19 seconds left, and the 26-23 double overtime loss to Stephenville in the 2005 quarterfinals at Texas Tech.

I still have the tape of the second half of the Andrews game when Tom says, "It can't get more exciting than this," and there are still four touchdowns to go. Listening to him set up that kickoff and the elevation in his voice when Taber breaks into the clear still gives me goosebumps.

Tom has always been good about judging whether the ball is past the first down marker on a measurement. At Tech, where the press box is 18 stories in the air, he speculated that the ball was "18 inches from a first down."

As we continued to talk and the officials pulled the chain tight, Tom asked me, peering through binoculars, "How short is it?"

"About 18 inches," I said with considerable admiration.

"Sure helps after I had that cataract removed," he said.

Tom and I umpired baseball (he once offered a loud grandmother a chance to come down from the stands and finish the game) and refereed basketball. We liked to "put the mustard" on basketball calls like our role models—Jerry Martindale, Harlon Voyles, James Kile, Keith Wormsbaker, Del Poss, Jack Scarborough, and Garret Harbison.

Tom dotes over his granddaughters—children of his daughter, Jenny Rosetta, and her husband Randy. They live in Baton Rouge, La. Mallory, now 14, insisted that "Santa Claus brought me this blanket" (intended for Tom and Linda) when she was about six and I played the Jolly One.

When Tom told Mallory that story would be in this book, six-year-old Darby asked if she would be in the book as well. When "Dee-Dad" said he didn't know, Darby crossed her arms and fumed, "I'm never gonna be famous."

Tom, who was named Man of the Year by the Chamber of Commerce in 2004, has been the first to call when I've had a crisis in my life. We both have survived tussles with cancer. We like to acknowledge each other at church—me in the choir and he on the third row west side—by tugging on an ear.

We're far removed from our Class of 1967 picture in which he, standing behind me, has a full head of red hair and I'm sporting a flat-top.

Almost half a century later, I have all the hair and he still has all the brains.

We've laughed together and cried together and unashamedly told each other "I love you" in emails and face to face.

Friendship doesn't get any better than that.

*   *   *

Lanny Voss

My pal: Lanny Ray Voss, Esquire

A man is truly fortunate if he has two or three really good friends.

Lanny Voss would fall into that category for me. We've been friends for more than 40 years since he came to Plainview to practice law after graduation from Texas Tech.

Voss and I have been known to combine our pitiful resources for lunch by sharing a sandwich, drinking water, and getting out with a small tip for around $5.

The great thing about Lanny is that we don't have to "build Rome" regardless of how long it has been since we have had a serious conversation. And our conversations can range from very serious and spiritual to the absolutely mundane and inane.

Lanny is a gifted teacher and speaker and has officiated many weddings and funerals.

Father of two sons, Lanny has loved my children as well, especially my daughter, "Baby Kayla," who is now 35. He got his own Kayla when oldest son Dax married Kayla Walker of Plainview.

One of our family's prized possessions is a video Lanny shot, complete with commentary, when my youngest son Brad was playing his youngest, Ben, in church league basketball almost 25 years ago.

I was coaching; our oldest son, Brandon, was officiating; and Kayla and her mom are also captured on video. Brad scored about 25 points that morning, including a couple of long 3's and a reverse layup.

My favorite "Lanny story" is about him serving as president of the student body at Howard Payne University in Brownwood. A "Passing of the Green" ceremony called for him to say a few words before each senior passed a green branch to an underclassman. Then he was to start the alma mater.

When Lanny began singing, no one joined in. So he started over and, again, no one tuned up. He figured everyone had ganged up on him.

Dr. Guy Newman, the president, looked at future Christian singing star Cynthia Clawson and asked her to begin the alma mater.

To his great embarrassment, Lanny had been trying to coax the audience into singing the Odessa Permian school song.

Can you sue yourself for mental distress?

*   *   *

Basketball magazine partners Danny Andrews and Garet von Netzer

Garet von Netzer: A great and long partnership

One of the most enjoyable associations of my life has been with Garet von Netzer, a tall, rawboned, hard-working native of Fredericksburg.

We started out as sportswriters in the early 1970s—he at the Amarillo *Globe-News* and I at *The Plainview Daily Herald*.

On a trip to cover a Floydada-Alpine football playoff game in Midland in November of 1972, it's my contention that I suggested we start a basketball preview magazine similar to *Top 'O Texas Football*. We discussed it quite a bit but it was Garet who called several weeks later and said, "Let's start that magazine we talked about."

We put $100 in a checking account, Garet made up the questionnaires, and we asked coaches in the region to help us promote a magazine to help a sport that will always live in the shadow of King Football.

That was the genesis for *Panhandle-Plains Basketball Magazine* that we published together for 38 years and continues to be published by Amarillo College communications teacher Mike Haynes and his sister, former Delta State and Wayland basketballer Sheri Haynes of McLean.

Working with Bob Tosh, a *Globe-News* employee who had a print shop in his garage, we got the first issue out early enough that we felt we should tell the coaches not to distribute them too quickly, lest they raise the ire of the head football coach.

The second issue was composed by another *G-N* employee, Seeger I. Jenkins, at his home in East Amarillo. We were so giddy from staying up nights working on that publication and seeing so many wrong type fonts, I dubbed Garet as "Lord Wrong Fontleroy."

The next few years, the magazine was "put together" at the *Canyon News*, owned by the late Troy Martin. He told me that Garet, a man of strong German heritage known for his frugal ways and wanting to cut costs any way he could, was "nothing but a damn Prussian."

I don't know for sure what that meant, but it didn't sound very complimentary.

That we were able to work together for 38 years was a testimony to Garet's incredible tenacity and, probably, that computers and email eventually made the project much less difficult.

After moving up through the ranks of the newspaper as sports editor, editor, general manager, and publisher, Garet retired in 2001.

We were honored to be inducted into the Panhandle Press Hall of Fame together in 2003. A U.S. Army veteran and former All-Big 8 hurdler at the University of Missouri, Garet also is a member of the Panhandle Sports Hall of Fame and a former Man of the Year in Amarillo, where he was involved in all kinds of organizations to promote his community.

I've nominated Garet—who was among the first to give girls equal coverage in sports and compiled the girls' all-state basketball teams for 15 years—for the Texas Basketball Hall of Fame.

Several years ago, Garet and wife Mardi moved permanently to the 750-acre ranch his father bought in 1949 for $69 an acre. It's worth about $10,000 an acre now but Garet, an honored conservationist, wouldn't sell it for love nor money.

In addition to raising a variety of sheep, he also conducts several hunts each year.

I never think of Garet, a former elder and Sunday School teacher at First Presbyterian Church in Amarillo, without recalling his favorite verse, Philippians 4:6-7: "Do not be anxious about anything, but in every situation, by prayer and petition, with thanksgiving, present your requests to God. And the peace of God, which transcends all understanding, will guard your hearts and minds in Christ Jesus."

A Prussian, maybe. A peaceful, thankful one, no question.

* * *

Cary Eaves

Cary Eaves: A blossoming relationship

Interesting how a casual relationship early in life can blossom into a deep one through the years.

I met Cary Eaves when he was shy, though talented, young pitcher for the Plainview High baseball team. He was a sophomore when I was a senior.

He matured into a dependable righthander. I'll never forget his masterful four-hit, 1-0 shutout of archrival Monterey at Jaycee Park in the spring of 1968. Ronnie Fudge—a key player in a big Homecoming upset of Palo Duro (then coached by future PHS mentor George Kirk) the following fall—doubled in the lone run.

A year later, Cary was set to pitch in Pampa and the Bulldogs still had an outside shot at winning district. I convinced *Herald* Editor Jim Servatius to let me drive to Pampa to cover the game.

Bookkeeping cut a check for $30 but when I stopped to get gas, I discovered the check was made out to my friend Danny *Owen*. Shows how well I was known at the newspaper. I had to hustle back downtown, get a new check, and stop again for gas. By the time I got to Pampa, it was the fourth inning, and Cary didn't have his best stuff.

Cary graduated from West Texas State and returned to join his father Bill Eaves—one of the finest men I have ever known—in the insurance and real estate business.

He has been a strong community leader and supporter. But I admire him most for his commitment as a Christian. He's a fellow deacon and teaches a men's Sunday School class across the hall from my class. It's euphemistically known as "The Young Men's Bible Class," even though most of the members are 70 and up. I can't even shame them into "promoting" to my fast-dwindling group.

Cary was the dedicated arrangements chairman for the Go Tell Crusade at Bulldog Stadium three years ago that resulted in more than 1,100 decisions, including more than 500 professions of faith in Christ. The Lord and "Kingdom Business" are never far from Cary's mind and conversation.

The best thing that ever happened to him was being discovered on a local tennis court by the lovely Sally Dillman, a Wayland student from Canadian, who says, "The first time I ever saw Cary, I knew he was the man I was going to marry."

God has blessed them with three fine children—Jonathan, Timothy and Cary Catherine—and their first grandchild this fall.

Sally is a Wayland trustee, and they have endowed a scholarship at the university.

That's another relationship that has really blossomed.

* * *

Danny with Vestal Goodman, "The Queen of Gospel Music"

Crossing paths with some famous folks

It's been my good fortune through the years to meet some famous folks in various places. Being in the newspaper business facilitated some of those opportunities. Not being afraid to talk to telephone poles and fire hydrants never hurts, either.

In 1989, I got off the shuttle at DFW Airport and tennis star Arthur Ashe was standing on the curb. I slowed down, cocked my head, and said, "Sir, if you're not Arthur Ashe, you're certainly missing a golden opportunity."

He nodded as if to say, "You know it and I know it, but please don't call any attention to me." (By the way, Paul DiPasquale of Richmond, Virginia, who sculpted the bronze statue of Jimmy Dean for the museum being built at Wayland in his honor, also created a statue of Ashe, a Richmond native).

When I went into an airport gift shop after encountering Arthur Ashe, there stood former Dallas Cowboys star Tony Dorsett, who agreed to autograph my airline ticket. In a moment, he was standing out on the concourse with folks passing by, none apparently recognizing him, or snubbing him since he'd been traded to Denver.

I met motivational speaker Zig Ziglar in the men's room of Prestonwood Baptist Church in Plano several years ago and told him we ran his column in *The Herald*. He didn't seem overly impressed.

When *Leap of Faith* was shot here in 1992, I got 15 minutes with the star, comedian-actor-singer Steve Martin, at an old barber shop in the Weksler Building next to the Quick Lunch (now the Broadway Brew), which underwent quite a bit of remodeling for the movie.

I found Martin very personable. We had met briefly earlier in the day when I took some papers featuring the movie's caterer to the old Bob Hooper Motor Co. at Seventh and Ash where the cast and crew ate lunch.

As I started to leave, Martin, who was seated near the door, said, "Hey, you're the guy from the newspaper." I was flattered. Apparently he was at least looking at *The Herald* while staying in the home of Mike and Suzy Hutcherson in Westridge.

At a Dallas hotel, I interviewed John Schneider, who played Bo Duke on *The Dukes of Hazzard*, to promote a movie, *Eddie Macon's Run*, that he made with Kirk Douglas in Laredo.

Banker Jeral Miller made my day by asking if I'd like to introduce Baseball Hall of Famer Nolan Ryan when he was here stumping for George Bush for governor.

You know, we're both about the same age, both grew up in Texas, both played baseball, and we're both right-handed. As comedian Yakov Smirnoff used to ask: "Is this a great country or what?"

I got to meet such sports notables as Dallas Cowboys coach Tom Landry, former Cowboy and NFL coach Dan Reeves, several other

Cowboy players who came to Plainview for special events, Texas Rangers announcers Eric Nadel and the late Mark Holtz, Hall of Fame baseball player Harmon Killebrew, Pittsburgh Steelers quarterback Terry Bradshaw, University of Texas football coach Darrell Royal, and national championship women's basketball coaches Geno Auriemma of Connecticut and Gary Blair of Texas A&M. Gary brought several Dallas South Oak Cliff teams to the Plainview Queens Classic tournament.

I didn't get to meet him but got to hear colorful baseball pitcher/TV announcer Dizzy Dean sing "The Wabash Cannonball" at a golf tournament banquet in Lubbock.

My favorite story, though, was meeting three celebs while on a trip to California in 1993. Publisher Rollie Hyde had asked me and Carolyn to host a *Herald*-sponsored cruise out of Los Angeles to Catalina Island to Ensenada, Mexico.

As we were strolling through Los Angeles International Airport, I saw a guy with a University of Texas orange-colored leisure suit and a cowboy hat with a feather in it walking with two other folks.

When we got to the baggage area, I told Carolyn, "That guy over there is an actor. I'm going to find out who he is."

I walked up to the man and said, "Pardon me, sir, you're an actor aren't you?"

Turns out he was Wings Hauser, about my age and a veteran of films (mostly horror movies as I later found out) and a recurring role on the TV show *Roseanne*.

He decided to introduce me to his traveling companions: "This is Linda Blair," he said as the tiny actress from the super scary movie, *The Exorcist*, extended her hand (I later found out they were dating at the time), "and this is Rich Little," the impressionist whom I had seen on *The Tonight Show* many times.

Little looked like he had been in a tanning bed for a month and had greasy, slicked-back hair and very dark sunglasses.

"Mr. Little, I'd just like to say that of all the talent I've ever seen, I'd like to have yours," I gushed, alluding to his ability to mimic others so believably.

You would have thought he would say something like, "Well, that's very nice of you," or just, "Thanks." Instead he replied, "Well, man, I wish you had my problems, too."

Turns out he was going through a very messy divorce and decided to let a total stranger know how he was feeling. I thought, "These folks are real people with real problems."

One of my real blessings came about 10 years ago when Bill Gaither scheduled a "Homecoming" concert at the United Spirit Arena in Lubbock.

Having attended a couple previously, I wrote several of his regulars for interviews and wound up doing three—Jake Hess, lead singer for the famed Statesmen and Imperial quartets; tenor Larry Ford (a Levelland native who was at Wayland with comedian Dennis Swanberg for a concert in 2010); and the Queen of Gospel Music, Vestal Goodman.

As we concluded our visit on the phone, Vestal asked, "Danny, when am I gonna get to meet you?"

How about Friday night?" I suggested. She gave me instructions to identify myself to her crew and we would meet after she and her husband Howard and Johnny Minick performed.

In a tunnel at the arena, Vestal visited with Carolyn and me for several minutes, then put her hand on my shoulder and prayed for me.

I think the hair stood up on the back on my neck for an hour.

*   *   *

It really is a small world after all

In 1978, when the Flying Queens were in Los Angeles for the national tournament, Tom Hall, Carolyn and I took an excursion through Beverly Hills, then had about four hours to spend at Disneyland.

I went to an ice cream stand and there stood Frank Bass, who later would drive the bus to hundreds of athletic events for Wayland, and his wife Wanda, the woman I said I'd choose for my second mother. This was April, not exactly big vacation season.

That song at Disneyland that gets in your head, "It's a Small World After All," really is true.

In 1987, Carolyn and I returned to the Mayflower Hotel in Washington and saw a sign that said "Baylor Night in Washington." I was certain I'd know someone in that meeting and, soon, my favorite Wayland history professor, Gwin Morris, emerged from the room. Gwin, who was instrumental in the creation of the Museum of the Llano Estacado, will soon join the Wayland Board of Trustees.

Several years ago, *Herald* Publisher Rollie Hyde and his wife Jeri and Carolyn and I ate lunch at the Carnegie Hall Delicatessen in New York City.

There you sit at long tables, sometimes next to total strangers, as we did that afternoon. Two older women who said they were from Florida asked us where we were from and we said, "Plainview, Texas."

"Did you know Dr. (A.A.) DeSouza?" one inquired about a former Plainview physician. "I really didn't know him, but I went to high school with Jeanette (his daughter)," I said.

Turns out the women were her aunts.

On a shuttle in Albany, New York, an airline pilot, finding out we were from Plainview, asked if we were familiar with the Lyles Scale Company just south of Dulaney's Auto Parts.

"It's just a couple of blocks from my house," I told the pilot.

"A.B. Lyles is my father-in-law," he said. Unfortunately, I never met him.

In 1996, the Hydes, Carolyn and I, and Circulation Director Frank Silvas were in California for a Hearst meeting. After taking Frank's wife to catch a plane in San Jose, we stopped in Morgan Hill for lunch.

At a place called the Way Better Cafe, the proprietor, Stoksie Vaughn, handed out little cards as he prepared our sandwiches. My favorite was "Stop Global Whining."

I wrote a column about Stoksie and mailed it to him. He framed it, and when a friend came into the restaurant, he showed it to her. Turns out it was Plainview native Linda Ayers Tarvin who ran a stationery store in Morgan Hill.

Linda told me a woman came into her store and they discovered they both were from Plainview. The customer was the daughter of

Albert Garrett, one of the owners of Cloverlake Dairy Foods. "My daddy (Manuel Ayers) worked for your daddy," Linda said.

On a trip to San Francisco several years later, Carolyn and I were waiting for the boat to take us to Alcatraz prison. I struck up a conversation with a fellow who turned out to be a "sod farmer" in Michigan but also grew potatoes for Walker Brothers Produce in Plainview.

I love the story former PHS golf coach and Houston School principal Tommy Chatham tells about going into a T-shirt shop on Malibu Beach in California with his wife Tonei and son Tad.

The woman behind the counter heard them talking and asked, "What part of the South are you all from?"

Tommy said "Texas" and elaborated "Up in the Panhandle area," when the woman inquired "What part?"

The woman informed them that "I have a friend near Lubbock. You wouldn't happen to know Martha Chatham, would you?"

"I guess so," said a shocked Tommy, "that's my mother."

"Well, you must be Tommy and that has to be Tad," the woman said, noting that she had corresponded with her friend for many years but had never met Martha's family.

There are dozens of T-shirt shops on Malibu, and the Chathams just happened to wander into the right one.

The most amazing story I ever heard was about the late Fred Garrison, longtime Texaco distributor in Plainview, visiting with a fellow passenger on a plane about to leave Logan Airport in Boston.

Soon the other man said, "You're from Texas aren't you?" When Fred acknowledged he was, the man said, "I think I can tell you where you're from—somewhere between Silverton and Quitaque."

Fred about fell out of his seat at that revelation because he grew up in Silverton.

"How in the world would you know that?" asked Fred, totally baffled.

"There is a distinct speech pattern for folks in that part of Texas like no other in the state," explained the man, who turned out to be a linguistics professor.

When Fred's son, Gary, related that story, I wrote a column and called Texas Tech to see if they had a linguistics professor who might elaborate. Seems like someone in the English department said she didn't know if they had such a professor, and no one called back.

So, I still don't know, but find that a fascinating story.

* * *

Gene Shelburne

Beware: Someone is always watching you

For our 35th anniversary in 2004, Carolyn and I took a cruise to Alaska with some of the money my dad left me when he passed away six months earlier.

Our college friends, Bill and Sue Coward of Granbury, also were celebrating their 35th and invited us to join them.

I'm sure my daddy, who gained most of his savings in CDs from high interest rates when Jimmy Carter was president, was spinning in his grave at the money we spent.

One of my favorite memories of that trip was of spotting Gene Shelburne, minister of the Anna Street Church of Christ in Amarillo for more than 40 years. His column has run on Friday's Religion Page in *The Herald* for more than 20 years.

Gene, by the way, was nice enough to edit this book before it went to press.

Several years ago, Gene wrote a great column about how Glenn Dillard, then head of the truck shop at Cargill Meat Solutions and now owner of West Texas Woodfire Grill, stopped to help him with his broken-down car, worked on it for more than an hour, and refused any payment.

Gene was headed into a store in Juneau as we were boarding a bus on our way to catch a boat for a whale watch and a salmon dinner. Unfortunately, I was far enough away that he didn't hear me hollering his name.

That was on Sunday. By Thursday in Ketchikan, I saw four ships docked end to end and spotted Gene and his wife Nita at the end of the pier.

I sneaked up behind him and said in the deepest voice I could muster, "Gene Shelburne, this is the Lord speaking. What are you doing in Alaska?"

We had a good visit and Gene wrote a column about being careful how you act any time and any place because you never know who might be watching when you least expect it.

*   *   *

My brother claims his brother knows everyone

It's always been my nature to talk to anyone who'll listen.

Not long before she died, my mother gave me some report cards from Hillcrest Elementary she had saved. My second grade teacher, Hazel O'Bannon wrote, "Danny tends to talk too much."

Guilty as charged. But I've met a lot of neat people by not being afraid to strike up conversations with total strangers, maybe remarking about their cap or calling the name of their hometown's sports mascot when they tell me where they're from.

In 1994, when Plainview's boys won the 4A state championship, we left my brother's house in Round Rock and in a few minutes pulled up at a light beside Gene Glaser, Jr., whose father formerly was minister at Garland Street Church of Christ. Gene, Jr. was a former minister at Broadway Church of Christ in Lubbock. I didn't really know him all that well, but we waved at each other like old friends.

At the El Arroyo Restaurant, I saw several coaches I knew, drawing a hug from Amarillo Palo Duro coach Gerald Tucker, and we were seated next to folks I was acquainted with.

Of course, at the Frank Erwin Center, it look liked half of Plainview was there.

After the game, Guy and I were walking to the car when a black woman approached us. I stopped and gave her a big hug. It was my dear friend Kathleen Jackson, whose husband, the late Walter Jackson, was pastor of Emmanuel Church of God in Christ.

"Who was that?" my brother asked with a puzzled look on his face.

"Oh, that's our sister. Didn't Daddy ever tell you?"

Kathleen and I have had several laughs about that through the years.

That caused my brother to write an email titled, "My brother knows everybody."

Reader's Digest reported several years ago that there's a 1-in-20 chance that you'll have something in common with anyone you meet if you talk long enough.

I'm doing my best to lower those odds.

*   *   *

Mike Parker

Mike Parker and the Amazing Challenge

My friend Mike Parker used to give me grief about claiming to know somebody just about everywhere I go.

In the late 1990s, several of us from First Baptist loaded up on a bus and headed to Texas Stadium in Irving—home of the Dallas Cowboys—for a Promise Keepers rally for Christian men.

"I bet you don't see anybody you know," Mike insisted as we stopped to eat at Luby's Cafeteria in Wichita Falls. Little did he know that Leroy Daniels, owner of the restaurant, and I served on the *Baptist Standard* board together for several years.

I quietly asked an employee if he could ask Leroy to "make over me" when I got to the end of the line.

Mike couldn't believe it but wasn't smart enough to leave well enough alone when we stopped at Wyatt's Cafeteria in Dallas to eat supper, offering to buy my meal if I saw someone I knew.

When we went to check out, the young lady behind the counter asked, "Where are y'all from?" we told her and she said, "Hey, I'm from Plainview. My folks still live there."

"Who's your dad?" I inquired.

When she told me, I said, "Aw, we had him on the cover of our Hispanic paper the other day wearing a big sombrero."

The look on Mike Parker's face was priceless. I wasn't too hungry that evening so he only had to pay for a glass of lemonade.

Just by the luck of eating at the right place, I put Mike Parker in his.

Sometime later, Mike told me he was going to Hawaii and was in the DFW Airport early one morning when he spied actor-martial arts champion Chuck Norris, star of *Walker, Texas Ranger*.

Mike said he went over to him and said, "Mr. Norris, I know you get a lot of requests, but would you let me take a picture of my boys with you?"

Norris willingly obliged. Only Mike Parker had no film in the camera, as it turned out . . . or didn't turn out, as fate had it.

I rode him hard, making sure he knew I was skeptical of that story since he had given me so much grief.

* * *

Meeting Moses at a Rangers game

About 20 years ago, our church had a Father-Son trip to visit Texas Stadium and take in a Texas Rangers baseball game.

I made a non-monetary wager with my pastor, Travis Hart, that I would see somebody I knew before he did.

No luck at Texas Stadium, but that night I stood on the concourse at the Rangers' park, certain I would be able to boast to Travis. Sure enough, the sister of our former youth minister, Phillip Golden, came riding up on the escalator.

I couldn't wait to tell Travis, who was seated in the stadium. Just as I walked to where he was sitting, he crowed, "I just saw Moses."

Pretty sure he wasn't referring to *the* Moses of Bible fame, I asked, "You talking about Mike Moses (former superintendent of Lubbock schools and by then Commissioner of Education for the State of Texas)?"

Travis acknowledged that was the one.

"Doesn't count . . . you have to know them," I countered. "I just spoke to Phillip Golden's sister."

Anyway, I headed back out on the concourse and, lo and behold, here comes Mike Moses. So I walked over, introduced myself and asked a favor: "Would you come meet my pastor?"

I promise this was his response: "What do you want me to do, act like I know you?"

When we walked back to where the Plainview group was sitting, I said, "Hey, Travis, I want you meet my friend Mike Moses."

He looked astonished, like watching *the* Moses part the Red Sea.

Turns out there was someone in our group that Mike Moses did know—accountant George Meriwether. They went to school together at Stephen F. Austin University in Nacogdoches.

Travis and I were both amazed.

*　　*　　*

Bub, K. Y., Gene & Willie: Great Oltonites

About 40 years ago, Olton hosted a regional baseball tournament and invited several of us from Plainview to umpire—Jimmie Chennault, Buddy Dodson, Tom Hall, and me, as I recall.

That's when I met three great guys—postmaster D. M. "Bub" Holt, Texaco service station owner C.J. "K.Y." Givens, and banker Gene Trotter. They were in charge of the summer baseball program in the Lamb County community 25 miles west of Plainview.

Bub Holt was the P.A. announcer, and I got a hoot out of his gravelly voice.

The first varsity basketball game I ever officiated, my partner was Bub Holt. When I arrived to pick him up for our short trek down to

Spade, he was wearing a striped shirt that looked at least two sizes too small, a pair of very tight black slacks that had been sewn up due to a tear near the right pocket, and a pair of black high-top tennis shoes.

He said he hadn't refereed in a couple of years and apparently had been pressed back into service. "I'm very embarrassed about this uniform," Bub apologized.

One night he accompanied me and Tom Hall to Spade and insisted we come in and have some of his wife's delicious peach pie when we returned through Olton.

Well, it reminded me of that sign in a cafe window that said, "Pie like Grandma made: 50 cents. Pie like Grandma *thought* she made: 75 cents."

Frankly, the crust was hard as a rock, but we obligingly ate the pie as Bub repeatedly apologized: "I'm very sorry; this is the worst pie I've ever seen."

K. Y. unwittingly helped me out one day so I could go get into trouble.

I was scheduled to referee a basketball doubleheader in Morton—a community to which I had never been before. But I was pretty sure I had seen a sign not far from Levelland that said Morton was 12 miles away.

I had left Plainview a little late and my car was overheating. So I stopped at K. Y.'s station in Olton and he put in some antifreeze. Alas, when I got to that aforementioned sign, it said "Morton 26." And that turned out to be 26 very winding miles.

By the time I arrived, it was almost halftime of the girls' game. I apologized profusely and went on to work the boys' game for future Abilene Christian University coach Tony Mauldin. Not surprisingly, I was never invited back to Morton.

Gene Trotter was a quiet but friendly fellow. His wife, Mozelle, became a good friend. She has written a column and stories for the Olton *Enterprise* for years and serves on the board of the Runningwater Draw Care Center in her community.

Another really fine Oltonite was Willie Green.

When my friends Hope English and Phyllis Wall and I went to Olton to judge the Miss Sandhills Contest in the summer of 2006, Willie and his wife Jean hosted a luncheon for the contestants.

When we arrived, Willie met us at the door and said something I will never forget: "Welcome, it's an honor to have you in our home." We felt like royalty.

Mozelle Trotter told me that when she could no longer help Gene get in and out of bed as his health declined, Willie Green and his son Nick came to her home every morning and again every evening to help Gene.

That's the kind of folks who live in Olton, just indicative of the many great people in West Texas.

*   *   *

Marshall Formby

Marshall Formby: A very colorful character

One of the most colorful characters in Plainview's history passed away in 1984.

Marshall Formby packed a lot of living into 73 years. Marshall looked like he slept in his suits, and his hair, combed straight back, might not always be well coiffed.

His glasses were often slightly skewed and he had a crooked little smile. He looked and acted like a "character." Maybe he worked at it.

Marshall tried his hand at many different things and was successful at most. Associated with a law firm in the Skaggs Building for more than 30 years, he had been editor of *The Toreador* at Texas Tech, founded *The Plainview Tribune*, a weekly farm-oriented newspaper, and was elected Dickens County Judge. He later wrote a book about the folks there called *These Are My People*.

He also served in the Texas Senate and would have been happy to know that his nephew, Robert Duncan, served as Hale County's senator in Austin and a few months ago was named the new chancellor at Texas Tech.

Marshall was chairman of the Texas Highway Commission, was a regent at Texas Tech, served on the Texas College and Universities Coordinating Board, was a Rotary District Governor, and served for many years on the Central Plains Regional Hospital Board.

Marshall was foursquare about one thing: The financially struggling hospital ought not to fall into the hands of "strangers." He eventually lost that tussle.

I think I first heard of Marshall when he was running for governor in 1962 against some formidable foes—a fellow named John Connally and incumbent Price Daniel, and finished third behind those gentlemen, respectively.

Supporters threw a barbecue dinner at the old City Auditorium and my dad took me along. I don't recall a thing about the speech, but the barbecue was good.

Marshall taught a Sunday School class for older men—"reprobates," I think he called them—at First Baptist Church for several years. I suspect it was one part gospel, one part politics, one part sports discussions, and one part Marshall Formby philosophy.

I don't know how much good it did the members' spiritual lives, but I bet they got a little smarter each week. After all, someone said Sunday School is "where we all come together and pool our biblical ignorance."

It has been my privilege to teach the Formby Class for the past nine years but, sadly, through folks passing away, becoming incapacitated, or moving, it has dwindled from a good Sunday of 25 to a low of four during bad weather.

One of Marshall's law partners, Graddy Tunnell, a charter member of the group, told me, "Danny, you can kill off a class faster than anybody I've ever seen."

At least most of the regulars stay awake, including my faithful class president Buddy McGehee and secretary Don Smith.

And they're more directly encouraging than longtime member Jake Finney who used to tell me on the way out the door, "We appreciate your efforts." He didn't say he liked the lesson, just "thanks for trying."

Marshall Formby was fond of telling his preacher, Carlos McLeod, "Carlos, I enjoyed that sermon today—*both* times."

Marshall was a devoted Rotarian and created a little invention that blew air through a tube, causing the American flag to wave as the club recited the pledge.

Being an old newshound, Marshall wasn't bashful about calling me to suggest an idea for a story or photo.

Also, being a reader of *The Baptist Standard*, the journal of Texans of that denomination, and knowing I was a board member, Marshall called and asked me to lunch at the Far East Restaurant.

He sported a bright red plaid tam-'o-shanter on his head and, soon, a goodly portion of his lunch on his shirt and tie.

He said he wanted to nominate me for the Baptist Communications Award and was certain I would be chosen for that honor. He mustered several letters of recommendation—including one from my new minister, Dr. Fred Meeks, whose remarks were so flattering I didn't even recognize whom he was writing about.

Marshall died a few months after our meeting. Long story short, I didn't receive that honor until 10 years later, thanks mostly to a 13-part series I wrote about my mission experience in the Ukraine. But he probably would have been happy anyway.

His widow, the late Sharleen Formby Rhodes, donated his papers to Texas Tech and made a $250,000 gift to the College of Mass

Communications from the charitable Formby Foundation to help train the next generation of West Texas journalists.

Marshall's name also appears on a room at Tech's Southwest Collection/Special Collections Library.

I bet Marshall Formby would smile that quirky smile and be happy about all that too.

*　　*　　*

Pete McDonald

Pete McDonald: President of American junk

If ever there was a "larger than life" character, it was the late Robert E. "Pete" McDonald, owner of McDonald's Trading Post that was featured on several television programs.

Pete stood 6-4 and proclaimed himself as "225 pounds of creepin' torment."

He was tall and lanky as a youth and said he took the famous Charles Atlas body-building course. After six months, he wrote to the company and said, "Dear Charles, I've finished the course, please send the muscles."

Pete and his wife Evalene, one of the finest women God ever created, went on a cruise and met a man who introduced himself as "President of American Airlines."

"Glad to know you," said Pete, "I'm president of American junk."

I loved the signs outside his massive store that said, "All cash—no payments to make for the rest of your life," and, "If we don't have it, you don't need it."

I also liked the signs inside the store like "Free gum under stools and counters." My favorite was "Please do not throw cigar and cigarette butts in the urinal as it makes them soggy and very hard to light."

Pete basically had one price for merchandise—his—and wasn't much for dickering. When a fellow complained about a light globe being too expensive, Pete fired it in the trash and said, "I think you're right!"

Another guy said, "Pete, let's go back there and look at that fire hose." Pete said, "Hell, I've seen it a million times. You go back and there and drag it up here, and we'll haggle over the price. If you don't like it, I'll drag it back."

He could tell the wildest tales, including the explanation for a leg injury: "I was working on the roof and tied one end of a rope around my waist and the other end to the back of Evalene's car. She drove off and drug me halfway to town before she realized what happened."

One summer he bought a huge crate full of assorted nuts and bolts. He hired several friends of his sons, "Little Pete" (known as Larry later in life) and David, to sort out the shipment. Every night when I'd go to the baseball park, all I could see on the field was nuts and bolts.

Daddy and I were sitting in his front yard one summer evening when Pete rode up on his bicycle. He launched into some big windy and, about 10 minutes later, rode off. I don't think Daddy and I said a word other than, "Hi, Pete."

My favorite story about Pete is the time Jimmy Neff was teaching the Formby Sunday School Class of which Pete was a faithful member.

He frequently sat on a love seat behind the teacher and might not always pay rapt attention to the lesson.

Jimmy read the Bible passage about King David's attendants providing a virgin to sleep with him to keep him warm in his old age.

As Jimmy started to expound, Pete interrupted, "Wait a minute, wait a minute, what did you just say? To think, all this time we've just been sending flowers (to ailing class members)."

That was Pete McDonald.

* * *

Davis and Peggy Horne

The Hornes: Salt of the earth family

I've never enjoyed being around two people more than Davis and Peggy Horne, longtime pillars of St. Alice Catholic Church as well as the Lubbock Diocese.

I think I first encountered the Horne Herd—Davis and Peggy had eight children—when I took a picture of them lined up beside their old blue limousine. When I arrived, they were having lunch and it looked like an ox was on the table. I have never seen so much meat in my life.

A favorite mental picture for me is Davis, who served on the Plainview school board for several years, standing at the top of the bleachers at Babe Ruth Park watching one son play while keeping an eye on another at the adjacent Little League park.

Peggy, who passed away in 2013, was the happiest person I think I've ever known. If she wasn't laughing or smiling, you knew something had to be drastically wrong.

John Horne followed in the footsteps of his Uncle Bob Horne (who later played at Navy) by quarterbacking the Bulldogs in the mid-1970s and also was a standout golfer. He went on to play at the University of Houston and briefly on the PGA tour.

At Houston, he was a teammate of future pro stars Fred Couples and Blaine McCallister as well as Jim Nantz, the lead announcer for NFL football, NCAA basketball, and pro golf for CBS Television.

In fact, Nantz says in one of his books that John hollered out to a CBS sports executive at the Houston Open, "This guy wants a job." Nantz was hired as a "gofer" and, as they say, the rest is history.

John's sister, Ann, coached Dallas Lake Highlands, led by future pro Justin Leonard, to the boys' state golf championship in 1987.

When I was facing lymph node surgery for cancer in 2009, I went by the Hornes to visit. As I started to leave, Davis put his hand on my head and said the prettiest prayer you've ever heard.

I told him it was better than the pope praying for me. Better, in fact, because Davis Horne is a wonderful friend. I am not acquainted with the pope.

*   *   *

Fort Shea on Southeast Ninth Street

Two of my neighborhood friends were Mike and Larry Shea, who lived on Southeast Ninth, a block from our house.

Their dad, J. L., was the Gulf distributor and had a big train set in his garage. Their mom, Gay, was our leader in Cub Scouts and that's as far as I ever got in Scouting. One day she was cleaning out her cabinets and found a can with no label on it, so she decided she'd cook whatever was in the can and serve it to us neighborhood kids. Glad it turned out to be pumpkin instead of cauliflower.

Mike and Larry, who later drove an Army surplus ambulance to Plainview High School, were enamored with things military and had hundreds of toy soldiers spread all over the bedroom floor.

They also dug a huge "foxhole" in the backyard and may even have flown a Nazi flag from the TV antenna pole. I know Mike had a German helmet.

One day the brothers got into it over something and Mike fired a rock and hit Larry in the head. We had to enlist my mother's help to patch Larry up. She had to squeeze into the bathroom past a protruding washing machine.

I hate to say Mike was "fat and lazy," but the shoe fit. He also wore a pair of glasses that were constantly dirty and also taped up because the ear piece had come loose.

He got knocked down, or tripped, during a football game in his front yard and lay there for several minutes as the contest progressed.

Another time, he convinced me that he would not make me pay for a "hot" Coke if I drank the whole thing, which I did.

My most memorable story about Mike was the day he and I were playing catch in the front yard of Cleone Purcell, mother of the lovely Pebble and Patti Purcell, who both were cheerleaders at PHS.

I tossed a ball to Mike and it bounced up and hit him in the lower anatomy, causing him to double up in pain and fall to the ground.

He lay there moaning for several minutes. I was helpless other than to apologize. I mean what can you do when a guy gets hit where he got hit?

Finally, Mike began to crawl on his stomach maybe 30 yards to the alley, then got up and walked through the back gate and into his house.

If nothing else, Mike Shea was a good soldier.

* * *

First organist at Garland Street?

A guy I always enjoyed being around was the late Perry Walker, mainly because he laughed at all my stories. A dapper dresser, I think Perry wore a suit and tie when he mowed his yard.

One night I was headed to Olton to referee a basketball game and realized I had forgotten to pack a belt. So I stopped at Perry's house on the Olton Highway and asked if I could borrow something to keep my pants up.

I was determined not to try and find some shoelaces to string together as one of my officiating partners, John Smith, did one night in Bovina.

Perry opened a dresser drawer stocked with seven or eight belts and said, "Take your pick."

But when I got to Olton, Coach Jimmy Rich told me he didn't have me down to call that evening. That was fine with me because opera star Terry Cook of Plainview was in town for a concert. I knew where I was headed.

In addition to leading singing at both Churches of Christ here as well as at Broadway in Lubbock, Perry was an accomplished organist. I joked at his funeral that he told me he aspired to be the first organist for Garland Street.

We both knew Hell was probably going to freeze over before that would happen.

*   *   *

A rather odd but funny story when Keith tells it

Another guy I like because he not only laughs at my stories, he gets tickled at his own is Keith Longbotham.

A singer, guitarist, banjo player and songwriter, Keith graduated from Plainview High and Wayland and later wound up pursuing a musical career in Nashville, including gigs on the Grand Ol' Opry, the Nashville Network, and Opryland.

A music minister still much in demand for programs all over the country, he headlined Wayland's Homecoming banquet several years ago and he and several friends—including former singing cohorts Travis and Amy Thornton of Plainview—entertained at the 2014 Chamber of Commerce Banquet.

Keith loves to tell a story about a guy whose parents named him "Odd." The man hated his name because he took so much kidding all his life.

He instructed his wife at his passing to just put the dates of his birth and death on the tombstone.

For years, people walking through the cemetery have stopped, looked at the tombstone, and remarked, "That's odd."

*   *   *

Teacher goes outside the book for life lesson

I was touched by the nice letter we received at *The Herald* several years ago from Sharon Woodall King of Federal Way, Washington, about her former teachers, the late Floyd and Florence Montgomery.

The Montgomerys, who taught in Plainview for many years, never had children of their own. They passed away after moving from their home on Travis to spend their last days at the old Care Inn on St. Louis Street.

Mrs. King's letter reminded me of the impact teachers have on young lives, sometimes even in ways they would never remember. I can think of how each of my teachers at Hillcrest Elementary—Lena McWilliams, Hazel O'Bannon, Hazel Hale, Lois Weatherall, Mayme Lou Rayburn, Nell Saul, and Dell Brown—positively influenced my life in many ways.

Not long before I received that letter, my friend David Milstead (he and his dad Eldon Milstead owned Milstead Hardware on South Date and I called him the Mayor of Seth Ward) told me a most poignant story of how one of his teachers made a point that has stuck with him to this day.

When David was in the late Perry Willingham's sixth-grade class at the old Lamar Elementary at Fifth and Date, the kids frequently teased a student named Mattie Hargrave.

Mattie was a large girl and wasn't very pretty. She lived in Seth Ward and, in a community where a lot of folks would have classed themselves as "poor," Mattie came from a very poor family. She became an object of occasional ridicule by other students.

Flynn Hargrave, a yardman with little education, did the best he could to make ends meet for himself, his wife and four children, although one of the boys, Robert, was only with the family for a while in the summers because he lived in a home for the mentally handicapped in Mexia.

But when the doors of Ninth and Columbia Church of Christ were open, you could find Flynn, Edna, James, Edna May, and Mattie Ethel Hargrave front and center.

Edna was closer to my age, and she always carried herself with an air of dignity that belied her general state in life.

Eventually Mattie found that a nursing career would lead to much better economic circumstances. She was an LVN trainee when I spent a week at the local hospital in 1975 after a car wreck. I'm glad it wasn't beneath her dignity to attend to some of a patient's most basic needs.

A nurse for more than 40 years, she became an RN in the Cardiac Care Unit of Northwest Texas Hospital in Amarillo.

I wish I could stand before God right now and say I never made a disparaging remark about any of the Hargrave clan, but I don't think I could do that with a clear conscience.

That's why David Milstead's story just about broke my heart.

David says Perry Willingham told the class: "Boys and girls, it's time this teasing of Mattie stopped. She's a sweet girl."

He had Mattie stand by his desk and then asked each student—one by one—to come and apologize to her for the way they had treated her. There must have been some flushed faces and stinging ears.

David said Mattie accepted the stammered apologies, and a group of humbled students learned a lesson for life because Perry Willingham reached outside the textbook that day.

*　　*　　*

Wilda Redin

Get your stomach off my counter

Although she has been associated with the Wayland Flying Queens for more than 65 years, I haven't known Wilda Hutcherson Redin very well until the last several years.

What a lovely and classy lady.

Wilda has played "second mama" to hundreds of Queens through the years, opening her home and heart to the players.

Now past 90 (sorry, sometimes you just gotta tell a woman's age, even at the risk of bodily injury), she is still sharp and feisty.

She gave me some jackets and bow ties after her first husband, team sponsor Claude Hutcherson, passed away in 1977.

Wilda loves to make peanut brittle, and a couple of years ago even showed me and Carolyn in her own kitchen just how she does it.

I was watching intently but obviously my pooching stomach was encroaching on sacred territory because Wilda said with mock sternness in her voice: "Danny, don't lean on my counter."

That has become a running joke.

I got back in her good graces by bringing her a sack of a different kind of nut so she could make pecan brittle.

Her husband, Harley Redin, former coach of the Queens, was the delivery man and told me he might sneak a few pecans for his two pet squirrels.

I'm kind of glad I didn't hand the pecans over to Wilda in person. I might have leaned on her counter and gotten in trouble all over again.

*   *   *

Hope I don't go to Hell . . . I've already been there

Mike Parks was the owner and chief barbecuist for the Chuckwagon Restaurant on the Dimmitt Highway before it closed several years ago.

Mike was a personable fellow who took his job seriously. One of its occupational hazards was being near a hot "pit" much of the day.

Mike also had a voice that sounded like he had swallowed gravel most of his life.

One day he came out of the back area of the restaurant where he had been cooking. He was dripping with perspiration and decided aloud: "I sure hope I never do goduh Hell, 'cause I think I aw-ready been there."

On the other side of that observation, I met a new Wayland football player from the East Texas community of Colmesneil, Texas, not far from Lufkin.

"Not as much humidity here as what you're used to, huh?" I asked him.

"No sir," he said, "I don't even sweat in practice here."

*   *   *

What color did you say that building was?

Rex Ramsower, longtime owner of Ramsower's Furniture, has always been an independent kind of guy.

In the early 1980s, Texas started a Main Street Project designed to upgrade central business districts, then mostly located in downtown areas.

Plainview was one of the first cities to have a Main Street program.

The director, a woman who shall remain unnamed, did quite a bit of research on downtown buildings and suggested to Rex that he paint his building in the 700 block of Broadway dark green since that apparently was the original color.

Never one for any kind of bureaucracy, Rex told me, "I painted it lemon yellow just to spite her."

*   *   *

Centenarians Era Tooley and Mayes Osborne in 1996

Sweet moment: Centenarians share a kiss

E. Mayes Osborne, longtime manager of the Higginbotham-Bartlett Lumber Co., and father of Ethel Ramsower, lived to be 106 years old.

When he passed away in 2002 he was one of only four World War I veterans in Texas. He had served as a machine gunner in France.

Mayes was a former city councilman, a Mason for more than 60 years, deacon at First Baptist Church, and trustee at Wayland for more than 30 years. In the mid-1960s, he donated the home he built at Sixth and Milwaukee to serve as the President's Home for Wayland.

A fellow church member, Era Tooley, also turned 100 in 1996. At age 90, she told me, "You probably don't think I ought to still be driving."

I told her, "Mrs. Tooley, if you can still drive safely, I think that's just fine."

When they had her 100th birthday party, Mayes Osborne came in to the church parlor and asked, "Era, you ever been kissed by a hundred-year-old man?"

Mayes planted a good one right on Era's cheek.

I captured a picture on that occasion—a very sweet moment.

*   *   *

Bud Cason's unlucky Chevy on road trip

In the spring of 1971, Plainview was chasing the school's first UIL state boys' basketball championship.

Less than a week after the Bulldogs beat El Paso Bowie and Wichita Falls Rider at Abilene Christian University on the same day for the regional championship, it was on to Austin.

Tom Hall, *Herald* circulation assistant Bud Cason, and I piled into Bud's 1969 Chevy Impala and headed for the state's capital city.

While Tom and Tut Tawwater had done PHS games all year, they were sidelined by UIL rules that gave exclusive tournament rights to Diamond Shamrock. Future Texas Rangers broadcaster Dick Risenhoover was mikeside at old Gregory Gym.

As Bud slept in the backseat, Tom backed out of a convenience store in Brownwood and into the concrete surrounding the store's sign. Bud sat bolt upright but Tom assured him the damage was minimal— just a partially caved-in trunk.

At the Sheraton Crest Hotel, Bud actually crawled out on the ledge of our room. I promise, he had not been drinking, but the thrill of adventure summoned him, not the thought of suicide for what Tom had done to his car.

Sadly, the Impala was to sustain another "mark." As I pulled out of the Sheraton Crest parking garage, I got a little too close to the adjacent white-over-lime green Lincoln Continental, putting the slightest crease in the left front panel of that lovely automobile.

"What are we gonna do?" I moaned.

"Get the hell outta here!" Tom loudly advised from the back seat. We did, Lord forgive me.

The next evening, after Plainview lost 58–55 to Houston Cypress-Fairbanks, I decided on impulse to forego staying at the far-outdated Stephen F. Austin Hotel with Tom and Bud and make the all-night trek back to Plainview with fellow-*Herald* employee Ben Thompson and his family.

But the Impala was to take one more hit. As Tom and Bud drove down Guadalupe, a car in the adjacent lane—driven by a fellow who perhaps had a little too much alcohol—swerved into Bud's vehicle.

As the drivers got out to assess the damage, the initiator of the collision asked rather indifferently, "Did I hurt your car?"

Bud, ever courteous and not wishing the other fellow possible embarrassment with his two female companions, said, "No, but your pants are unzipped."

Maybe Bud was lucky *he* didn't suffer any damage.

*   *   *

Paul Lyle

Slain by the jawbone of an ass

One of my favorite people is Paul Lyle, a longtime Plainview attorney who retired several years ago.

My wife worked for the law firm of Day, Owen, Lyle, Voss, and Owen for several years and, knowing Paul there and from church, I saw him quite often.

Paul, a highly intelligent man with many interests, approached me about writing a brief daily column called Vocab-Lab, choosing a word for the day, its meaning and how to use it in a sentence. He did that for a year or so.

I hadn't been editor of *The Herald* long before Paul—no doubt seeing if he could get a rise out of me—offered this curt appraisal of my column writing: "Why do you use so many adjectives in your column? Why don't you just get to the point?"

I was taken back a bit and stewed on it for a few days. The next time I saw him, I said, "Paul, you'll have to forgive me. I'm a little slow.

The other day, you said I use too many words. Some people say you're a pompous ass. They should just say you're an ass, is that right?"

He just offered a slight grin and staggered off.

Which reminds me of what Carlos McLeod, his pastor, declared after a similar critique by Paul: "I'm like the men killed by Samson . . . slain by the jawbone of an ass."

*   *   *

Harold Dye

Unusual book title saves a man's life

I became friends with Dr. Harold Dye, former editor of *The Baptist New Mexican newspaper* and writer for the *Open Windows* devotional guide, when he did morning meditations at Glorieta Baptist Conference Center in the late1980s.

His son, Lee Dye, was the science editor of *The Los Angeles Times*, and through him Dr. Dye was able to meet the world-famous astronomer, Carl Sagan, an avowed agnostic.

He said it was sad that Carl Sagan knew all about the universe but did not know the Creator of the universe.

Dr. Dye told how a book title saved his life.

His personal doctor happened to be close by when Dr. Dye went into cardiac arrest at a hospital. The doctor was giving him chest compressions and suddenly blurted out, "She tore my heart out and stomped that sucker flat."

That was the title of a book by the late great humor writer Lewis Grizzard. Dr. Dye said he got to laughing and his heart began to beat again. I wrote a column and sent it to Grizzard, who, coincidentally, died of a heart attack several years later.

There's no record of whether anyone yelled out the name of one of his books to try and save his life.

NEWSPAPER STORIES

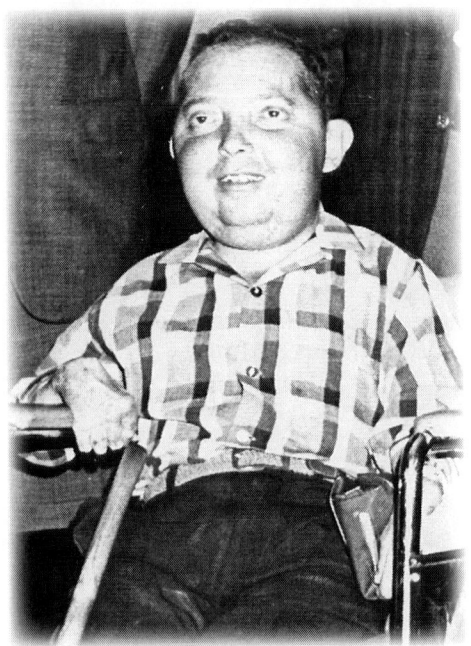

Robert Ramey "Bob" Hilburn

Bob Hilburn: My mentor and role model

My mentor and role model for the professional vocation I would have
for almost 40 years was Robert Ramey "Bob" Hilburn.

I had met him while covering PHS football for the *Bulldog Barker* as
a junior and even made some trips with him to out-of-town games. Of

course, he was always accompanied by a fellow *Plainview Daily Herald* employee or two to help him get to the press box.

Watching huge Runt Burch carry little Bobby up the 27 steps of Bulldog Stadium was always a touching sight.

You see, Bob Hilburn was pretty much confined to a wheelchair since childhood due to rheumatoid arthritis. His father, Herb Hilburn, who served as editor of *The Herald* from 1919–65 and was a part owner at one time, spent thousands of dollars on treatment for Bob. He reportedly was the first child in America treated at the Mayo Clinic with cortisone for his ailment.

Bob, blessed with an indomitable spirit, went on to graduate from Plainview High and join the staff of the *Daily Texan* at the University of Texas, even doing a stint as managing editor.

A jokester and prankster, Bob pulled a good one on a future novelist and magazine editor, Willie Morris.

Morris started as wire editor of the *Daily Texan*. His duty was to pull the first paragraph of the top six Associated Press stories of the day. One day he came in about half asleep but was thrown into a tizzy by this mock bulletin:

> **WASHINGTON (AP)—The Pentagon has announced that the Soviet Union has launched an attack on the United States.**
> **(MORE)**

Morris raced to the pay phone, called his folks in Yazoo City, Mississippi, and told them to get in their boat and get out into the Gulf of Mexico.

Mr. Hilburn paid for another young man to attend UT and help Bob get around campus and to his various other activities. The landlady at their rooming house was none too happy when she found breakfast dishes in the bathtub, eggs floating in the water.

Bob went on to graduate *summa cum laude,* but the university withheld his diploma for a time since he decided not to attend Commencement.

Bob loved sports and betting on same. Or betting on any kind of game, even if money wasn't involved. One of his favorites was seeing how long it took to get from the city limits of Plainview and seated at the Silver Grill in downtown Amarillo. Bob let out an unprintable expletive when a journey to Amarillo was stymied by a red light at a new signal recently erected in Tulia.

When Baylor upset Texas in 1963, Bob had to sit outside *The Herald* and hawk pencils after losing a bet with Baylor graduate Graddy Tunnell.

My big break came in the spring of 1967 when *The Herald* decided to publish a special edition commemorating the 60th anniversary of Hale County. Bob was assigned to do a number of stories, particularly about the hospital.

He called to ask if I might be interested in covering the Bulldog baseball team, of which I was a member.

Is the pope Catholic?

I jumped at the chance and eventually landed a job in August as a reporter and photographer, a month before I started school at Wayland. I also began to work in sports.

Bob amazed me with his ability to knock out stories and a weekly column or two, using his spindly index fingers to pound away on an electric typewriter.

Bob taught journalism courses at night at Wayland, and he'd sometimes let class out early so he and I could head to the Granada for a movie. He loved Roadrunner cartoons and always cheered for Wile E. Coyote, moaning loudly as the hapless varmint would be the victim of a falling safe or pick up a stick of dynamite that was about to explode.

One night, as we were putting on his jacket, a bone in one of his arms snapped. We went to the old Medical Center out on St. Louis Street. Dr. Joe Horn, his friend and Toastmasters buddy, told him, "Bobby, your bones are so thin I can hardly get an X-ray." He wound up dictating stories to news side assistant Betty Hingst until the arm healed.

A mid-morning coffee break was still the norm in the 1960s, and someone would push Bob to Blair's or Robinson-Herring for java. Bob got a kick out of advertising salesman Joe Don Hancock—later editor and publisher of the twice-weekly *Plainview Reporter News*—being the recipient of a deposit by a passing pigeon, saving Bob from the indignity.

Bob, who loved to fish at Greer's Ferry in Arkansas or take in a game in St. Louis on occasion when that was the closest venue for major league baseball, also was a huge model railroad buff. A building across from the home he shared with his father was a treasure trove of railroad trains and memorabilia.

I spent most of my first semester at his house, sleeping on a rollaway at the foot of his bed. A nightly contest was to see who would get in the last word before one of us fell asleep. I usually was the winner.

Sadly, Bob's health began to fail in the summer of 1968. He had to curtail a trip to Europe with a nephew and niece, intending to purchase items for an antiques and gift shop he planned to open.

In late August, Joe Don Hancock and I drove to Dallas to see the Cowboys play the Green Bay Packers in an exhibition game at the Cotton Bowl.

Bob would have loved that trip. We paid a woman a dollar to let us park in her vacant lot as she pulled back a bedspring to allow us entrance. At the game, a rather inebriated young woman, seeing the Packers come onto the field in colors she recognized, yelled at the top of her voice, "Go Baylor!" Every Baptist in the house ducked their head.

When Joe Don and I arrived home late on Sunday afternoon, Carolyn gave me the sad news that Bobby Hilburn had passed away.

My mentor and role model was gone at age 36. I loved that little guy and owe him more than I could ever repay.

*   *   *

Millie Bishop

A logical conclusion, but just not correct

Because I spent almost 40 years in the newspaper business, most folks think I majored in journalism. A logical conclusion, just not correct.

Since Wayland didn't offer a journalism major, I minored in that field as well as English while majoring in history. Thus, most of my journalism background is in "on the job" training.

My first introduction to journalism came in the sixth grade in 1960-61 when my teacher, Nell Saul, decided to publish a weekly mimeographed newspaper for Hillcrest Elementary.

Foreshadowing the future, I was the sports editor, which consisted of reporting the scores of schoolyard basketball games.

When I decided to take journalism at Plainview High School as a junior, I told advisor Millie Bishop, who became a dear friend and also was the mentor for future Herald colleagues Doug McDonough, Gordon Zeigler, Bobby Hall, and Cynthia Gregory, that I wanted to be the sports editor for the *Bulldog Barker* newspaper.

I always said that I wanted to be a sportswriter in the worst way and several friends decided "you certainly succeeded at that."

My high school newspaper assignment gave me a chance to write a column called "The Spectator's Side," a name I adopted for my column when I became sports editor of *The Herald*. In addition to serving as sports editor of The Barker for two years, I also did similar duty for the *Plain View* yearbook as a senior.

At Wayland I was a reporter for the *Trailblazer* my first year and editor the last two, introducing a couple of firsts—a 12-page edition and paid advertising. My advisors were former Herald reporter L.D. Brown and then Joe Provence, who almost 40 years later would be my predecessor in the alumni office at Wayland.

While at *The Herald*, I had opportunities to move to the sports departments of the Amarillo and Lubbock newspapers and to become editor of the *Friona Star* and the *Floyd County Hesperian*.

To be honest, I liked Plainview and enjoyed being a big fish in a small pond. The weekly newspaper jobs would have required selling advertising and working in the darkroom to develop pictures and I had little or no background in either and even less desire to learn.

When Jim Servatius decided to take a new post in Midland, General Manager Jim Oswald called me at home on July 4, shortly after we had put out an early edition, and asked if I'd be willing to take over as editor.

After I literally picked myself up off the ground, it was an easy decision.

So, there you have a little history.

*   *   *

Plainview Herald building at 820 Broadway

Blessed with great *Herald* colleagues

In 39 years at *The Plainview Daily Herald*, I worked with well over 300 people. God blessed me with a lot of talented folks in the news department, including some who had very little formal training in journalism but liked people and had a knack for the writing.

I'm sure I'll miss some, but here are a few I worked with for a long time in a business where longevity isn't always the norm. Some are mentioned in other stories.

*   **Charlotte Thurman**, our news department assistant who could type faster (and with almost no mistakes) on any device you put in front of her. She was our Mother Superior, counselor, and friend . . . always in a good mood.

*   **Doug McDonough**, current editor of the paper, who worked his way from Farm Editor to News Editor to his present post. Dependable and dedicated as the day is long, he has won many awards for headlines, and his "Looking Back" feature on Sunday has been a great addition to *The Herald*.

*   **Myrna Smith**, "women's editor," worked many nights and taught me a lot about life by our frequent conversations.

* **Marie Harris**, regional editor for us and a regular columnist ("Marie's Malarky") for the *Tulia Herald*, she made terrific ham dip and "Texas Trash."
* **Dalton Wood**, news editor and quipster extraordinaire, he also was one of my journalism instructors at Wayland. He was saxophonist for the popular "Old Masters of Swing."
* **Richard Orr**, a tenacious reporter who did the difficult stories; he took a lot of flak he really didn't deserve but also got some from liberal columns that he did deserve.
* **Nicki Logan**, Lifetyles Editor for more than 25 years, built a great following with a lively weekly column and devoted community service.
* **Kevin Lewis**, easily the most gifted person I ever worked with. He was a quiet, hardworking sports editor who could have made a living as a sports photographer. I'm glad he was my successor as editor at *The Herald* and is now my Wayland colleague as sports information director.
* **Gary Ott** moved from general assignments to news editor before moving on to Midland where he served as editor and an excellent column writer for the *Reporter-Telegram*.
* **Phillip Hamilton** did two stints with the paper as a reporter and editor and now is editor and publisher of the *Olton Enterprise* and the *Hale Center American*.
* **Richard Porter** could take a complicated agriculture issue and make it understandable. He also took some excellent photos, especially of the outdoor world.
* **Gordon Zeigler**, a fellow 1967 graduate of PHS, showed his diversity as a reporter, photographer, special projects editor and finally in the advertising department.
* **Three current Wayland colleagues**: Sports editors Bobby Hall (Executive Vice President and Provost) and Jon Petty (Director of Public Relations) and reporter-photographer Teresa Young (former PR director and now Director of Annual Giving). They all did great work.

*   Special friends include Ben Thompson, Bill Rushing, Joe Billy Frye, Jerry Ticer, Carol McGill, Rosemary Gonzales, Sandra Sims, J.R. Ruiz, Frank Silvas, and Frankie Hembree who worked in press, production, circulation and accounting areas.

*   The Herald also has been blessed with some great freelance columnists such as John Perry, Carole Bell, Louise Harper and the late Yolanda Godsey Rodriguez.

*   *   *

James Thomas: Herald Publisher 1979-90

James Thomas embodied "Dedicated Service"

If ever a man lived up to the motto he created for his business, it was James Thomas, publisher of *The Plainview Daily Herald* from 1979 to 1990 and then publisher emeritus until his death in 2008.

Not long after succeeding Jim Oswald as the chief executive of the newspaper, James added "Dedicated Service" to the masthead.

As an advertising salesman for a decade before his promotion, James was all about service for his customers and, by extension, the entire newspaper.

James relaxed the dress code a bit in the summer but preferred all males to wear a tie lest they be thrown in the same barrel with slovenly media types of non-print persuasion.

James was almost always congenial, but his face could turn bright red if he got angry as he did on rare occasions. One day a prominent businessman came by and told me a merchants' boycott of *The Herald* was imminent because of some unpopular story.

When I told James, he said, "I wouldn't worry too much about those guys. They can't even get organized for Dollar Day."

James—and it was never "Jim"—was a native of Seminole, Oklahoma, where he claimed his family was "too poor to paint and too proud to whitewash."

I loved to hear his stories about local school bus drivers transporting kids to Sunday School and church at First Baptist; about his father the fire chief and his mom, who worked in the school cafeteria; and his military stories (he was at Pearl Harbor for 3 1/2 years)—about being embarrassed because he didn't have any money to put in the offering plate at church, and about arriving home on leave late at night and his mother whispering, "There he is!" when he stepped onto the porch.

James, who was named Plainview's Man of the Year in 1986, was a devoted Rotarian, and served on all kinds of local boards for the betterment of the community including the Chamber of Commerce, Wee Care Child Center, Hale County Chapter of the American Heart Association, Meals on Wheels, South Plains Better Business Bureau, Plainview Crime Stoppers, Texas Press Association, West Texas Press Association, and Panhandle Press Association. He was a big supporter of Faith in Sharing House food pantry.

James received an honorary doctorate from Wayland for his tireless efforts to promote the campaign to finish and furnish the Mabee Resources Learning Center libraries.

He was proud to have put on an extra push by the newspaper to encourage Sam Walton to locate a new distribution center in Plainview after it appeared we were out of the running. He joined in a hula dance with other community leaders at the Ollie Liner Center when Walton decided on Plainview.

But his real love was his family and grandchildren, and he talked about them often. Bob served as Chamber of Commerce manager in Slaton and later worked for the NCAA, while Janie has been a Methodist minister's wife.

James loved my kids too and made a baseball uniform for my oldest son. One of my favorite pictures is of James standing in front of New York Yankee great Joe DiMaggio's locker when we visited the Baseball Hall of Fame in Cooperstown, New York, during a Hearst trip in 1984.

Another passion for James, who worked for 12 years for C.R. Anthony stores and then was in advertising in Tulia and Dumas, and for Polly, who worked for JC Penney after they moved to Plainview, was teaching Sunday School at First United Methodist Church.

They started out teaching the fifth grade but moved to first graders pretty quickly and taught for more than 30 years.

James always had a good supply of candy, and it pleased him no end that older kids would come by his room on the way to worship to get a piece of candy from their former teacher.

Polly told me that James literally forced himself to go to work many days when his crippling arthritis would have caused lesser men to give up.

To be closer to family, the Thomases moved to Santa Rosa, California, where James died July 25, 2008, at age 84. Polly told me that in the last couple of weeks of his life, James told her, "Don't ever be afraid to die; it's so beautiful."

He's buried not far from Charles Schulz, the creator of one of his favorite comic strips, "Peanuts."

Like the strip's lead character, Charlie Brown, James Thomas was just a good man.

*　　*　　*

Rollie Hyde: Herald Publisher 1990-2005

Rollie Hyde: You're going love this guy

When James Thomas was nearing retirement as publisher of *The Plainview Daily Herald*, Hearst officials asked if I was interested in the job.

I "sneaked around" for several months, visiting other Hearst papers in Texas to get a feel for what that job entailed but quickly realized with no business background I had no business trying to run the newspaper.

The economy wasn't so hot at the time and a couple of fellow Hearst editors who had been promoted to publisher had failed miserably. That didn't exactly boost my confidence.

Anyway, it was certainly a great decision when Rollie Hyde, advertising director for *The Midland Reporter-Telegram*, was named publisher in August of 1990, a post he held for 15 years.

We never had one cross word in that time, and I loved him like a brother. He had a great sense of humor and a big laugh that could be heard all over the building.

He also had such a good heart for the community. The annual Cowboy Days and Cattle Drive was his idea, and that has become a great tradition for Plainview.

Named Plainview's Man of the Year in 2000, Rollie was president or chairman of the Industrial Foundation, Chamber of Commerce, Rotary Club, United Way, Wee Care Child Center, and Community Concerts, and vice chairman of the Hale County Hospital Authority.

Rollie was the 120th president of the Texas Newspaper Association, serving from 1997-98, president of the Panhandle Press Association in 1995-96 and inducted into its Hall of Fame in April 2005, past president of the Oklahoma City Ad Federation and Corpus Christi Ad Federation, and former member of the Texas Tech University Journalism Advisory Council.

Professionally, he received the Frank Mayborn Award for community service from the Texas Daily Newspaper Association and the Harold Hudson Award from the West Texas Press Association for lifetime service.

Sandra Aven succeeded Rollie as publisher. I only worked with that energetic lady in that post for six months before moving to Wayland. She made a great observation: "Rollie was always interested in his people and how he could help them grow, both personally and professionally." I know he was happy to see Sandra succeed him.

As with James Thomas, I was blessed with another Oklahoman who allowed me to run the news side with encouragement and support. Rollie admitted when he applied for his first newspaper job at the Anadarko *Daily News* that "I wasn't positive I could tell the difference between a news story and an ad."

Over the years, he worked at newspapers in Oklahoma City, Borger, Canyon, Corpus Christi, Fort Worth, and Davenport, Iowa. He came up with a lot of creative ideas to spur advertising as well as circulation.

Though born in the same town as Baseball Hall of Famer Johnny Bench, Rollie cared very little for sports. Camping was his thing. So was having a project, whether it made any money or not.

Even before he retired from *The Herald* in 2005, he bought a place down at Roaring Springs but spent a lot of his time chasing loose livestock. He also bought several cars from far-off places. I never figured out how he made any money by the time he drove them home.

Carolyn and I enjoyed Hearst newspaper trips with Rollie and his personable wife Jeri to San Francisco, New York, Tampa, and New England twice. On one trip to New York to see Hearst's advances in technology, I conversed on a new-fangled thing called the Internet with, of all people, someone in Olton, Texas.

One of my favorite "Rollie stories"—and I told it at his funeral—was the time we were driving from Monterey to San Francisco and Jeri was talking, talking, talking (probably while I was taking a breath).

Finally, Rollie looked over at her and said, "Did you ever hear about that guy who killed his wife because she talked all the time?"

We all busted up laughing.

After retiring from *The Herald*, Rollie joined W.B. Grimes and Co., as a senior associate for the Mountain States and Southwest regions. Among the top tier of American newspaper brokers, he compiled a remarkable average of one newspaper sale every 10 days for a full year.

Rollie passed away on Nov. 11, 2013, in Oklahoma City at age 76.

My predecessor as editor of *The Herald*, Jim Servatius, worked with Rollie at the Midland paper, and Jim told me when Rollie was bound for Plainview, "You're going to love this guy."

He was absolutely right.

*   *   *

Jim Servatius...Herald Editor 1965-78

Jim Servatius: Refreshingly arrogant

I first met Jim Servatius, editor of *The Plainview Herald* from 1965-78, when I began writing sports as a high school senior in 1967.

Jim cared absolutely nothing about sports, despite having four boys, but he reluctantly went to their games. Mainly, he preferred hunting arrowheads in New Mexico.

He pronounced his name "Sir-vay-tus," though any number of people would say "Sir-vay-shus."

Jim had come to Plainview by way of a news stint in Vernon after selling advertising for the San Antonio *Express-News*. While in that city, he also taught dance lessons at the military bases.

After years of wanting to see him prove what a great dancer he alleged to be, I finally witnessed a bit of ballroom dancing demonstration with the wife of our head of newspapers.

In retrospect, it did not impress me that he would have advanced far on "Dancing with the Stars."

I always said Jim was "refreshingly arrogant."

Early in my career, I angered the grandfather of Kevin Whisenant, who went on to become an accomplished builder in Plainview. I happened to mention young relief pitcher Kevin as making an error in a pivotal inning of a Little League game. It was not meant to impugn his talents, only one of several events in a bad inning for Plainview.

Franz Pannell called me up at home and told me in no uncertain terms that I had besmirched his grandson's good name and demanded a retraction in the next edition.

He wanted to know who my boss was and I said, "Jim Servatius." Not satisfied, he wanted to know the name of the owner of the paper. "That would be James N. Allison, Sr. in Midland."

Mr. Pannell showed up at *The Herald* office in the old building at Eighth and Broadway on Monday morning and spelled out his case against me.

Jim had no office in those days, just a desk by the side door, so I was able to hear the conversation. After what seemed like a long time, Jim finally told Mr. Pannell in a rather dismissive tone: "I think your interpretation is loose and extreme."

Mr. Pannell then asked, "Well, what can I do about it?"

Jim's option: "There's the advertising department over there. You can buy an ad."

Mr. Pannell left without taking Jim's advice. Sometimes finances can get in the way of defending a family's honor.

Maybe it also illustrated the old bromide: Never argue with people who buy ink by the barrel.

Jim wrote some clever headlines including one for a story I wrote about a fellow who thought he might have an authentic Stradivarius violin:

Egad, a Strad?
Well, maybe

Jim smoked like a fiend—lighting one off another—picked his teeth with his letter opener, and cleaned his ears with a paper clip. Otherwise, he was an elegant man.

Jim was also possessed of an explosive temper—often yelling on the phone at one of his four sons, then slamming down the receiver.

It made him none too happy when Larry, the youngest, took a family car and headed off to Portland, Oregon, to see an older brother—Mike or David, or was it Steve?

Jim once told me, "Danny, you remember everything that's ever happened to you. I can't remember anything. One time Ann (his bridge-addicted wife who stood about 4 feet, 8 inches tall) said, 'Jimmy, do you remember that Christmas when David got that little toy elephant and was so excited?'

"I told her, 'Hell, Ann, I don't even remember which one David was.'"

Thirty years ago, we were in New York City on our way to Albany for a Hearst Editors and Publishers meeting and decided to visit the World Trade Center. We went to the very top floor.

After lunch, as the elevator doors opened, Ann asked innocently, "Is this elevator going down?"

"Hell, Ann," Jim said in mock disbelief, "we're 110 stories in the air, where do you think it's going?"

At the famous Highland Inn in Carmel, California, some years later, Jim sternly warned Ann to not get in the in-room hot tub without his direct supervision.

Jim could say volumes with a raised eyebrow and baleful stare, and I was recipient of both upon asking if I might possibly have a day off since as sports editor I was putting in 55-60 hours a week.

"I'm shocked and surprised that you would ask that," he said, a tinge of sadness in his voice.

I slunk back to my desk and never made that request again.

Well, some of the best advice I was ever given was delivered by Jim Servatius before he departed to become assistant editor and later editor of *The Midland Reporter-Telegram*.

"Don't sit behind that desk and pontificate (on the editorial page or elsewhere). There's always somebody who knows more than you do."

Boy, did I ever find the truth of that statement.

*   *   *

Wendell Holloman checks copy from the Associated Press wire

David Bryant   Mike Wall

The *Daily Herald's* "Three Musketeers"

I've often pondered whether people who are "characters" decide to become newspaper reporters or the nature of the business turns newspaper reporters into characters.

I worked with three early in my journalistic career. You might have called David Bryant, Mike Wall, and Wendell Holloman "The Three Muskeeters" . . . or perhaps "The Axis of Evil."

To say that David Bryant was his "own man" would be a major understatement. Like many creative people, he could be mercurial in his temperament—enormously engaging at times, downright surly at others.

I worked with David, who died in the 1973 tornado, for six years. He was a reporter and *The Herald*'s chief photographer when I started at the newspaper. At the time of his death, he was in charge of editing copy and laying out the paper as News Editor.

David's first love was photography and he was darn good at it. His "This is Plainview" series on familiar landmarks is still a classic because the photos were taken from unusual angles or were just brought to life in ways that only those who see things the way others don't can do it.

In early 2014, I had the picture of Paul Aday making the winning layup against Lubbock High in that famous televised playoff game in Bulldog Gym in 1964 blown up and framed for the gym lobby.

David said he was so disgusted—thinking the Bulldogs had lost after turning the ball over with five seconds to play and trailing by one point—that he turned the strobe off on his camera.

When Phil Stephenson flew out of nowhere to intercept a pass and toss it to Aday under the Plainview basket for the winning score, David said he instinctively wheeled and shot almost from the hip. Fortunately, there was enough charge in the camera strobe to capture the photo.

In it Paul Aday is stretching high to put the ball on the backboard and half a dozen fans on the floor have their fists clinched, each with a leg lifted in unison—almost like a chorus line.

Mike Wall was an introspective guy who wrote a beautiful book of poetry called *Sails*. He only lacked one course to have his degree from Texas Tech. He succeeded David as News Editor.

Wendell, who was the Farm Editor much of his time at *The Herald*, banged away on his typewriter with just his index fingers. He once wore a pair of Pepto-Bismol pink and baby blue cowboy boots to work and also showed up in a pair of velour slacks in a light shade of purple.

Editor Jim Servatius told him to never wear those pants again. So he dyed them pea green.

Those guys worked a 48-hour week so it seemed they were always around—except when they were sneaking out to the Holiday Inn for an extended coffee break, at which they were caught by General Manager Jim Oswald and properly chastised.

One Saturday, they collaborated on about 100 derogatory one-liners about the sorry state of the old *Herald* building:

* *The Plainview Daily Herald*—member of the Armstrong Everlast Tile proving grounds."
* *The Plainview Daily Herald* has received the Flint Ink Corp. award for most ink used in one year. Second place: *The New York Times*."

Editor Jim Servatius was not amused. Nor was he the time he ordered a general clean-up of the premises by the news staff. David got so mad he cleaned out everything in and on his desk (including, I think, some valuable file materials), polished the desk, and stuck the phone in one of the drawers.

For a time, David and Mike had a side business called, appropriately, Bryant-Wall Photography in the 300 block of Broadway. Mike was going through a divorce, so he slept in a big cardboard box at the studio.

They hired me to photograph a wedding at the Nazarene Church. It was one of the few times I have ever perspired on the job, fearful I would mess up the pictures and suffer the wrath of David Bryant. Thank God that didn't happen.

I guess cash flow wasn't a big issue for David. He once had seven uncashed *Herald* payroll checks in his wallet.

He was one of the first people around here to have a video camera. He would mimic the way I walk, then show me on camera that he wasn't exaggerating.

David was a good and thoughtful writer, penning insightful prose on "If I Were the Prince of Peace" in response to an essay by national commentator Paul Harvey called "If I Were the Devil." Harvey used it on a broadcast in September 1973.

I never think about David without recalling a warm spring evening in 1968.

David's wife, Rita, was sitting next to me in a Wayland journalism class taught at the Flores Bible Building by the late *Herald* Sports Editor Bob Hilburn.

With Bob in mid-lecture, Mike Wall bursts into the room, looks around frantically, then opens a door and runs into the next room. Before we could react, David runs in, shouts, "Where did he go?" and rushes through the same door.

I'm thinking: "Mike has been running around with Rita and David's gonna kill him."

Several gunshots ensue and a handful of students look at each other in shock and disbelief. Then, Mike and David emerge from the adjacent room, smile, and walk out.

Hilburn turns to the class and says, "Now, write about what you just witnessed."

It was amazing the discrepancy in details, including how many shots were fired. A great object lesson unforgettably delivered. I wonder now if it was David's idea.

It certainly was his idea to join REACT, the local storm-spotting team. He was at his post at 4:15 a.m. April 15, 1973—a forward observer—on the edge of excitement and disaster.

REACT still gives a scholarship in memory of David C. Bryant.

Mike passed away from a heart attack while editor-publisher of *The Hart Beat* newspaper, and Wendell is the last man standing, working, at last report, for a supermarket service station in Austin.

Gosh, I miss those characters.

*   *   *

Mary Lees, the Classified Lady

Mary Lees: The right wrong person to ask

One of the all-time great characters at *The Herald*—and we sure had our fair share in my nearly 40 years there—was Mary Lees, daughter of Wayland founder Dr. James Henry Wayland and wife Sarah.

Mary, a "free spirit" who had created some havoc while attending her daddy's school, worked in Classified Advertising, that counter being located at the front of the old building at 801 Broadway.

Mary was about 4-feet-10 and looked like an elf with frizzy hair.

Walter Frye, the press foreman, was replacing a fluorescent light bulb near her desk when he dropped it. A couple of shards struck Mary in the back of her leg. She looked down, saw a little blood, threw up her hands and screamed, "My God, I've been shot!"

Mary took a classified that was printed thusly: "For sale—two Palomino billy goats" (rather than filly colts).

But the classic story is about the guy who came into the office about 1 o'clock one afternoon and inquired if the paper was off the press yet.

"No," Mary said, "but it won't be long."

Making conversation, she asked if the man was abreast of a fairly sensational local trial about which Mary was quite interested.

"Have you been keeping up with that trial? I think they were going to come down with a verdict today," she asked.

"Yes, ma'am," the man replied.

"Well, did they hang the sonofabitch?"

"No, ma'am," the man said, "they acquitted me."

Mary jumped up from her chair and ran to the back of the building, hiding out while the acquitted laughed out loud.

*   *   *

I Stand Amazed in the Presence . . .

Newspaper reporters like to come up with clever leads to get the reader's attention.

Two of the best I ever saw were written by John Anders of the Dallas *Morning News*. They concerned SMU's inventive Flying Wishbone formation developed by Coach Hayden Fry—kind of a combination of the vaunted Wishbone running attack with some passing thrown in.

Passing and the Wishbone would not have been something Darrell Royal at Texas would have invented. Darrell K. said, "When you throw the ball, three things can happen, and two of 'em are bad."

SMU opened the 1971 season with Oklahoma and John Anders wrote: "SMU's Flying Wishbone got caught in some kind of colossal holding pattern over Norman here Saturday. In this case, Oklahoma was the holder and SMU definitely was the holdee, 30-0."

The next week, he wrote: "SMU's Flying Wishbone got hijacked again here (Columbia, Missouri) Saturday. This time it was Missouri that held the gun to Peruna's head and switched the controls from automatic pilot to self-destruct."

With SMU still floundering in late season, a Dallas *News* head asked testily: "What next, Hayden?"

Well, notwithstanding that former *Herald* News Editor Dalton Wood declared my 87-word lead on a Petersburg-New Deal playoff game was "the worst example of journalism I've ever seen" (mainly because you had to take three breaths to be able to read it straight through), I liked my lead on a story in advance of a Wayland basketball game with Bethany Nazarene.

That school, now known as Southern Nazarene, is located in suburban Oklahoma City and once was a rival of Wayland in the Texoma Conference and later in the Sooner Athletic Conference.

Then known as the Indians—but later changing to Crimson Storm amidst the angst over nicknames related to Native Americans—Bethany was led by 6-8 Jeff Jantz who averaged 17 points and 8 rebounds a game.

Thus my lead: "There is no truth to the rumor that the Texoma Conference, comprised mostly of church schools, is going to adopt as its theme song 'I Stand Amazed in the Presence of Jantz the Nazarene.'"

It was obviously a play on the old hymn, "I Stand Amazed in the Presence of Jesus the Nazarene" (proof, folks of that denominational stripe contend, that Jesus was "one of us").

However, since many *Herald* readers weren't familiar with that hymn, that clever lead went right over their heads.

At least it wasn't the worst piece of journalism Dalton Wood had ever seen.

*   *   *

Charlotte Thurman...Herald's Gal Friday

Slip of the tongue and typewriter: Forgive us our sins

Typographical errors and Freudian slips are the bane of reporters and broadcasters, some of which are a bit too graphic to repeat.

Charlotte Thurman, longtime *Herald* newsroom assistant, got a kick out my story that said a certain player wouldn't be able to play because of a bruised *thing*, rather than a bruised thigh.

I was broadcasting a Wayland basketball game during my college days. We were on KVOP and without benefit of commercial sponsorship, so I just had to keep talking during breaks in the action.

Wayland's Ted Welch went up for a rebound with a College of Santa Fe player and landed an elbow in a strategic location below the beltline.

The poor guy hit the deck, writhed in pain, and literally crawled off the floor. All I could think of was that Bill Cosby skit about playing football on television and being advised by the camera crew, "Do not touch certain areas of your body."

Trying to gingerly describe what had happened, I decided, "He got it where it hurts."

Larry Smith, a former Wayland player who was doing Bulldog basketball at the time, was sitting next to me and fell over on the bench laughing.

(By the way, Bill Cosby did a show at Wayland's Hutcherson Center in the early 1970s. He played tennis in the afternoon and that evening talked about painting a Studebaker, equipped with an airplane engine, with pink house paint.)

One of the all-time great miscues appeared in a *Herald* obituary written by Nicki Logan. It said, "She is survived by three *sins*."

Shortly after the paper was printed, some men came into *The Herald* requesting several copies. They, as it turned out, were the *three sins* and took it good-naturedly.

In fact, years later, one came up to me after a funeral at Northwest Church of Christ and asked, "Do you recognize me?"

I had to admit I didn't.

"I'm one of the three sins," he said.

We both laughed. Nothing else needed to be said.

*   *   *

Dealing with complainers and know-it-alls

It always took a lot to get my blood pressure up when I was at the newspaper. But two men, long deceased and who shall remain unnamed, had that special ability to fire up the boiler.

One would regularly call up to complain about city and county government decisions, railing on about this and that, sometimes berating me in the process. In his later years, his wife got to yelling in the background when he'd call.

He said he quit going to church years before because, "All those preachers do is preach 'pink tea' sermons." Not enough hellfire and brimstone, I guess. Older folks seemed to like those kinds of sermons, especially since most of them never dreamed they might be aimed at them . . . just at "sinners."

One Monday morning, Phil Hamilton, now editor and publisher of the *Olton Enterprise* and the *Hale Center American*, said, "Mr. So-and-So called and thanked me for the story on page 1 yesterday. He said he knew I had to run the story around you to get it in," alleging my reporter had to sneak the story past me since I wouldn't have run it otherwise.

You remember Jackie Gleason threatening his wife, Alice, on *The Honeymooners*? "Bam, zoom, Alice, you're goin' to the moon!"

That's how my blood pressure skyrocketed.

I picked up the phone and dialed the man's home. When he answered, I bellowed, "Mr. So-and So, Phil Hamilton says you called and thanked him for running that story and said you knew he had to sneak it past me. Let me tell you, nothing gets in this paper without my approval" (not totally true, to be honest, but not that story).

"Sir, you call me up and berate me and every elected official in town. I listen to your criticisms, and I have been nothing but courteous to you. I don't want you to ever call here again. Do you understand me?" I asked, voice rising even louder. "I don't want you to ever call this newspaper again!"

WHAM! I nearly broke the phone slamming it onto the cradle. Then I immediately thought, "Well, that was certainly nice, wasn't it?"

I called his daughter and told her what I had done and asked if she thought an apology would do any good. She said her father was probably glad he got me riled up, but if I thought I should apologize, I probably should.

So, I fired off an apologetic letter. But I don't recall if he ever phoned again.

The other chap made a habit of regularly writing letters decrying the stupidity of the American public to believe anything that proceeded out of the mouths of politicians—especially those in Washington.

We didn't have a policy about how many letters we'd accept in any given time period or that they couldn't be on the same subject.

So, one day, this old fellow wanders in with another letter in hand, immediately wanting to know, "Where's my previous letter (that hadn't run)?"

"Oh, I've got that on the backburner," I said, hoping the deluge would stop.

Looking down at my desk, he spied the *Lubbock Avalanche-Journal* with a headline that mentioned a legislator from the region.

"Well, you always have room for the crooks," he opined, referring to said politician.

Bam, zoom . . . look out for another moon shot!

"Yeah," I retorted, "and know-it-all SOBs (and I didn't use an abbreviation) like you coming in here and telling me how to run the newspaper."

His eyes glazed over and he staggered out the door, perhaps thinking I was about to do him bodily harm.

As with the other gentleman, I thought, "Well, that certainly was a Christian thing to say." So I wrote him a letter of apology, too. But that may have dried up the letters as well.

The closest I ever came to thinking I was going to get whipped by an irate reader concerned a fellow who didn't want his marriage license announcement to run in Public Records.

I told him I was sorry, that when we decided to run Public Records back in the 1970s, we would run them all or none at all. Oddly enough, the first time we ran them, a *Herald* employee was being sued for non-payment at a local jewelry store.

The guy, leaning on my desk, told me I could hold the information out of the paper. I told him I couldn't but that he could go to Tulia and get a license (I don't even know if that was legal) but that the *Tulia Herald* would probably run it, too.

That didn't help his demeanor one lick. "You can hold it out if you want to," he insisted.

"I guess I don't want to," I said as he glared and walked out of my office.

Making a smart remark to him might have resulted in bodily harm to me.

* * *

Anonymous letters: Humorous and curious

I got a few anonymous letters in my 28 years as editor of *The Herald*, some pretty funny, some pretty hurtful.

One that I look back on as encompassing both emotions was a missive from somebody—I suspected a certain person but could never be sure—who took me to task over stories about a rift between Central Plains Hospital and Central Plains MH-MR Center.

"You're trying to drive a wedge between the two organizations," the handwritten communication declared.

We felt the hospital board was actually meeting "off the record" to make some decisions. When I called the venerable attorney for the hospital to express that sentiment, "Judge" H.M. LaFont, who practiced here for nearly 70 years, said tersely, "I don't agree." End of conversation.

After the opening salvo, the letter writer got personal: "It was a sad day when you were named managing editor—a boy trying to take a man's place. Bring back Jim Servatius."

This, of course, referred to my predecessor, who had departed a couple of years earlier to eventually become editor of *The Midland Reporter-Telegram*.

I was 31 at the time, but the "boy" title stung a bit. However, it became more humorous as I got older—and that didn't take very long, either.

Another letter asserted that my daughter was the "dirtiest player" in Little Dribblers basketball. Hey, she was shorter than many players and had to defend herself with a sharp elbow or two. And there was that time she slammed the ball down and got a technical foul. But "dirtiest player"? C'mon.

But the two anonymous letters that puzzled me most came in December of 2010 and 2011. I suspected they were from an older woman and said essentially the same thing. I paraphrase:

"Why do you always have to be front and center in the choir at First Baptist Church? Are you as unhappy as you look? You wear your clothes too tight. You need to wear looser-fitting clothes. You need to smile more."

As I surveyed the congregation the next week, I didn't see anyone that caused an "Ah-hah, there she is" moment. Maybe she watched our services on cable television.

So, when people ask, "Did you get a lot of critical letters when you were at *The Herald?*" I have to say, "No, actually, I've gotten more criticism from being in the choir at First Baptist Church."

Which reminds me—and many stories remind me of other stories—of a recollection by the late Plainview mayor Gene Ridlehuber about a fellow Hillsboro resident.

The father of Jack Loftis, former editor of Texas' largest paper, the Hearst-owned *Houston Chronicle*, was sent to prison in the 1930s for bootlegging.

When he got off the train, someone asked, "Henry, are you going back to Huntsville?"

"Not unless it's for singin' too loud in the First Baptist Church choir?"

If so, I hope he smiled a lot and wore loose-fitting clothes.

*   *   *

Danny Andrews: A rich, white elitist?

I tried not to respond to most Letters to the Editor unless they just made a statement that needed to be refuted.

I got one from someone that said: "Danny Andrews allowing an elitist rich white person's comments to be published in Line One shows what side his bread is buttered on. The 'not my son' letter writer shares the same paradigm of patriotism as the Bushes and others who used their political connections to make sure their sons protected America from Austin or some military court.

"I'm sure Danny Andrews can come up with some reason for allowing the comment to be published, and I'm waiting to hear it so I can see how really shameless he is of being a rich and white elitist."

(EDITOR'S NOTE: The person who called in the comment is a blue-collar Anglo man. We recognized the voice though we don't have Caller ID for Line One. Since the caller did not violate Line One guidelines, his comment was used. Danny Andrews admits only to being white.)

* * *

Herald's Line One: A decided inconsistency

For several years during my time at The Herald, we ran "Line One," allowing readers to call in and respond to specific questions. Later, it was pretty much an "open forum for comments on subjects of interest to our readers."

I had friends who berated me for "running that trash" and asked "why do you allow people to make anonymous comments to Line One but you won't run a Letter to the Editor without their name?"

"A decided inconsistency," I would admit.

One of my favorite responses was to this question: "As Bill Clinton begins his second term, what advice would you give him?"

A man with a slow West Texas drawl had this to say: "I'd tell him to lay off the cards and the cigars and the liquor and the women and just be a good president and go to church."

But the best one (slightly edited) was this, that didn't run in that 1996 edition: "I'd tell him to have that birthmark removed from his (a certain vital organ) before Paula Jones (who was alleged to have had an affair with Clinton while he was governor of Arkansas) has a chance to go on TV and give a description of it. I think he'd just be better to cut it off."

Ouch!

* * *

Tenuous relationship with *Herald* cameras

Herald cameras and I never had a great relationship, and it was mostly my fault.

We got off to a rocky start. As a new part-time *Herald* reporter in the summer of 1967, I was assigned to take a picture of young probationers raising the flag on the courthouse square.

As I turned on the sidewalk at Fifth and Broadway, the strap of a Roliflex camera caught on the fire hydrant and the photographic contraption was jerked from my grasp. Fortunately, it seemed none the worse for wear.

Several years later, I was walking down the alley behind *The Herald* with a Roliflex mounted on a "pistol grip." To my absolute horror, the camera—apparently not tightly screwed to the grip—took a header to the pavement, resulting in smashed dials.

I had a camera stolen from my car (which I insisted was locked) and what I called a "point-and-shoot" digital camera literally went flying out of my hand onto the red brick street in front of the newspaper. You would have thought I intentionally threw it.

I was never a great photographer but captured a few I was proud of:

* PHS footballer Gary Covey diving for a ball in the foreground. The photo looked like a genie rising out of a bottle.
* A Morton player blocking a ball off the square of the backboard with an Olton player, hands up, looking as shocked as everyone else in the house.
* A horse and rider silhouetted by the light of a Feris wheel at the rodeo grounds
* A liquor bottle lying near the tire of a car used in the "Broken Dreams" presentation to PHS students to discourage drinking and driving.
* Doug Douglass leaning over fellow World War II veteran Gene Ridlehuber's wheelchair as they were bundled up against the cold at a Veterans Day service.

Sometimes you just get lucky—especially if you don't break the camera.

*   *   *

Devil's Beverage plays a role in incidents

A former *Herald* colleague, who shall remain anonymous, had his issues with John Barleycorn, especially when his wife was out of town receiving medical treatment.

Knowing she was about to be gone, I reminded my friend to "keep your nose out of the bottle." He feigned a puzzled look and I added, "You know what I'm talking about."

Sure enough, a couple of days later, he came staggering down the back hallway of the newspaper. Moments later, I saw him talking to his bosses in one of their offices.

I went back to work for a while and thought I ought to see what was going on, but the aforementioned office was now vacant. So I headed to the newspaper circulation department at the back of the building and opened the door just in time to see Production Director Ben Thompson and Ad Director Jack Overby struggling to hold the inebriated man's hand—in possession of a large pistol—toward the floor.

Funny what you'll do under duress. Publisher James Thomas recently had suffered a heart attack, and I was afraid the present situation might cause him to have another.

"Get out of here!" I screamed at James. "You get out of here right now!"

Ben managed to wrestle the gun from the man. My heart says he really meant no harm. Reality may have said otherwise. We left his pickup—shotgun in the seat—locked up on the parking lot and transported the man to Central Plains MH-MR Center.

Somehow, though, he managed to walk out of the building and down to a convenience store at 24th and Dimmitt Highway, convincing another fellow to drive him home.

Several years later, after his wife had passed away, he called me at home and said he was going to do himself in. He was clearly several sheets in the wind.

I quickly drove to his house and found him sitting in the middle of the living room with three shotguns lying next to the front door. He said he needed a drink. I told him that was the last thing he needed. He kept insisting, and my resistance finally wore down.

We headed to the Austin Heights community where a purveyor of alcoholic beverages was not found to be at his home, liberally protected by iron bars. Another stop proved fruitless as well. Finally, my friend spotted a couple of guys in a car on Austin Street and purchased a pint of whisky.

As I sat in my car, I looked across the street and spied a former standout Plainview High School basketball player sitting in his car. This is the same enterprising chap who charged friends a certain amount to let them in through a dressing room window so they could see sold-out games at Bulldog Gym in the early 1970s.

I meekly waved. He waved back, and I drove my friend back home so he could further drown his sorrows.

I then beat a fast path to *The Herald* and told James Thomas exactly where I had been and why I had been there in case any lurid stories got back to him.

Some tales are just too wild to make up.

* * *

I'm dictating, ma'am, but I'm no dictator

Two skills I learned as a young employee of *The Herald* was reading upside and backwards in the old "hot type" days and dictating stories over the phone way before laptops were invented.

I also learned to basically compose stories in my head, coming up with a "lead" paragraph and then looking at my notes to give scoring summaries. This was quite helpful if you were trying to beat a deadline.

In the days well ahead of that wonderful invention called a cell phone, I stood at an unenclosed phone booth across from the Treasury Department in Washington, D.C., dictating my story the day after a Flying Queens game in the national tournament in State College, Pennsylvania. Some fans had made a day-trip to the nation's capital.

Another time I used a pay phone in a restaurant somewhere in Kansas to dictate a feature story on a bus trip by Wayland fans to the national men's basketball tournament in Kansas City.

But that practice drew the ire of some folks when I didn't make arrangements to use a phone at Pauley Pavilion on the UCLA campus (even the one I used to broadcast a game) when the Queens played in the national tournament in 1978.

I had to wait a while to use a pay phone (remember those?) outside the arena and then launched into a rather lengthy story back to *The Herald*.

I sensed unrest behind me, and a woman gave me "what for" when I finished the call.

I started to just walk off but I went back and told her, "Ma'am, I'll probably never see you again, but I'm sorry. I'm a sports writer from Texas and was calling in a story to my newspaper."

The woman was very apologetic.

I was just dictating and didn't want to come off as a dictator.

*   *   *

Make that "Boxene," with one X

One day I was dictating information for our Back in Time feature to our faithful Gal Friday, Charlotte Thurman.

I was giving her the name of Charlie Cook for an item about his and Rushia's son, opera singer Terry Cook. I said, "He is the son of Charlie—*ie* (rather than *y*)—and Rushia Cook."

When I proofread the copy, it said: "He is the son of Charlie I. E. and Rushia Cook."

I couldn't wait to call Charlotte at home because over the previous few years we'd gotten such a big kick out of a similar misunderstanding.

We sent a reporter out to take a picture that included the very personable Lucile Davis. When the reporter wrote the picture identification, she listed our friend as Lucile Juanell Davis.

We questioned the reporter about Mrs. Davis' middle name, which we had never seen before. She insisted that was the name Mrs. Davis had given her.

Later, it dawned on us: Lucile has only one *l* in her name. When she told our reporter what her name was, she said, "Lucile—one *l*—Davis and the reporter thought she said *Juanell*, meaning her middle name.

For years after that, we'd see our friend and say, "Hello, Lucille Juanell."

On a related note, John Walker, our sports editor from 1984–87, signed his correspondence to us with the unusual name of "Boxene."

John was a big railroad buff. Someone nicknamed him "Boxcar" and for his "going away party," I ordered a cake that was to say, "Good luck, Boxcar."

Unfortunately, my handwriting is generally indecipherable (I should have been a doctor), and the person at the bakery put the name on the cake she thought she saw on the instructions.

I.e., "Boxene," one X.

*   *   *

Sorry, we don't have a Saturday paper

Seems like at least once or twice a year I'd pick up a ringing phone on Saturday at *The Herald* and the caller—usually an elderly woman—would say, "Honey, I didn't get my paper today."

I'd always try to be polite: "Ma'am, I'm sorry, we don't have a paper on Saturday."

Long pause: "Is this Saturday?"

"Yes, ma'am."

"I'm sorry, I thought it was Sunday."

"That's OK, we'll try to get the paper to you tomorrow," I'd say.

One Saturday morning, the Rev. Walter Griffin, who pastored United Baptist Church for 28 years, came into the office seeking a Sunday paper. He was dressed like he was on his way to church.

"This is Saturday, Brother Griffin, did you think it was Sunday?" I quizzed.

His expression said, "You're kidding, aren't you?"

"This isn't Saturday?" he asked tentatively.

"No, sir, you've got 24 more hours to work on that sermon."

*　　*　　*

This interview is going nowhere fast

A year or so before I left *The Herald*, a woman in the nursing home at Hale Center turned 100.

It was our habit to do stories on centenarians, so I trekked to our neighboring community to meet her. But the folks at the nursing home said they really knew very little about the woman, even where she was from originally.

I sat down next to her and asked, "Did you grow up around here?

"I don't have to tell you anything," the woman replied.

"Well, we're off to a good start," I thought before posing another question: "Did you work in the public?"

"That's none of your business," she said sternly.

"Well, did you belong to a church?" I queried.

"I damn sure did," she insisted.

About that time, the administrator came over and said, "You better come with me. I think she's about to hit you."

The oldest person I ever knew in a nursing home was Louie Horne, a resident of the old Care Inn. She lived to be 107.

One night, the late Floyd and Florence Montgomery, former Plainview school teachers, were going to lead the singing, and I was going to give the devotional.

I could hear Mrs. Horne hollering as they brought her down the hall, "Kill him! Kill that old devil! Cut his head off!"

When she arrived in the commons room, I told her, "Mrs. Horne, you shouldn't talk about Floyd Montgomery like that." Floyd just grinned.

Mrs. S.C. (Margaret) Horan—mother of Roger Horan, former owner of Hale County Spraying Service—was spending her last days at Plainview Healthcare at 24th and Yonkers.

One morning I said brightly: "Hello, Miz Horan."

"I don't have to talk to idiots like you," she snapped.

Roger's buddy, Alton Carmichael, ate that up when I told him, and now when I see him I can just expect him to say, "I don't have to talk to idiots like you."

*   *   *

A new *Herald?* When your conscience freezes over

In the mid-1970s, a fellow named Jim Ramsey came to work as a reporter at *The Herald*.

Jim seemed to work every Saturday night when usually not much was going but a reporter had to be on duty to "hold the fort" in case any newsworthy event took place.

Since I worked sports every Saturday night, Jim and I had numerous conversations, usually as he munched on a Butterfinger, washed down with a Dr Pepper.

Nearly every Saturday night, he'd call a woman friend who was a reporter for the *Christian Science Monitor* based in Boston. Jim himself was a Christian Scientist.

For some reason, he always called me Mr. Andrews.

One night he asked, "Mr. Andrews, do you think we'll ever get a new building?" deciding correctly that our 70-year-old facility was pretty outdated.

"Jim, do Christian Scientists believe in Hell?" I asked.

"Well, we believe it's a state of mind," he responded.

"I'll tell you what. We'll get a new building when your conscience freezes over."

"Ah, very good, Mr. Andrews," Jim praised.

HEARST STORIES

**Danny Andrews with President George H.W. Bush
at the White House Oval Office in 1991**

A personal message from the president

Not in a million years when I was a kid growing up out in the Hillcrest neighborhood in southeast Plainview would I have dreamed of one day being in the presence of three sitting presidents of the United States and one soon-to-be occupant of the Oval Office.

But, because of the influence of the Hearst Corp., owner of *The Plainview Daily Herald*, I was afforded that privilege.

The final visit was in early summer 2000 at the Governor's Mansion in Austin. George W. Bush, of course, was running for president, and he asked a typical West Texas question when I introduced myself and told him where I was from: "Y'all get any rain up there last night?"

During that meeting, he excused himself to take a call from Dick Cheney—the man he would eventually choose as his running mate.

I have a picture of all four visits to the White House—sitting across the table from Ronald Reagan, shaking hands with George H. W. Bush and Bill Clinton and standing next to George Bush, who appears to be singing. I tell people looking at the photo display it's obvious what he's singing: "O, Danny Boy."

The first visit of Hearst editors to the White House was in 1982 when Reagan was in office. Most of us didn't actually get to meet him that day. He came in, we stood, he nodded, and we all sat down.

I recall that trip for three specific reasons: At DFW Airport, some guys backing far right-winger Lyndon Larouche for president were soliciting funds and asked what I thought his chances were. I forthrightly asserted something like "a snowball's chance in Hell."

They were none too pleased to hear that assessment, and when they asked what my profession was and I admitted "a newspaperman," one groused that "that's the problem with this country—the media controls everything."

On the way into Washington, we passed a guy protesting media dominance with cardboard signs and other wonders—including himself clad only in underwear and wrapped in cellophane.

And, on the return flight, airplanes were being "de-iced," just a month after the Air Florida plane had crashed into the 14th Street Bridge over the Potomac, killing 74 of 79 on board plus four motorists. That doesn't exactly engender confidence.

As was the custom at the White House, we sat around an oblong table in the Cabinet Room, each poised to ask a question as it fell our turn. Unfortunately, I was always seated far enough away that our 45-minute to 1-hour session ended before I got to pose a query about some ag-related issue.

A white-coated attendant set a cup in front of Mr. Reagan, who drew a pen-like instrument from his pocket and squirted something into the cup—artificial sweetener or perhaps an extra shot of caffeine to keep him from nodding off.

After the session, William Randolph Hearst, Jr., seated next to the president, asked if he could have the piece of paper on which Mr. Reagan had been doodling.

We got a transcript of the meeting, which ended with Mr. Hearst and Mr. Reagan uttering unintelligibly.

Mr. Hearst: Mmmm . . .

The President: Errr . . .

Our next visit was in 1991 when George H. W. Bush was in office. He spent about 45 minutes with us and then asked, "Would you fellows like to see the Oval Office?"

One by one, we posed with the former Midland resident, shaking his hand under a picture of George Washington. He gave each of us a presidential tie clasp.

Five years later, it was Bill Clinton's turn to meet with Hearst editors. As it happened, I was the first to shake hands with him as he emerged from the Oval Office.

After the meeting, he hung around a few minutes, making small talk. As he started past me, I said, "Mr. President, I bring greetings from Brian Harbour" (his former pastor when he attended Emmanuel Baptist Church while governor of Arkansas; at that time Dr. Harbour was pastor of First Baptist Church in Richardson).

Mr. Clinton lit up like a candle and said, "Hey, man, where do you know him from?"

"Oh, I've been in some Baptist meetings with him," I said, possibly fudging the truth a bit.

"Well, the next time you see him, give him my regards," Mr. Clinton said. "He's a great man."

Earlier I had handed to an aide seated behind me a note that said: "Mr. President, my pastor (Travis Hart) has stolen messages from your former pastor," alluding to "Brian's Lines," a series of sermon outlines by Dr. Harbour. The aide grinned and said, "I'll give this to him."

When I got to Dulles Airport later that afternoon for the flight home, I called Brian Harbour's office. The secretary said, "I'm sorry, he's in a meeting right now."

"Well," I said, "could you tell him I have a personal message from the President of the United States?" Soon, Dr. Harbour came to the phone and we chatted a moment.

The next month, the Baptist General Convention of Texas was held in San Antonio. Dr. Harbour happened to be assisting with registration, and when I introduced myself, he said, "Hey, I appreciated you calling me. We spent the night in the White House about three weeks ago."

After Mr. Clinton's dalliance with Monica Lewinsky, *Newsweek* magazine ran a series of questions about that scandal, and one was: What head of state did he keep waiting while he was having a tryst with Monica in the White House?

The answer was President Zedillo of Mexico.

Well, guess who was in town that day and guess whose entourage of limousines was just down the street when we exited the White House?

"Hmm," I thought, "*before* or *after* our visit?"

Come to think of it, the President did seem pretty happy when he came out of the Oval Office.

*   *   *

Pin the head on the editor: This is no game

Ever play the game, "Pin the Tail on the Donkey"?

I sadly admit I won a prize at a birthday party because my blindfold slipped down and, after taking some "air stabs," pinned the tail on the donkey.

And that story relates to this story.

In 1980, not long after purchasing *The Midland Reporter–News* in a package deal that included *The Plainview Daily Herald*—as well as some other papers shortly thereafter—The Hearst Corp. decided to send its editors to New York for a special project.

The company planned to produce a slick softback book that included photos of editors, publishers, TV executives, magazine editors, etc. to show off its growing publications empire.

We were delivered to lunch and the following photo shoot in blue limousines, and I distinctly remember the rather cocky editor from Edwardsville, Illinois, saying he didn't feel obligated to run the weekly column by William Randolph Hearst, Jr., editor-in-chief of the papers.

I can assure you we were running it in Plainview. That was long before I heard the term, "You can't fix stupid."

Mr. Hearst was unabashedly a fan of Ronald Reagan (soon to be elected president), and I said often that "Ronald Reagan could have committed an indiscretion in the middle of 1600 Pennsylvania Avenue and Mr. Hearst would have hailed it as a great humanitarian effort."

Just an aside here: To show the independence of Hearst newspapers in the 1980 election, five endorsed Ronald Reagan, four endorsed incumbent Jimmy Carter, two endorsed independent John Anderson, and two abstained from promoting anyone for the White House.

The photo session was held in a fourth-floor studio in Greenwich Village, preceded by lunch. I'll never forget the lunch because Bob Danzig, recently promoted to head of newspapers for Hearst, lamented to me that two *Herald* staffers were checking into possibly organizing a union.

At that time, Bob was dealing with 13 unions at *The Boston Herald-American* that eventually was closed by Hearst because it was losing a reported $1 million a month.

All those Herald staffers did was get raises held up for six months while the National Labor Relations Board investigated.

Like I said, you can't fix stupid.

For the photo shoot, we editors (13 of us at the time) were positioned on platforms of various heights—some seated, some standing—like you see in college yearbooks. An accompanying numbered drawing would identify each man. This was shortly before Hearst, now a very diversified company, hired its first woman editor.

The photographer had to back his camera out into the hallway to be able to get all of us in the picture. The editor from Seattle forgot to bring a pair of black shoes so he went to a local shop and paid $300. I could not fathom anyone paying that much for a pair of shoes. Besides, they didn't even show up in the picture.

My predecessor at *The Herald*, Jim Servatius (editor in Midland) and I enjoyed a couple of days in New York. We stayed at the Essex House on Central Park, and Jim and I ate at the famed Tavern on the Green in the Park and at Mama Leone's Italian restaurant and took in the sights of the Big Apple.

Anyway, several months passed and no sight of the publication. Maybe 18 months later, it arrived in the mail.

I opened it and perused the photo of editors. There I was in a rather casual pose, wearing a dark blue suit borrowed from my father-in-law. The suit bag I carried onto the plane and hung up at the front in the days when you could still do that must have weighed 200 pounds.

Instantly I thought, "What is Harry Rosenfeld (the editor in Albany, New York) doing on the front row? And where is Reg Murphy (editor in San Francisco who had earned some notoriety when he was kidnapped while serving as editor of *The Atlanta Constitution-Journal*)? And who are those other chaps I know weren't there for the photo shoot?"

It became obvious that with turnover at several papers, a little "creative editing" had to be done before publication in the days well before Photoshop allowed you to manipulate pictures that didn't look like they had been messed with.

Harry Rosenfeld's head was put on the body of Reg Murphy (who had gone to *The Baltimore Sun*), Harry's body contained the head of the new editor of Hearst's *Baltimore Herald-American*, and the new editor in San Francisco on the back row had what appeared to be a halo around his head.

It wasn't long before *Time Magazine* ran the picture on Page 3 with the title "Pin the Head on the Editor."

I've lost my head several times in my life, but I can truthfully say I had my own in that picture.

*   *   *

Finding some important "lost" photos

When Hearst editors visited with President Bill Clinton at the White House in 1996, a young woman was snapping photos.

As with my two previous times to the Cabinet Room, I expected some pictures to show up in a few weeks. Months passed, no photos.

I called The Hearst Washington Bureau and they explained apologetically that the photographer had some camera problems.

"Great," I grumbled to myself, "it's not every day you get to go to the White House and then have no pictures to prove it."

Probably three months later, I was conducting one of the quarterly clean-ups of my office when I found a FedEx package on my credenza.

I started to trash it, thinking it was some press release I wasn't interested in. But when I opened it, much to my surprise there was a photo of me shaking hands with President Clinton, along with several pictures from other meetings Publisher Rollie Hyde and reporter Teresa Young (now my colleague in Advancement at Wayland) were a part of.

When I called the Washington Bureau to report finding the pictures, someone said the photographer was able to capture a few pictures before the camera malfunction. Happily, I was closest to the door when President Clinton arrived to meet with us . . . and happier still I didn't throw away the evidence.

That photo is in a display with President Reagan and both Bushes in my office. A friend who was no fan of Clinton's took a look at the picture and said with an air of disgust: "Look, he's not even gripping your hand."

"Aw, that's not really President Clinton," I said with a straight face. "It's just a cardboard cutout. You slip your hand into the cutout and it makes it look like you're shaking hands with the president."

Nope, as Coke says, it's the real thing.

*   *   *

"High cotton" day in Washington, D.C.

The 1991 trip to Washington for Hearst editors and publishers was a great one, culminating with editors meeting with President George H. W. Bush.

Sorry, not enough room in the Oval Office to include the publishers—the financial "big dogs" at all newspapers. Guess they found out where they ranked in the eyes of the Big Man.

Come to think of it, it was a stupendous day.

We started with breakfast at the Capitol with Speaker of the House Tom Foley, moved on to the FBI to meet with Director William Steele, to the Pentagon to meet with the Assistant Joint Chief of Staff, to the CIA to meet with the Acting Director, and finally to the White House.

On the bus ride to the White House, Chuck Lewis, an ex-Marine and chief of the Hearst Washington Bureau, said his press colleagues were both impressed and envious that he had managed to put together a one-day agenda of such magnitude.

As I told Chuck in West Texas terms: "Man, we're in high cotton today."

*   *   *

Bob Danzig

Bob Danzig served Hearst with great sagacity

Bob Danzig was general manager of Hearst Newspapers from 1978 until his retirement in 1997. The newspaper side had great growth and profitability during his tenure.

A gifted motivational speaker who does that full-time now around the country, giving his profits to charities, Bob grew up in six foster homes. He wrote a wonderful book about his experiences—make-believe conversations with himself about living pillar-to-post but how he turned negative experiences into positives.

From Hearst meetings through the years, I have several vivid memories of Bob, who always looked like he stepped out of *GQ* magazine.

I have a picture of him giving a "blessing" to a kneeling Herald Publisher James Thomas (who never called him "Bob," but always "Mr. Dan*zing*") at a meeting in Chicago.

Bob had an expansive vocabulary and, during a meeting in Albany, New York, used of the word "sagacity" to describe a law firm's relationship to Hearst. I glanced around the room and you could see guys mouthing the word, wondering what it meant (wisdom and good judgment).

At our meeting at the University of Missouri in 1990, he used the word "bifurcation" to describe the diversity of channels because of the expansion of the cable TV industry. (Repeat 1984 Albany reactions with slightly new cast.)

In 1987, he sent a note to editors encouraging the use of color ("spot" or otherwise—boy did we do some horrendous things with spot color in the days before we had the capability to use full-color photos anywhere except Page 1) and mentioned "over the weekend, I was reading Machiavelli . . ."

Since my reading material was a lot less deep than his, I had the greatest desire to write back and say, "Dear Bob, as I was reading *Sports Illustrated* over the weekend . . ."

Bob had the uncanny ability to No. 1, stay awake during afternoon sessions when some of us were fighting to keep from nodding off and, No. 2, succinctly summarize the speaker's main points.

A real "ladies man," Bob sent nice flowers to Carolyn on the rare occasions when I did something noteworthy.

And I'll always appreciate Bob Danzig for his comments at several Hearst meetings that caused me and James Thomas to nearly bust our buttons when he'd mentioned "our little jewel in Plainview, Texas."

There would be little bifurcation of opinion that Bob Danzig served Hearst with great sagacity.

*   *   *

Harry Rosenfeld

That's straight out of the horse's mouth

One of the most colorful Hearst editors with whom I was acquainted was Harry Rosenfeld, the man in charge in Albany, New York.

He had been the Metro Editor of the *Washington Post* and worked directly with Bob Woodard and Carl Bernstein when they were cracking the Watergate scandal of the mid-1970s that brought down the Nixon administration.

Harry wrote a wonderful book called *From Kristallnacht to Watergate*, detailing his family's oppression in Hitler's Germany before they emigrated to the U.S., and his experiences at the *Post*.

At the 1984 Hearst Editors and Publishers meeting in Albany, Harry lined up Gov. Mario Cuomo as one of the speakers. It was just a few months after Cuomo had been the keynoter at the Democratic National Convention in San Francisco and wowed everyone.

During a Q&A, Mary Ann Dolan, editor in Los Angeles and the first woman to break the all-male bastion of Hearst newspaper editors, asked something like, "Don't you think (Democratic vice presidential candidate) Geraldine Ferraro is a bit disingenuous to say she knows nothing of her husband's real estate dealings?"

Cuomo said he high regard for her as a lawyer and went on to say that "Tippy and I went out to Logan and lobbied Fritz to take her as his running mate."

He didn't say, "Speaker of the House Tip O'Neill and I went out to Logan Airport and lobbied Vice President Walter Mondale . . ."

I thought, "That's coming straight out of the horse's mouth."

I was tickled at a meeting several years later in Washington when then-Gov. George Pataki said that during the Cuomo administration there was a highway project "making 10 inches a day."

I asked Gov. Pataki during a Q&A session if he might be interested in joining up with another George—Bush of Texas—to form a Republican ticket.

"I like George Bush very much," he responded with a grin but without committing.

One of my favorite "Harry" moments was in Houston in 1992 during the Republican National Convention when we were all asked to share an idea from our papers.

I showed off "The Readers' Page," contributions of various kinds by our readers that has been running monthly in *The Herald* for about 25 years now.

Never afraid to express his opinion, Harry scanned a page and asked—with only a slight air of incredulity—"Danny, do your readers actually like this drivel?" To which I responded, "I guess so, Harry, they keep sending it in every month."

I still wish I had worked on getting Harry to come to Wayland for a Watergate perspective.

During our dinner at Woodrow Wilson's home one evening, a wag in the audience asked Len Downie, editor of the *Washington Post*, "Now, refresh my memory, who was Deep Throat?" several years before the man's identity as Woodard and Bernstein's inside source was identified.

Had a name been revealed and it was the truth, I suspect I would have thought, "Straight out of the horse's mouth."

*   *   *

Dapper Don Forst's surprising revelation

I was sorry to read of the passing in January of 2014 of Don Forst, former editor of *Newsday* and later the ultraliberal *Village Voice* in New York.

After Hearst sold *The Boston Herald-American* in 1982 because it reportedly was losing a million dollars a month, Don was sent to some of the small papers to share editorial ideas.

I had only been around him once or twice but liked him (double-breasted suit, white snap-brim hat, shiny shoes, and all) and wanted to share a word about my Christian faith with him, not knowing until he mentioned during our session, "This is probably all you need, a New York Jew trying to tell you how to run your newspaper."

I thought, "Dear Lord, you didn't tell me Don was a Jew. How am I going to broach the subject?"

The next morning, he's sitting in my office, waiting to leave to catch a plane, likely thinking, "I've gotta get out of this one-horse town."

James Thomas, our publisher, came in and handed Don a Chamber of Commerce brochure while I was on the phone and Don politely thumbed through it. When I got off the phone, the first thing out of his mouth was this: "Danny, this looks like a very religious community," having noted we had 65 churches in town.

Well, if I ever wanted an entree to a "faith conversation," that was it. I politely and briefly shared my faith in Jesus Christ.

Don listened very intently and responded, "Danny, I didn't know you were so dedicated. It might interest you to know that my father-in-law was Harold Okenga (Ah-ken-gay)."

Dr. Okenga was a leader of the reformation movement in the 1930s when some theologians felt Harvard, Yale, etc. were becoming too liberal and later was a big supporter of Billy Graham and the *Christianity Today* magazine.

Don continued: "My wife is a professional photographer and shoots a lot of nude photography, and I'm sure he thinks, 'A Jewish son-in-law and a liberal daughter . . . why me, Lord?'"

*　　*　　*

Phil Bronstein

Don't mess with Phil . . . or Komodos

Phil Bronstein was the editor of Hearst's *San Francisco Examiner* and later the *San Francisco Chronicle* after the *Examiner*, the corporation's flagship paper, was merged with the larger paper in 2000.

He later left the paper to become chairman of the board for the Center for Investigative Reporting.

Phil, a former foreign correspondent for the *Examiner*, was nominated for the 1986 Pulitzer Prize for his coverage of the downfall of the Ferdinand Marcos regime in the Philippines.

A ruggedly handsome guy with salt-and-pepper hair, mustache, and goatee, the Georgia native favored cowboy boots and gospel music.

Phil, who has been married four times, also favored a beautiful blonde actress by the name of Sharon Stone. She gained fame for such pictures as *Basic Instincts*, *Casino*, and *The Quick and the Dead*.

In 1997, when Bob Danzig retired as general manager of Hearst Newspapers, a dinner was held at the Whitney Museum in New York City.

Sharon Stone happened to be filming a movie in New York, and Phil brought her to the dinner. He didn't introduce her around, but they did walk past me and I silently prayed, "Lord, don't let me slobber on myself."

They married in 1998 and moved into a $7 million mansion in Marin County, across the Golden Gate Bridge, and later adopted a little boy from Texas and named him Roan, after Phil's father.

Phil and I were visiting one morning in San Antonio before he caught a cab to the airport. We talked about his new son, and he got a kick out of a story I told him about my oldest son.

When Brandon was about five, we were driving down Columbia when he asked, "How old is Mimmaw?" referring to my wife's mother.

"She's 52," I said.

"No, how old is she?" he asked again.

"I said she's 52."

"I don't want numbers," Brandon insisted. "How old is she in the face."

No offense to Phil, but I figured that marriage would last as long as Sharon Stone wanted it to—about five years as it turned out.

Phil, who once crawled across his office desk to punch a guy with whom he had a disagreement, showed up in scuba gear at a San Francisco lake in 1996 to assist in capturing an escaped alligator, but the cops turned him away.

In 2001, Sharon Stone rented the Los Angeles Zoo for his private birthday bash. The adventuresome Phil found his way into an enclosure for Komodo dragons and suffered severe damage when one of the huge reptiles—apparently mistaking his white tennis shoes for a rabbit—took a bite out of his foot.

Advice: Don't mess with Phil Bronstein . . . or Komodo dragons.

*   *   *

W.R. Hearst Jr.

W.R. Hearst, Jr.: Living in a famous father's shadow

I was only around William Randolph Hearst, Jr.—son of the newspaper empire's founder—four times during my newspaper career.

Mr. Hearst shared the coveted Pulitzer Prize for reporting in 1956 for his interview with Soviet premier Nikita Khrushchev and associated commentary. He also spent four decades as editor-in-chief of the Hearst newspaper chain.

The first meeting was when Mr. Hearst hosted editors and publishers for lunch in August 1979 at the white 3-story bougainvillea-draped ranch house at San Simeon, California, just down the hill from the famous Hearst Castle.

Wearing a camera around his neck, he greeted arrivals and made small talk. He joined us the next day in Monterey for a meeting briefly interrupted by the tremors of an earthquake about 150 miles down the coast.

We got to take a tour of San Simeon, and Mr. Hearst, who said he hadn't visited "The Castle" in some time, wandered onto a carpeted area, earning a gentle rebuke from a tour guide.

He looked around when the guide turned his back and playfully shuffled his feet on the carpet as if to say, "This is my house and I can stand on the carpet if I darn well please."

The next time was in October 1980 at the Continental Plaza Hotel in Chicago, the only hotel I've ever stayed in that had a television in the bathroom.

I especially remember that because I was sitting in the tub watching *The Mary Tyler Moore Show* when a maid walked into the adjoining bedroom and announced, "Housekeeping."

She had towels or something, and I hollered, "Just put them on the bed, please."

Mr. Hearst and the very gentlemanly Joseph Kingsbury-Smith (Washington Bureau chief) arrived late in the evening, and I heard the desk clerk say he didn't have a reservation for them.

I thought Mr. Hearst might say, "Do you have any idea who I am?"

The next morning, our meeting was repeatedly disrupted by the persistent banging of men working on the awning outside the hotel.

Finally, having his fill of the noise, Mr. Hearst excused himself. He was gone for several minutes and returned with the satisfied look of a man who had exercised a bit of power as the noise ceased.

However, that look faded quickly as the banging resumed with greater fervor, to which Mr. Hearst snorted, "Damn union man."

My next encounter came in 1982 when Hearst editors met with President Reagan at the White House. Jim Servatius of Midland and I exited our cab about the same time Mr. Hearst, attired in a heavy coat with fur collar, got out of his taxi. I later had my picture made with him in the hotel.

The last meeting was in 1991—the same year his book, *The Hearsts: Father and Son*, was published—when editors met with President George H.W. Bush at the White House. By then he was in poor health and rather frail.

I shook hands and introduced myself and he said in a decidedly Eastern accent, "How are you-uh?"

Mr. Hearst, who died in 1993 at age 85, said, "I lived in my father's shadow all my life."

*   *   *

Program provides some educational PEP

When Hearst editors met with President Bill Clinton in 1996, our trek to Washington also included lunch at the famous New York Press Club.

The speaker that day was Secretary of Housing and Urban Development Henry Cisneros, Mayor of San Antonio from 1981-89.

Cisneros had spoken to a gathering in Plainview near the end of his mayoral term about a coalition in San Antonio that provided assistance with college education costs.

That was the impetus for Don A. Williams, a Plainview CPA, to go about organizing the Plainview Education Partnership that continues to provide 30 hours of tuition free to Wayland Baptist University.

Plainview High, Plainview Christian, and homeschooled students must maintain a B average and 95 percent attendance for their last two years of high school to qualify.

The founding funds came from the United Way (of which PEP is still a member), Chamber of Commerce, Industrial Foundation, and the Hearst Corp.

All three of my children, along with hundreds of others, have benefited from PEP.

At the luncheon, I told Cisneros, "Mr. Secretary, I want to personally thank you for the idea that saved my family probably $10,000."

May I say that compliment kind of "pepped" him up.

*   *   *

A major tornado brews in Iran
(I wrote this column in 2004.)

You may have noticed a story in last Tuesday's paper about how Iran's exiled crown prince is plotting nonviolent insurrection from his home in suburban Washington where he has lived for more than 20 years.

Reza Pahlavi, now 41, got a lot of attention in this neck of the woods in the late 1970s and early 1980s when he was taking fighter training at Reese Air Force Base in Lubbock.

He lived in a well-guarded home in the 2100 block of Slide Road.

Of course his father, the Shah of Iran from 1941-79, was overthrown by the fundamentalist Muslim followers of the Ayatollah Khomeini. The Shah fled from country to country and spent a brief time in the New York for cancer treatment before he died in Egypt in July 1980.

In May of 1987, Hearst editors and publishers gathered in Washington, D.C., and one of our speakers was Reza Pahlavi. The deposed Shah's son arrived under tight security since there was a price on his head.

I was standing in one of the meeting rooms of the Mayflower Hotel when an official-looking man came up and said, "Sir, could you step out of the room for a few minutes?"

I was told by one of our group that they were going to sweep for bombs or other explosives. I figured the crown prince had armed guards at the doors, probably sporting Uzzis.

What a nice feeling.

Accompanied by his wife, the handsome Pahlavi told us he had smuggled into the country a videotaped message that was played on one of the television stations.

He implored his countrymen to overthrow the Khomeini regime that had been responsible for kidnapping 50 Americans and holding them hostage for more than a year, releasing them on the day Ronald Reagan replaced Jimmy Carter in the White House.

When we departed Lubbock very early one morning for Washington a couple of days earlier, someone said a tornado had done some damage in the area, but we didn't get any details.

As Carolyn and I passed through a receiving line, I said, "Your Majesty (that's what he's officially referred to by his supporters), we live in Plainview, near Lubbock, and drive by your old home from time to time."

"Yes," Pahlavi beamed, "was there any, uh, any damage from the, uh . . ."

"Tornado?" I interjected as he made a swirling motion with his right hand, struggling to find the word.

"I really don't know," I told him, amazed that he knew something about what was going on around his old stomping grounds.

Pahlavi says he is preparing cassettes and pamphlets for distribution in remote areas, using the same tactics as the dour, bearded Khomeini, who sowed his own revolution with cassettes.

He knows there is still a big reward waiting for anyone who could kill him—an individual or a hit squad. Pahlavi argues that a democratic government is the best means to unite his country but wants a referendum so Iranians can decide for themselves.

"It's not about the past. It's not about me. It's not about the monarchy," Pahlavi says. "It's about the people."

Maybe they need a good, well-placed tornado.

*   *   *

Al Gore: Let me share this with you

During a Hearst meeting at the Mayflower Hotel in Washington in 1987, we heard from Senator Al Gore of Tennessee, who was running for president.

He lost the Democratic nomination that year to Michael Dukakis, who lost to George H.W. Bush in the race for the White House. Twelve years later, after "hanging chads" and Supreme Court decisions, Gore eventually lost out in the finals to George W. Bush.

Several times during his speech to Hearst editors, Gore said, "Let me share this with you."

After the meeting, I shook hands with the senator and said, "You're a Baptist aren't you?"

He seemed a bit taken aback but replied, "Yes, why do you ask?"

"Oh, a friend of mine (the late attorney Marshall Formby) says all Baptists like to say, 'Let me share this with you.' Why don't they just say, 'Let me tell you something'?"

Gore just grinned and went on to share with others in the room.

*　　*　　*

Maybe Sam Donaldson can investigate

In 1982, when Hearst editors were invited to meet with President Reagan at the White House, we stayed at the Mayflower Hotel in Washington.

I told my colleague Jim Servatius of Midland that the man I'd most like to meet from the national media was ABC reporter Sam Donaldson.

Lo and behold, when we started to go out for dinner, there sat Donaldson in the hotel lobby, having a drink with friends shortly after his Sunday night newscast.

I apologized to him for interrupting "but just wanted to say how much I enjoy your work."

He said thanks and, as I started to walk off, he added "I have a ranch in El Paso." He now has several ranches in Lincoln County near Ruidoso.

More than a decade later, a New York trip included a visit to the United Nations building. We Hearst folks each had our picture made with U.S. Ambassador Bill Richardson, later the governor of New Mexico, but I never got my photograph.

I think I'll call Sam Donaldson to investigate this egregious oversight.

On second thought, considering some of the ethics issues Richardson had, maybe I should leave well enough alone.

*   *   *

Hearst nixes two-column pictures of brides?

One thing I particularly appreciated about *The Herald* being a part of the giant Hearst Corporation for almost 30 years of my time there is that we had no interference with the news operation and only one "intervention" with an editorial decision.

While Publisher James Thomas and News Editor Gary Ott, ardent Democrats, thought we ought to endorse incumbent Jimmy Carter in the 1980 presidential election, the Hearst "higher ups" favored Republican Ronald Reagan, mainly because they saw him as pro-business.

We endorsed Reagan, as did four other Hearst papers, but four went with Carter, two with independent John Anderson and two chose not to endorse, showing the independence of Hearst papers.

I was tickled when the mother of a bride-to-be was not happy with our decision to reduce engagement photos from two columns to one in the Lifestyles section, certain that this directive had been made by the Hearst Corporation.

I could just envision someone in an obscure office at Hearst headquarters in New York surveying *The Herald* and saying, "Hmm, I think we need to send a directive to Plainview insisting they save space by reducing engagement photos to one column."

*　　*　　*

Was the brother really a "brother"?

Carolyn and I got to go to San Francisco in 2000, 2001, and 2003 when I was chosen to help select Hearst Fellows—bright young journalists who would do 4-to-6-month stints at Hearst newspapers.

We were delighted to have Mary Vuong and Wyatt Buchanan on our staff in 2002 and 2003, respectively. Mary is now an independent writer after several years as a feature writer for *The Houston Chronicle*, and Wyatt was a reporter for the *The San Francisco Chronicle* from 2004-13 and is now an editor at *The Arizona Republic*.

One morning we decided to eat at the famous Mel's Diner near our hotel. Just as Carolyn started across the street a little ahead of me, the light changed so I backtracked to the curb.

Just then, a slender black man attired in a brown suit and carrying one of those big early-day cell phones, came walking toward me at a brisk pace.

"Say, man, can you help me? My car got hijacked last night and I need some gas," he said. Since he still apparently had his vehicle, I assumed he meant he had just been robbed.

Nonethless, I pulled out a $10 bill. He asked if I had a card so he could mail a repayment and asked where I was from. "Plainview, Texas," I said, insisting he didn't need to send any money.

"Hey, man, I'm from San Antonio. I was born at Brook Army Medical Center."

Ah-oh, instant connection: "I was born at Baptist Hospital in San Antonio," I said.

"I go to St. John's Baptist Church," he said.

Ah-oh, connection two: "I go to First Baptist Church in Plainview."

Well, since we were practically kin, the guy asked if I could spare $20.

I fudged and said that was all I had.

He smiled and headed off up the street . . . either to find a gas station or to fleece another sucker.

That's OK, I figured it was worth a column and didn't mind spending a few bucks, just in case the "brother" was a brother.

And a Texan to boot.

*   *   *

Homeless them, but helpless us

It is not uncommon in America's major cities to see or even be confronted by homeless people.

Among the first I ever saw were a man wearing a black suit and white socks lying face down in Battery Park at the tip of Manhattan and another, wearing a heavy coat, lying in the doorway of Carnegie Hall.

On a trip to the nation's capital, I walked down The Mall between the Lincoln Memorial and the Washington Monument one morning. A young woman, sleeping near a tree, suddenly rose, pulled up her skirt and relieved herself. I was embarrassed for her, and I was embarrassed for me.

Not long after, I passed a young man in military fatigues near the impressive Korean War memorial. He asked if I could make a donation to homeless veterans. I'm sure my first thought was, "This guy is just a panhandler."

I fished a dollar out of my pocket and dropped it into his bucket. As I started to walk on, he said in the sweetest voice I've ever heard, "God bless you, sir."

I felt about two inches tall.

On a San Francisco street corner, a fairly well-dressed black man spoke loudly to no one in particular. "Folks say they ain't got no money. I understand. Everyone has they problems."

That evening, Carolyn and I were going to take in a Golden State Warriors basketball game, riding the Bay Area Rapid Transit system that runs beneath the San Francisco Bay, connecting 'Frisco and Oakland.

As we stared at the instructions, a young woman came up and asked, "Do you need some help buying your tickets? I'm homeless, and I make some of my money by helping people buy their tickets."

We were more than happy to pay a little extra for her assistance.

She was homeless, yes, but not helpless like us.

*   *   *

Better take stock in this exchange

In October 1997, Hearst editors met in The Big Apple and visited the New York Stock Exchange.

We were split into small groups and assigned to a broker on the floor of the Exchange.

Our broker asked where we were from and when I said, "Plainview, Texas," he asked, "Do you know Frank Gabriel?"

Not only did I know the local haberdasher—co-owner with his brother Max of Gabriel's Department Store for more than 30 years—I also wrote the Sunday "Brothers Gabriel" column in The Herald that saluted local individuals, accomplishments, and activities for more than 10 years.

"I went to school with him at Baylor," said the broker, acknowledging that Frank also had served on the board of the Hankamer School of Business at their alma mater.

Another thing about that meeting: The head of the Exchange told us, "We predict a slight uptick in the market until about April and then a leveling off."

Exactly a week later, the market took one of those heart-stopping dives, proving that even the "experts" don't really know.

*　　*　　*

I think you won . . . I know you won

When Frank A. Bennack, Jr. retired as chief executive officer of The Hearst Corp., the company threw a big bash for him at the Lincoln Center in New York on Memorial Weekend 2002.

Herald Publisher Rollie Hyde and wife Jeri and Carolyn and I flew in for the formal affair, Rollie and I taking along our rented tuxedoes.

As we were not far from landing, an attendant announced a trivia contest for which a nice New York travel guide would be the prize.

"What former New York mayor is the namesake for one of the city's airport?" was the question.

Several people—including me—hollered the answer: "Fiorello LaGuardia." Actually, I may have been the only one giving the first name of the city's 99th mayor from 1934-45.

A flight attendant handed a woman several rows in front of me the travel guide, but another came back to my seat and said rather assuredly, "I think you were the winner."

"Thanks," I said with a smile, happy that I knew the answer.

Momentarily, she returned and said again, "I'm pretty sure you won." She returned a third time with something in a gray plastic bag and said as she handed it to me, "I know you were the winner."

It was a bottle of champagne. We held onto that bottle for two or three years before a New Year's toast.

Thanks to the Fiorello—Italian for "Little Flower"—for the prize. Salud!

* * *

George Irish

Bet I see someone I know before you do

George Irish served as president of Hearst Newspapers from 1997–2008 after stints as publisher of the newspapers in Midland, Beaumont, and San Antonio.

One of the nicest compliments I ever received came from George when I told him the day of the terrorist attacks on New York's twin towers that I had hawked papers in the middle of the street near Fifth and Quincy.

"Way to go, Danny," George said in a conference call with other editors to see what they had done regarding coverage of that dreadful day.

Obviously at least one motorist wasn't so impressed, calling the police to say I was impeding traffic. A policeman asked if I could move to the curb. It was OK; I was about out of papers anyway.

I asked George if he was afraid to walk the streets of New York City at night.

George said, "No, I would be more afraid walking on the streets of Plainview at night," owing to the fact we only had three working streetlights on Broadway at the time.

When George was publisher in Midland, we were on the same flight home from a meeting in Albany, New York, in 1984. As we walked into the DFW Airport, I looked at him and said, "George, I bet you a quarter I see someone I know before you do."

Being from a much bigger city and figuring the chances of him seeing someone were a lot better than mine, George accepted the challenge.

We walked along, "rubber-necking" the whole way and it looked like neither of us would have to pony up a coin with George Washington's likeness.

But just as we were about to part company, I spied the familiar face of a man walking up to a ticket counter. "Hey, Ervin Graham," I hollered and waved to a Plainview farmer and agribusinessman.

Then I looked at my companion and demanded with a grin, "Give me that quarter, George."

I'm not sure he did, but George treated me to a nice lunch across the street from Hearst's beautiful headquarters building in Manhattan four years ago after having an employee take me on a tour.

That lunch cost a whole lot more than quarter.

SPORTS STORIES

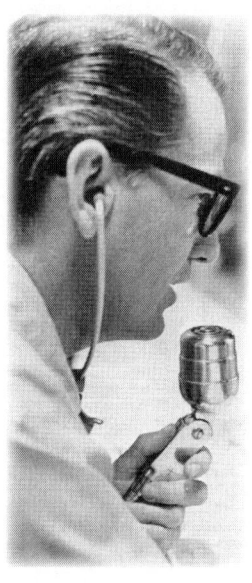

Tut Tawwater broadcasting
Bulldog basketball

Tut Tawwater

Tut Tawwater: The Voice of the Bulldogs

A man I envied as a youth for what seemed to be the ideal job was Tut
Tawwater, the Voice of the Bulldogs.

A World War II prisoner of war and later a telegrapher for the Fort Worth & Denver Railroad, Tut went to work as an advertising salesman at the eight-year-old radio station KVOP in 1952.

He would go on to be the play-by-play announcer for Bulldog football for 37 years before retiring after the 1989 season. The home radio booth at Greg Sherwood Memorial Bulldog Stadium is named in his honor. He also did PHS basketball and baseball games through the years.

In the mid-1950s, he "re-created" Plainview Ponies minor league road, watching a Western Union ticker spit out play-by-play as he called the action over recorded crowd noise, hitting a cigar box with a pencil to simulate bat meeting ball.

I spent many a Friday night listening to Tut's signature opening line: "Good evening, football fans, Tut Tawwater along with B.D. Perkins, here to bring you a broadcast as the Plainview Bulldogs host the Pampa Harvesters."

When I was in college, Tut was nice enough to let me do several Wayland basketball games on KVOP, sometimes after Plainview games, as the Pioneers had to share Bulldog Gym with the PHS squad.

I was a broadcaster wannabe, and he also let me help him on some Bulldog basketball games by keeping stats

I went to him after I had started at Wayland and told him about my friend at West Texas State, Tom Hall, who also was an aspiring broadcaster.

As it happened, after college Tom went to KVOP as a disc jockey and worked alongside Tut on football and basketball broadcasts in the early 1970s and eventually occupied his seat at Bulldog Stadium starting in the early 1990s.

Tut and I broadcast a youth boxing tournament one night at Wayland's Hutcherson Center, but about the time we got the flailing combatants' names right, the bout was over.

I remember going with Tut, his sidekick Billy Don "B.D." Perkins, and a couple of high school "spotters" to the final Plainview High football game in Kermit in 1970.

The best part of that otherwise four-hour trek to a place I was pretty sure God didn't even know existed was the pre-game meal at a local eatery.

I figured Plainview—fresh off an 8-7 upset at Bulldog Stadium that almost cost Lubbock Coronado the district championship—would whip up on Kermit and finish a dismal season at 3-7.

Instead, the Bulldogs fumbled four times inside the 20 on a cold, windy night and lost 18-13. It was the last time I saw a game with a clock that had hands instead of digital numbers.

Tut, who was the third Chamber of Commerce Man of the Year honoree (in 1958), has been president of several organizations, and led about every fund drive imaginable in Plainview, is past 90 now but has had perfect attendance as a member of the Noon Lions Club for more than 60 years.

He also taught through the Bible in his Sunday School class for many years at First United Methodist Church.

Oh, yeah, about that name "Tut." He was born Wilton Lewis Tawwater in Quanah the same week King Tutankhamun's tomb was discovered in Egypt in 1922. An uncle took a look at the newborn and declared him "King Tut."

A great friend—he still calls me "D. A." for Danny Andrews—Tut Tawwater is royalty in my book

* * *

Jimmie Chennault...here's the call

Logical response: So, what's the question?

One of my dearest friends—in and out of the officiating business—was the late Jimmie Chennault.

If you refereed a basketball game with Jimmie, he would make 70 percent of the calls. He didn't let much get past him, and that's why, during playoff season, you might walk into a gym where two games were scheduled, and Jimmie would be working both. He was much in demand by coaches. He called in the girls' state tournament for four years.

A legendary story has it that Jimmie made a call a coach didn't like, and as he was walking toward the scoring table to report the foul, the coach threw his coat in the air. Jimmie shot a glance at him and said, "If that coat comes down, you've got a technical foul."

It did and he did.

Jimmie worked a lot of Wayland Flying Queens games, especially when big name schools like Texas Tech and Texas came to town in the mid-to-late 1970s when Dean Weese was the coach and the Queens could beat up on fledgling NCAA programs.

Not accusing Jimmie of being a "homer," but I always said Dean Weese could be standing on a chair, waving a towel, and Jimmie would run right past him. On the other hand, Texas Coach Jody Conradt or Stephen F. Austin's Sue Gunter could stand up and clear their throat and Jimmie would give them a technical foul.

Jody told me several years ago that Sue (retired from coaching LSU) told her not long before she died that "I'd like to go back out to Plainview and play Wayland one more time if Jimmie Chennault wasn't refereeing."

One night Jimmie was supposed to be at Lubbock Roosevelt to call a playoff game but was held up by a prolonged game in Muleshoe where he was working earlier in the day.

As the fans stood in the gym lobby, wondering if Jimmie was coming, I told Kit McDaniel, longtime clock operator at Hale Center, that I would be glad to fill in if we could find a uniform and whistle.

Kit left little doubt where he stood on that idea: "We've seen some of your stuff before."

Jimmie—a former All-Navy softball player, who allegedly felled a runner heading for home with a throw that hit him in the head—also was a good umpire, and we worked many games together.

One summer afternoon, several mothers must have had collective PMS because they rode us—Jimmie, in particular, since he was working the plate—the whole game.

As we were walking off the field, Pat Thompson, a real estate agent, accosted us and said forcefully to Jimmie: "I wanna ask you a question!"

"OK," Jimmie said.

Thereupon, Pat launched into a tirade, allowing as how "that was the worst umpiring I've ever seen . . . blah, blah, blah."

After about 30 seconds, Jimmie asked with a straight face, "So, what's the question?"

One spring, he took me to the old Lubbock Christian University baseball field to work some games for Larry Hays, who gained legendary status as coach at LCU and Texas Tech.

I was umpiring the bases when a pitch rode in tight on the LCU first baseman, who stood about 6-4, 260. He started into his swing, but hunched his left shoulder and the ball hit him.

Because the catcher jumped up and blocked Jimmie's view, he looked to me for help.

I raised my right arm to signal "Strike!"

Larry Hays howled in protest from the dugout.

"Larry, the bat was already in the strike zone before the ball hit the batter," I yelled back from my post between second and short.

"Well, I've never seen that before," Hays declared.

All I could say was, "Neither have I."

Come to think of it, that's probably why I was never invited back to umpire college baseball.

*   *   *

Dean Weese

Dean Weese offers instruction
to his team

Don't come down here and brag on that one, ref

One of the greatest basketball coaches in American history is Dean Weese—mentor for the Wayland Flying Queens from 1973-79—attested by the fact he is a member of the Women's Basketball Hall of Fame in Knoxville, Tennessee.

Dean, a native of Higgins in the Panhandle, amassed an incredible 1,207-197 record (an 86 percent winning average) in a 42-year coaching career.

At Wayland, Dean compiled a record of 190-30, five appearances in the AIAW national tournament, including twice in the semifinals, four National Women's Invitational Tournament titles in Amarillo, and two national Amateur Athletic Union crowns,

In 15 years at Spearman High School he was 444-76 and won state titles in 1966, 1971, and 1972 as well as 13 straight district championships.

In 19 seasons at Levelland, he was 551-85 with seven state 4A championships, including four straight from 1985-89, and 17 district crowns.

By the way, after leaving Wayland for a brief stint as coach of the Dallas Diamonds in the Women's Basketball League, Dean was going to take a job at Portales, New Mexico, because the UIL transfer rule would have made his oldest son, Todd, sit out a year.

At the last minute, the UIL ruled Todd could play elsewhere in Texas, and Dean took the Levelland job instead. The rest, as they say, is history.

Dean also served as an assistant to Harley Redin for the USA squad that competed in the 1971 Pan American Games and was selected as the 2000 National Girls' Sports Coach of the Year by the National Federation Coaches Association.

Dean is a feisty guy who was a pretty fair baseball player and better than average golfer. One weekend he parked his 1951 Ford under a tree in Perryton while he went to Oklahoma for a tournament and a huge hailstorm about beat the fenders off that car.

When Dean went to get gas before returning to Higgins, the service station attendant said, Son, I think you need a new car."

"Why's that?" Dean asked.

"'Cause you don't have any place to put any more dents on this one," the attendant chuckled.

Irritated by that remark, Dean threw the car, still running, into gear and roared off with the gas hose dancing in the air behind him.

I vividly recall the first time I ever saw Dean Weese. It was at the regional tournament at Lubbock Coronado when he was coaching at Spearman. He jumped up off the bench and yelled, "Leann Shieldknight, I'm gonna wring your neck!" after a future Flying Queen did something that displeased him. I had never heard a coach talk like that to a female player.

Leanne Waddell of the Flying Queens, who is married to veteran Texas Aggies sportscaster Dave South, thought her first name was "Dadgummit" because Dean so often yelled at her, "Dadgummit Waddell!"

I attribute to Dean Weese one of the best retorts I have ever heard. It has to be in the Snappy Comebacks Hall of Fame.

The Queens were playing the host team in the Old Dominion Tournament in Norfolk, Virginia, in 1978. Sheri Haynes (now co-publisher of *Panhandle Plains Basketball Magazine* that Garet von Netzer of Amarillo and I published together for 38 years) and an Old Dominion player scrambled for a ball heading out of bounds. A tall, slender older man I'd describe as "prissy," ruled the ball was last touched by Sheri.

He then blew his whistle and ran to the bench farthest from him, leaned over to Dean and said, "I'm sorry, I missed that call."

Dean skinnied up his nose and barked, "Hell, you been missin' 'em all night. I don't know why you'd come down here and brag on that one!"

One time at the Plainview Queens Classic—a women's college and high school girls' tournament held at Wayland's Hutcherson Center for 29 years, Dean's Levelland Loboettes (not Lady Loboes, he always pointed out) outscored Dimmitt 10-2 in the second quarter.

As Levelland's host, I was walking to the dressing room with Dean and asked him, "Did you know Dimmitt didn't score in the last seven minutes of the second quarter?"

Dean responded with a wink, "Well, that's either very good defense or very poor offense."

Like most coaches, Dean had a routine, and one was to bring back his starters in the last few minutes of a game, regardless of the score . . . and usually the Queens were way ahead.

One Friday night in 1975, en route to a 34-1 season, the Queens plastered Murray State of Tishomingo, Oklahoma, 99-29. The teams were scheduled to play again on Saturday night, but the handsome Native American coach, Melvin Imotochi—no doubt irritated with Dean's lack of "hospitality"—loaded his team on the van and headed for home.

I don't recall Dean's reaction when he found out the Saturday night game wasn't going to happen, but I suspect it would not be suitable for print.

I nearly got a letter jacket one year after officiating six games for Weese in Levelland. One season, our Plainview officials' chapter took to heart a new directive from the University Interscholastic League to crack down on coaches getting up off the bench regularly. It was known as the "Seat Belt Rule." Violators were to be assessed a technical foul.

Dean was leading Dimmitt by about 50 points and suddenly, just as I was approaching his bench, he got up and walked toward the floor.

Momentarily stunned, I blew my whistle and walked over to the scorer's table and reported to Dean's wife Jo Ann, the official scorekeeper: "That's a technical foul for violation of the bench rule."

Jo Ann didn't register any surprise, and I don't recall Dean protesting, but Jim Douglass, my co-official and veteran assistant alumni director at Texas Tech, came over to ask, "Whada ya got?"

When I told him our chapter had been calling the Seat Belt Rule pretty tightly, he just said, "Our chapter (Lubbock) hasn't been too strict on that."

I thought, "Heck, if I was going to stick Dean Weese with a technical foul, I wouldn't have waited until he was 50 points ahead. Let's just wipe that off."

So we did. And I never bragged on that one, either.

* * *

They sound alike, but I know the difference

Between games of the previous story, I was visiting with legendary Dimmitt boys' coach Kenneth Cleveland about the Seat Belt Rule and he said sternly, "If anybody gives me a technical foul for that, it'll be the last time he calls for me."

Kenneth's wife, Libby, a math teacher at Wayland for more than 20 years, has published two books in his memory, "Letters to Coach," remembrances of him by former players, fellow coaches, fans and others, and "Letters from Coach," his workout schedules, plays and instructions to players and parents.

Speaking of Kenneth, who won more than 800 games, three state championships and 27 district titles at Dimmitt, here's one quick story. En route to its second straight state championship, Dimmitt led Tulia something like 38-5 at the end of the first quarter.

I was officiating the game and as I started to hand the ball to future Plainview and Amarillo High head coach John Smith on an out-of-bounds play, John said a four-letter word starting with "S." I don't know why, he just did. So, I rang up a technical foul.

After the game, Kenneth came in to the dressing room to ask why the "T." When I told him what John had said, Kenneth defended him and said, "No, he said 'Shoot.'"

I told him, "Well, I know the difference in the two words."

End of discussion.

However, years later, John and I were visiting and he recalled the incident, not remembering that I was the one who had assessed the technical.

I suspect even he would have admitted he knew the difference in the two words.

*   *   *

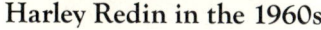

Harley Redin in the 1960s   Harley Redin at Hutcherson Center

Harley Redin: Great coach and a gentleman, too

It's practically impossible to mention women's basketball without thinking of Harley Redin, who I first met when I got a job working for the Wayland newspaper and handling sports information as well.

The 1936 graduate of Silverton High School and coach of the nationally-known Wayland Flying Queens had a profound influence on the game, not only as a coach but as a gentlemanly ambassador. Profanity was never a part of Harley's game.

A member of John Tarleton Junior College teams that won 88 games in a row, Redin would later coach the Queens to 76 of their national-record 131 consecutive wins recorded from 1953-54 through 1957-58.

From 1955-73, he directed the Queens to a 437-68 record (his first two teams were unbeaten) with six national Amateur Athletic Union titles and six second places, usually to archrival Nashville Business College.

Harley coached the U.S. women's team in the 1959 and 1971 Pan American games to gold and bronze medals, respectively, and in the 1964 World Championships and also coached all-star teams against Russian competition. Redin served on several Olympic and AAU rules committees that promoted the five-player game, the 30-second clock, and unlimited dribbling (theretofore, players could only dribble three times before having to pass). He also was among the first to use the full-court press and the fast-break offense (first using it in 6-on-6 competition).

A stickler for fundamentals and for good behavior on and off the court, he was cited by *The Plainview Daily Herald*'s Citizenship Hall of Fame for his promotion of sportsmanship.

Harley said he got only two technical fouls his entire coaching career, and about the only emotion he showed was pulling up his socks when things got tight.

Redin, who has two degrees from North Texas State University, came to Wayland in 1946 as men's coach and athletic director and held the latter title for many years.

He guided the Pioneers to a 171-97 record and four appearances in the NAIA national tournament from 1948-57. Between the Queens and Pioneers, he coached more than 40 All-Americans.

He also coached Hale Center's girls for two years in the early 1980s. I got to officiate one of his games at Hart. He was very polite, but may have pulled his socks up a time or two.

Harley was one of the 26 original inductees into the Women's Basketball Hall of Fame in Knoxville, Tennessee, in 1999 and also is a member of the Texas Sports Hall of Fame, Texas High School Basketball Hall of Fame, the Panhandle Sports Hall of Fame in Amarillo, an inaugural member of the Wayland Athletic Hall of Honor in 1992, and the Helms Foundation Hall of Fame.

He is a Distinguished Alumni of Tarleton, and he and his wife, Wilda Hutcherson Redin, were named Distinguished Benefactors of Wayland in 2007. The playing surface at Hutcherson Center is the "Wilda and Harley Redin Court."

The Atlanta Tipoff Club tapped Redin as the 2000 Naismith Women's Outstanding Contribution to Basketball Award winner for lifetime achievement, impact on the game of basketball, and honorable, exemplary service.

Also in 2000, Harley was selected as one of the 100 Sports Legends of the Texas Panhandle. He was named by *Sports Illustrated* as one of the top people in sports in Texas in the previous 50 years.

Wayland named its Athletic Hall of Honor for him several years ago, and a coaching award given by the university to outstanding alums since 1999 bears his name.

It's a shame that the only honor that has eluded him is the National Basketball Hall of Fame in Springfield, Massachusetts, for which he has been nominated several times.

Redin is proud of "just having the opportunity to be in on the ground floor of coaching student-athletes. We were probably the first college team that could compete with strict eligibility rules," he said. "There had always been AAU teams before, but all they had to do was just be amateurs.

"Sometimes I wish I would have hung around coaching a little longer," he said. "I got out just when women's basketball was really taking off."

A former banker, Redin published two books, *The Queens Fly High* in 1958 and *A Basketball Guide for Girls* in 1971.

A World War II veteran of the Marine Air Corps, Harley flew 38 bombing missions in the South Pacific. He served as a pilot for the Flying Queens, transporting them to their games for many years while coaching the team and for several years thereafter.

Perhaps his most auspicious achievement in later life has been serving as president of the International Downtown Coffee Club. At 95, he's the senior member of this group of cronies who meet each weekday at the Broadway Brew.

He often buys my coffee when I stop by to catch up on the latest efforts to solve the world's problems.

I told you he was a gentleman.

*   *   *

Greg Sherwood on the sidelines

Crowd hoists red dots in 1978 playoff game

Greg Sherwood helped Plainview's self-esteem

One of the smartest decisions a Plainview school board ever made was hiring Greg Sherwood as athletic director and head football coach in 1978.

Despite his successful record in Dalhart, in Liberal, Kansas, and, most recently in Spearman, moving a coach up from a 2A school was not a real easy choice.

Nor was hiring a man who stood 6-3, weighed about 400 pounds, and wore a dark blue leisure suit about the time those were losing their popularity.

Fortunately, the board looked past the outward appearance and saw the very big heart and character of this very big man.

I've always contended that I could have coached the 1978 Bulldogs to a district championship—something no Plainview team had ever accomplished since starting the grid sport way back in 1910.

That squad was loaded with talent—three running backs who gained between 800 and 1,600 yards, good receivers, outstanding offensive linemen, and a stout defense. It didn't hurt that Greg brought a virtual on-field coach in his quarterback son, Scott. He also recruited a staff of excellent assistant coaches as well. Greg's younger son, Stan Sherwood, also played for the Bulldogs.

That team went 11-2 and advanced to the state quarterfinals before bowing to the storied Odessa Permian Panthers on an ice-cold Saturday in Texas Tech's Jones Stadium.

"We had lots of great leaders on that team and a lot of depth. And I think our coaches were men of character you would want your son to play for," Sherwood said in an interview years ago.

From 1978-84, Plainview went 52-20, advanced to the playoffs four times and just missed going two other times. Greg introduced such slogans as "Angry Red, 'Nuf Said" and "Loyal to Effort." Red dots symbolized a new attitude as the resurgent Bulldogs proved that old saying true: "Nothing will bring a town together like a tornado or a winning football team."

Plainview also enjoyed great success in its overall athletic program during Sherwood's tenure. He was respected by his fellow educators, started a popular pep rally for the band the night before they went to contest, and he and his wife Jackie were active in the bus ministry at Garland Street Church of Christ.

A member of the Texas High School Football Hall of Fame and the Texas High School Coaches Association Hall of Honor, Greg served as president of the Texas High School Coaches Association and coached the North team to 7-3 victory in the 1985 Texas High School All-Star Game in the Astrodome. He was named one of the 100 Sports Legends of the Texas Panhandle in 2000.

His lifetime varsity coaching record was a 174-64-2. He was 63-36 in 10 years at Plainview, 48-10-1 in Spearman, and 41-9-1 at Dalhart.

Commenting on his reputation as an outstanding motivator, Sherwood said he took time to get to know his players, inquiring about their goals, their personal life, and their spiritual life. "I loved them and I think they loved me, and that's important."

After leaving Plainview, Greg served as athletic director for the Lubbock school district for 13 years.

In the fall of 2007, Plainview made official an act some believed should have been done years before.

Bulldog Stadium, which opened in 1956, was renamed Greg Sherwood Memorial Bulldog Stadium in honor of the man credited with forever changing the fortunes of Plainview football and improving a community's self-esteem at the same time.

Greg died Sept. 15, 2006, in Lubbock after a long battle with cancer. Appropriately, he passed away on a Friday—game night all over the state of Texas.

*   *   *

Thump-Ball sport wasn't for me

The only person I ever heard say they didn't like basketball was the late Robert Horne, manager of Rockwell Bros. Lumber Company at Fourth and Broadway and father of my friends, Davis and Bob Horne.

He derisively called it "Thump-Ball."

I have played, kept the scorebook and clock, handled the public address for, broadcast on the radio, reported on for the newspaper, and officiated Mr. Naismith's game.

Well, to say I "played" the game might have been an exaggeration. I didn't play it all that well to be honest.

I can't recall how many points I had as a seventh grader for Vernon Stokes, but I did net a mere 8 for Charles Lipscomb, one of my all-time favorite teachers, despite being a full-time starter in the eighth grade (hey, he liked me) and 26 as a freshman for Charles Thacker my final year at Coronado Junior High.

Coach Thacker, our unpaid "youth director" at Ninth and Columbia Church of Christ, was none too happy with me in a game at Tulia. After I had only run the floor a couple of times and, being unaccustomed to all that physical activity, I was gassed, and called a timeout. It was our sixth and resulted in a technical foul.

I do remember scoring 8 points in a tournament game at Estacado in early February 1964. It was the second-most important thing to happen in America that day. Some group called The Beatles showed up in New York that afternoon.

The day after football season ended in 1964, I went out for basketball. The next morning, I asked assistant varsity coach Harold Green if I might have a pair of shoes.

Coach Green gently confided that varsity coach Bob Clindaniel (apparently a very quick judge of talent, or lack thereof) felt I should concentrate on football.

A nice way of saying "Thump-Ball" is not your game.

*   *   *

Ronald Kersh

Going from goat to hero in just one week

If I could relive just one event in my rather checkered sporting past, I wouldn't hesitate to choose Oct. 21, 1965.

First, a little background.

Just a week before on the same Bulldog Stadium turf, the PHS Red Dogs, coached by Bill Mayfield and Floyd Murry, hosted Lubbock Coronado, in its first year of existence.

The Mustangs, who had chosen to play a JV schedule, stood 5-1 in district play and the Red Dogs were 5-0-1, a tie with Monterey being our only blemish.

Coronado brought 10 busloads of fans and band members to the game, so the attendance was about 4,000.

Now, I am on record as being the first Plainview player ever to score against a Coronado football team, and I made Wayland football coach Butch Henderson, former mentor at Coronado, aware of that tidbit when he came to the university.

I made a sliding catch on a 21-yard pass from Ronald Kersh in the north end zone in the first quarter.

Later, Roland McCutcheon, brother of future NFL star Lawrence McCutcheon, ran back an interception to give us a 12-0 lead at the intermission.

Though a senior, Roland was playing on the JV due to the funky UIL transfer rule that made him ineligible for the varsity when he transferred from Booker T. Washington—two years before full integration brought his brother to PHS.

So confident of a Plainview victory, a varsity player apparently went home and called KVOP to report the Red Dogs had won.

I think I had three other catches in that game and saved a touchdown by grabbing the face mask of a Mustang between two of his teammates who were about to level me.

We still led 12-7 with just over a minute to play with Coronado at its own 5-yard line.

But quarterback Gary Kirksey, now the pastor of City View Christian Fellowship in Lubbock, hit his big tight end over the middle. He shook me off like a rag doll and lumbered 57 yards before Roland ran him down. A couple plays later, umpire Bob Clindaniel (the varsity basketball coach) pulled a red flag out of his pocket and threw it in my direction for pass interference.

Seconds later, I lost my man, who caught a ball at the 1-yard line, setting up Coronado's winning score with about five seconds left.

I walked off the field feeling lower than the blades of grass I had helped plant on a work crew the previous summer.

Ah, but redemption was on its way.

The next Thursday, with the score tied 20-20 against Borger, Coach Mayfield called a first-down pass play in the fourth quarter.

I can still smell the damp grass as I split to the right at the south 35. At the snap, I raced about 12 yards downfield, made a quick fake to the sideline, and sprinted straight north.

Ronald Kersh lofted a perfect spiral that I caught over my shoulder around the Borger 35 and sailed home untouched for the winning score.

What I wouldn't give for a film of that play.

Absent that, I shall remain a legend in my own mind.

*   *   *

Don Williams   Ron Roberts

You're not gettin' paid to think

Don Williams was the head football coach at Plainview High my lone year on the varsity in 1966.

A former Texas Tech quarterback who walked like Matt Dillon due to a serious leg injury from his gridiron days, Don had come to Plainview from Littlefield in 1962 to replace Herman Smith. The Bulldogs had gone 1-19 under Smith and had lost 11 in a row before Williams arrived.

The Bulldogs lost at home by the horrendous score of 86-6 in the '62 season opener in Plainview. Smith had moved to Big Spring as an assistant, and the word was that he encouraged the head coach to run up the score.

Anyway, Plainview would go 0-10 in '62 and lose the first three of 1963 before ending the 24-game misery with a 20-18 win over Littlefield (*More on that story is elsewhere in this book*).

Don was an "old school" coach who probably liked most of his players but didn't bother to tell us very often. He chastised defensive end Richard Watson, longtime owner of The Fieldhouse Sandwich Shop, for allowing a certain teammate to block him out of the play in practice. Don called the blocker by name and alleged he's "the worst player on this team."

"Daddy Don," as some of his players called him behind his back, couldn't have been happy that we lost to his old school, Littlefield, 13-12 to open the '66 season. He nearly had a stroke when Pampa apparently called an audible and completed a pass to the 4-yard-line on the first play of the game, scored easily, and went on to win.

Finishing the year at 2-6-2, we tied Lubbock High, 15-15 at Lowrey Field, site of an earlier 9-9 deadlock with Coronado, playing its first varsity season.

We faked an extra-point kick and Ronnie Roberts passed to Bobby Bouldin for two earlier in the game, but Lubbock High did the same thing, completing the two-point pass in front of Roberts for the final points.

I must add here that the only reason I got to start four games at split end was because Bobby Bouldin abruptly quit the team in a disagreement with assistant coach Fred Dawson over how he should be rehabbing a knee injury.

This is the same Ronnie Roberts of Estacado Junior High who galloped like a racehorse down the sideline as the final buzzer sounded to beat my Coronado Red team when we were seventh graders.

We might have won by a small margin, but I cost us two points when I tried to help Lloyd Reese tackle Johnny Campbell in the end zone and only succeeded in knocking Lloyd off the Estacado quarterback.

As Lubbock High matched our trickery to tie the game, Don Williams—wearing a dark blue blazer and a white Stetson hat, jumped into the air, made a 180-spin and nearly crushed the walkie-talkie he held in his hand to communicate with coaches in the press box.

"I'll kill that Ronnie Roberts!" Don thundered.

When Ron came to the sideline, he made the mistake of prefacing his explanation of what had gone wrong by saying, "Coach, I thought . . ."

"S---, Roberts, you ain't gettin' paid to think!" Don interrupted.

True. Tacky, but true.

*   *   *

Prophetic utterance of a wrestling coach

James Kile, a member of the Panhandle Sports Hall of Fame in Amarillo, was an outstanding football and basketball official, in addition to being the wrestling coach at Amarillo Tascosa for many years.

James was a master at determining whether a measurement was needed for a first down and often put his pencil down within inches of where the chain would be stretched.

When a player recovered a fumble, James would pull him far away from the pile and pat him in the shoulder. "That helped the guys in the press box and made his mother proud," James said.

I first encountered James in the spring of 1966 as we Bulldog baseballers were waiting to take the field and eventually lose 4-3 in 14 innings in a game in which lefty David Gibbins struck out an amazing 25 batters in a duel with our southpaw Johnny Campbell, who had the best pickoff move I ever saw.

James said the Rebel gridders, working out in a park near the baseball field, were going to be so good in the coming season that "they aren't even going to tackle until the last week of spring training."

I thought, "What does this bragging old fart know?" The Red Dogs (of which I was a member) beat Tascosa's jayvee team, 53-6 the previous fall.

Well, six months later, after we pulled a trick play and Pat Buchanan ran a kickoff back 75 yards to make it 7-6, Tascosa went off and left us, 43-6 and went on to go 12-1 before losing to San Angelo Central at Dick Bivins Stadium in Amarillo.

The Rebels' offense was spearheaded by quarterback Monty Johnson, who followed his father and grandfather as a football player at Oklahoma, and wide receiver Danny Lester, who went on to star at Texas.

I was sent in to play safety late in the game and Lester came trotting out of the backfield as if the play didn't involve him. But when he got about five yards from me, he turned on the afterburners. I tried to grab him as he ran past me.

Danny Lester scored 32 points that night. Monty Johnson overthrew him by about six inches, thanks, I'm sure, to my slowing him down just a bit.

Otherwise, he would have had 38 points.

*   *   *

One homer wins a game, another stuns a fan

I only hit two homeruns in my organized baseball career.

One was the game winner for my City National Bank Giants, coached by genial postman Buddy Harriss, in the championship match of a 3-game playoff with the Cardinals in the summer of 1961.

Kenneth Scroggins threw a high fastball, and I swung over my head and launched a towering fly ball to left that fell over the fence, just out of the reach of my soon-to-be junior high buddy Lloyd "Buster" Reese.

This is the same Lloyd Reese who observed of a female classmate: "She's pretty in a grotesque sort of way."

I leaped and hopped around the bases and eventually collected a dollar from my maternal grandmother who asked me after the game if I had heard her yelling from the stands that she would reward me if I "struck a homerun."

My other round-tripper came in a junior varsity game in Nazareth on a windy spring afternoon in 1966. In fact, the wind must have been blowing about 40 mph for me to have launched a ball over the fence, which probably wasn't more than 300 feet away.

As I took off for first, an old German sitting on his car hood was so shocked he dropped his Budweiser.

I told that story to my friend Richard Entrekin of Hart at the Nazareth Senior Citizens Center several years ago. A native Nebraskan who worked at Farmer's Grain in Hart and later for Edmonson Wheat Growers for 25 years, Richard asked me, "What year did you say that was?"

"1966," I repeated.

"Couldn't have been me," Richard said with a wink, "I gave up drinkin' in 1965."

*   *   *

Lowlights of upper-level baseball career

I played one year of Babe Ruth baseball, one year of American Legion ball and two seasons at Plainview High, mostly on the JV squad as a junior. If they weren't so memorable, they would be altogether forgettable.

Our First National Bank Indians were so bad we might have gone 0-14 had I not called all the players earlier in the day and implored them to give their best that evening. We edged the White Sox, 10-9 to avoid being skunked.

The winning pitcher was Tommy Simmons, who otherwise worked behind the plate. Even on the mound, Tommy would yell, "Cut, batter!" when he turned a pitch loose.

I played every position except catcher that season which almost ended before it got started good when manager Barry McMennamy benched me in the first game after four errors at third base. I pondered quitting the team.

After the Cardinals—coached by Red Allen and led by the eminently talented black duo of Norman Smoots and O. B. Merlett—drilled the White Sox, 38-1 on a Friday night, we boasted that would not happen to the Indians. It didn't. We only lost 34-2 on Saturday night.

Anyway, I made the All-Star team, only because they had to pick someone from each team, no matter how poor they were. I did manage to get three hits in a tournament game against Groom, retired only when I ducked to avoid getting beaned but the ball struck the bat and rolled out to the mound.

In a rare varsity appearance as a junior, I ripped a pitch into the gap in right center and thought as I rounded second I might have a shot at an inside-the-park homer.

"Can I go, Coach, can I go?" I yelled as I raced toward third.

Coach Harold Green, daydreaming in the third-base box since we were already leading Nazareth something like 24-3, instructed, "Yeah, go in!"

My feet got tangled as I hit the bag and unceremoniously crashed shoulder first into the unforgiving ground. I believe there is still a divot at Bulldog Park to this day. Needless to say, my teammates thought that was quite hilarious.

More important to the 1967 Bulldogs as a scorekeeper than a third baseman or outfielder, I hit a paltry .125 and have the dubious distinction of taking a called third strike as the first batter up to start the season against Dumas and going down swinging as the final batter of the year against Monterey, despite Coach Jim Sears' encouragement to "go up there and finish your career on a high note."

I also may be the only Bulldog ever to have been pinch-hit for *twice* in one game, pitched by my former Hillcrest neighbor Roger Meester of Lubbock High.

I did credit myself with the winning RBI when a Palo Duro outfielder threw the ball onto the Jaycee Park screen behind home plate trying to prevent a runner from scoring and laid down a perfect bunt to put the winning run in scoring position in a 2-1 victory over Tascosa at Jaycee.

The absolute low-light, though, may have come one afternoon when we were working on pickoff plays and I was struck in the side of the head as I was diving back into second.

Tom Hall said it sounded like a bat hitting a telephone pole as I "dropped like a sack of potatoes."

I'm sure Coach Sears was happy I was not greatly impaired. He didn't have anybody near as talented as me to keep the scorebook.

*   *   *

Butch Flatt: More homers than Roger Maris

It is well chronicled that Roger Maris of the New York Yankees hit 61 homeruns in 1961 to break Babe Ruth's record of 60 set in 1927.

I was chasing Roger myself that summer but hit only 42 over the outfield fence at Jaycee Park, the target from which Hillcrest ragamuffins launched fly balls on our makeshift field in Broadway Park.

But Roger was no match for "Butch" Flatt, a big ol' strong kid who resided a block north of me with brother G. W.—better known as G-Dub—on Southeast Fifth.

Butch hit 102 homers that year and got quite a bit of exercise chasing the balls he hit over the fence on the occasions when he didn't order one of us younger guys to fetch them.

I still bear a scar on my right ankle where Butch spiked me with his metal cleats one afternoon. It wasn't intentional, but it bled and hurt nonetheless.

Butch was a mischievous sort, once almost causing me to inflict considerable pain upon myself. He encouraged me to hold a tiny plastic derringer while igniting a firecracker in the barrel.

At the last second, I decided that was not a good idea and put the derringer on the lattice work in front of our house. When the firecracker exploded, the white plastic handles blew off and the barrel split.

I'm not sure if that incident prompted my mother to take revenge upon Butch, who would one day become a Baptist preacher, but he sassed her and she sprayed him with the garden hose. Properly chastised, he slunk off to his house.

He may have hit 102 homeruns but my mother "hit one out of the park" with that feat, as far as I was concerned.

*   *   *

Wait a minute: JFK didn't win that game

I was saved from considerable embarrassment back in 1969 when the Wayland Flying Queens played in the national AAU tournament in Gallup, New Mexico.

That trip was particularly memorable because I met Dr. Bill Marshall, president of Wayland Baptist College from 1947-53. He was a pioneer in integration, accepting foreign students, and changing the school's mascot from Jackrabbits to Pioneers.

He also instituted a no-smoking policy, causing trustee and local attorney Frank Day to resign the board. Look Magazine did a story about it.

Dr. Marshall, who was then living in California, told a dramatic story about the Queens playing a Russian team. With Wayland down by a point, a much smaller Queen miraculously got the tip on a jump-ball. Another Queen raced down the court and let fly a shot. "The buzzer went off and the Queens lost," said Dr. Marshall, pausing for effect . . . "until the ball swished through the net."

After completing a second shortened broadcast back to KVOP because we got knocked off the air twice for some reason, I called in my story to The Herald. Then I went out and watched the championship game between John F. Kennedy College of Wahoo, Nebraska, and the

Queens' archrival, Nashville Business College. NBC had beaten the Queens soundly in the semifinals.

JFK was coached by a demonstrative fellow named George Nicodemus, who got ejected from a game with the Queens at Bulldog Gym for too vehemently criticizing an official's call.

George went down to the dressing room steps at the south end of the gym but kept peeking around the corner when the action would go to the opposite end of the court and the officials couldn't see him.

Due to a drop in enrollment and financial difficulties following the end of the military conscription draft in 1973, Kennedy College closed down in 1975 with a 6-24 record all-time against Wayland.

At Gallup, the scoreboard just had "Home" and "Visitor" rather than the names of the two teams.

Nera White, NBC's super-talented guard, seemed to be running around like the proverbial chicken with its head cut off, and I *assumed* NBC was on the ropes.

I had been half-heartedly watching the game with Alvin Redin, father of Queens coach Harley Redin, and F.G. Crofford, Claude's coach, who was considered as Harley's successor when he resigned a couple of years later, then decided to continue coaching.

When the final buzzer sounded, I walked to the press-hospitality room and dialed up the Associated Press to give them details on the Queens' game but also to report the score of the championship contest.

"First, I need to tell you that John F. Kennedy has stopped NBC's eight-year string of national championships," I told the person in Dallas.

Alvin Redin and F.G. Crofford both looked surprised and said, "JFK didn't win that game."

First I thought they were kidding but soon realized they weren't.

Uh, never mind, Dallas.

*   *   *

Saved from two near sporting disasters

I came very near death—or serious injury and embarrassment—a couple of times at sporting events.

In the spring of 1971, I went to the old W.T. Barrett Stadium in Odessa to watch Plainview's very talented trio of hurdler Randy Lightfoot, sprinter Zoe Simpson, and quartermiler Tim Son compete in the prestigious West Texas Relays.

Those guys went on to college stardom—Randy and Tim after winning at state: Lightfoot at Texas and Wayland, Simpson at Rice, and Son at Baylor.

Meet officials put up a fence around the track, allowing the athletes to compete and lounge on the football field.

It was a warm, lazy Saturday afternoon, and as I started to walk from the field back to the press box, I stepped onto the track just in time to see the entire field of the 880 bearing down on me about 30 yards away.

Thank goodness for that admonition when driving and crossing an intersection to "look both ways."

I sure wouldn't have looked good with cleat marks all over my body after causing a mass pile-up.

The second near-accident came seven years later at UCLA's famed Pauley Pavilion where John Wooden won so many games in his storied career coaching the Bruins.

For the trip to the women's national basketball tournament, I had bought a pair of new shoes, and as I sort of "skipped" down to the seats in the upper deck where other Wayland fans were seated, the slick soles felt like they were going out from under me.

In the briefest of moments, I could see my life flashing before me as I was headed for a tumble right over the rail a few yards ahead and a headlong dive into the seats below.

Suddenly, even before I had time to call out to the Lord for help, the scary descent ended.

I'm sure I looked around to see if anybody had noticed, then slunk meekly into a seat, thinking, "I sure won't do *that* again."

*   *   *

Run-ins with sports venue "Nazis"

I can bet you any sportswriter you ever talk to can tell you some horror stories about dealing with uncooperative gatekeepers and other "Nazis" at stadiums and arenas where they have been intent on covering games.

Press passes, notepads and cameras haven't been enough for some reporters to gain entrance without a hassle.

In 1968, new *Herald* Sports Editor Foster Johnson and I went to Vernon to cover a Plainview High football game. When we arrived at the press box—Foster in his Southwestern Oklahoma track sweater and I in my Plainview High football jacket—the press box attendant asked, "Are you boys covering the game for the high school paper?"

I didn't think we looked *that* young.

When I discovered there were no programs, I asked the man, "Do y'all provide programs for the press box?" His reply: "Yeah, I think they provide them down at the gate for 15 cents."

Foster, who nearly ran out of gas coming home from that game and went off and left his car running for two hours when we covered a Wayland basketball game at to Eastern New Mexico in Portales, raised the ire of a couple of Plainview boosters when he wrote in advance of the next year's PHS-Vernon game that much of Plainview's current success was due to the groundwork laid by Don Williams, who had resigned two years earlier.

I thought it quite ironic that the game wound up in a 16-16 tie.

My first year as sports editor in 1970, the press box attendant at Lowrey Field in Lubbock—obviously enamored with his own sense of power—first denied *Herald* photographer David Bryant entrance to get a cup of coffee because "he's not working press."

David had ridden to the game on his motorcycle and was so angry that he put his camera in my dad's car and rode back home without taking any pictures.

Next, the attendant decided that my "spotter," Mike Anderson, would not be admitted because "we don't allow high school boys in the press box."

I first thought he was talking about me. I still wasn't shaving every day, but I knew I had matured some since my encounter with the Vernon guy.

Mike had a district-issued press pass but that wasn't good enough. Since the same guy had given me grief the previous year when I apparently shook him up by showing up at the end of a playoff game to get some information, I was good and mad by now.

My dad came over from the other side of the field and was ready to get in the middle of someone.

Long story short, the athletic director was summoned and Mike and I were admitted with a bit of scolding for what was perceived to be a bad attitude.

But it was nowhere near as scathing as Editor Jim Servatius's phone call to the athletic director's office on Monday.

He was assured we'd never have such a problem again. I can assure you we didn't.

*　　*　　*

He doesn't know what Stan Musial batted in 1957

I think it's strange that a guy who had such trouble with math is so enamored with statistics.

I'm a big baseball fan and statistics are such a part of the history of the game.

When we played "sandlot" ball in Hillcrest, I usually kept score when no one else did.

And, because neighbor friend Mike Wadzeck and I collected baseball cards—until we got stupid and burned them in the alley trash can when we decided to "put away childish things" (those cards might be worth a lot of money now)—I became familiar with lots of numbers that stuck in my head.

I mean, why do I remember that Stan Musial of the St. Louis Cardinals batted .337 in 1957?

The Herald had a ton of Bulldog football stats compiled in a book after a summerlong project in 1965 by my brother and Walter Budd.

During Bulldog broadcasts, I frequently quoted some of those numbers—"Royce Coleman holds the school record for the longest run of 96 yards against Tascosa in 1978"—I could pull up from the cranial computer.

I was horrified when a new sports editor inadvertently threw that incredibly valuable resource away several years ago.

When Tom Hall was doing the morning show at KKYN, I'd call in to tell him and co-host Brandy Haines about stories that would be in that day's newspaper.

One morning we were discussing the many talents of my friend Eddy Curry, then-Minister of Education at First Baptist Church.

"He can paint, repair things, sew, make curtains," I bragged, quickly adding, "but he doesn't know important stuff like what Stan Musial batted in 1957."

OK, I just looked it up: "Stan the Man" batted .351 in 1957. He batted .337 in 1958.

Hey, even a statistics nut can be off a little bit.

*   *   *

Denzil McMillan   Joe Jacobs   Orville Wilhelm

Namesakes for Plainview summer baseball parks

Folks unfamiliar with the history of the Summer Baseball Program in Plainview may not recognize the namesakes for the three major parks in the South Broadway complex on the east side of Beech Street.

Babe Ruth Park is named for Joe Jacobs, a native of Whiteflat between Quitaque and Flomot, who was the Bell Dairy Products distributor. He served in several capacities for the program, operated by the Noon Optimist Club from 1969-2012.

Joe, who moved to McGregor, near Waco, several years ago, had many folksy sayings, including "larrupin'" for anything he felt was good—from food to outstanding plays on the diamond.

The north field is named for Denzil McMillan, longtime Certified Public Accountant, who was the official scorekeeper for the many post-season tournaments Plainview hosted. His sons, Ronnie and Tommy, came up through the program, then coached when their sons played, and were excellent groundskeepers to boot.

Tommy, now an assistant coach for the Wayland Pioneers and leader of Coaches Outreach Bible Study at Plainview High School, is one of the best men I know.

Denzil's admonition about proper conduct might not have been grammatically correct but fans usually followed it: "Do not criticize neither the players nor the umpires."

The south field's namesake is Orville Wilhelm who umpired in the program for more than 40 years. A man with few teeth and an ample stomach often covered by a white T-shirt, Orville tended to close his eyes and stutter if you got him rattled. His strike calls sounded more like "Streeeek!" and he might thrust his right arm out, then suddenly change the call to "Ball!"

But he was unfailingly happy, flashing a mostly toothless grin when I good-naturedly urged him not to call too many "Streeeeks" on my players when I was coaching.

Since he umpired almost all the time on the south field, it was appropriate that venue received his name.

Orville and Denzil are gone now, but I suspect if they have baseball in Heaven both men are at their posts doing a job Joe Jacob would adjudge to be "larrupin.'"

*   *   *

Harrell Weatherred

"You're not messin' with a rookie!"

One of the most memorable characters with whom I have ever been associated with was the late Harrell Weatherred.

A native of Kress, Harrell taught thousands of kids to drive via the local driver's ed program. I learned (and I use the term loosely) to drive as a high school freshman in 1964 when I was 15.

Harrell was president of our Plainview basketball officials association, was a football official, coached the PHS golf team for several years, and also ran the Optimist Summer Baseball Program for many years.

One year, Plainview was going to host a tournament. When a fellow from Pampa asked if certain rules would prevail, Harrell said, "Tell you what. We're hope you're happy when you come, hope you're happy when you leave. We're gonna play by Plainview rules. That's the way it's gonna be."

Harrell could be a cantankerous coot from time to time. He said, "I may be a horse's rear, but at least I'm consistent." To him, that was a badge of honor.

When Harrell assigned me to a game in Matador I always got tickled, because he transposed letters and it came out *Madator.*

One night, he and I reffed at that Motley County school. It might have been the night I attempted to blow my whistle only to discover it wasn't in my mouth, creating a rather unusual sound.

If you officiated with Harrell, he usually preferred that you drive. He'd slump down in the passenger seat, turn his head toward the window, and start talking and chuckling ever so often.

Best thing to do was just laugh with him since you probably had no idea what he was saying.

I have always tended to mumble, but I wasn't in Harrell's league.

During a tournament at Abernathy, I was walking past a Frenship player, headed to my spot under the basket while Harrell walked to the scorer's table to report a foul.

The kid said, "Sir, that other official said something to me, but I didn't understand what he said."

I told him, "Don't worry about it, son, we never know what he says to us either."

Harrell tickled me, too, when he called a "traveling" violation. He'd roll his arms and stomp his feet, shod in slightly built-up shoes, up and down.

One night, several of us went with Harrell to a district Little League meeting in Littlefield. On the way home—about the time we got even with the Coca-Cola bottling plant (now Casa Rica Tortillas) out on South I-27—his Mercury started sputtering . . . obviously out of gas.

Suddenly, Harrell began twisting the steering wheel back and forth, causing the car to rock violently.

Almost instantly, the sputtering stopped, and we headed on into town, eventually stopping at the Allsup's store at Fifth and Amarillo to fill up.

Happy that his maneuver worked, sloshing gas into the carburetor, Harrell announced with a laugh, "I'll guarantee you, you're not messin' with a rookie."

That became a mantra for several of us through the years.

*   *   *

"That's not a violation at the house!"

My freshman year at Wayland (1967-68), the Pioneers hosted New Mexico Highlands from Las Vegas.

Their coach, Dr. John Donnelly, was a stocky, balding, red-faced man, who believed the basket should be raised to 12 feet to discourage "dunking," had his players attired in black high-top tennis shoes worn only at that time by the Boston Celtics, had them practicing passing in a very robotic fashion, and had them shoot free throws underhanded (only Wilt Chamberlain was still doing that, if memory serves).

Anyway, early in the game, Harrell Weatherred, who matched Donnelly in stature and red-faced complexion, called a "spot violation" against the visitors, meaning the player inbounding the ball couldn't run up and down the endline as you can after a made basket. Nevertheless, the Highlands player did so and Harrell duly called a violation.

As Harrell got ready to hand the ball to a Wayland player, he was tapped on the shoulder by Donnelly, who had marched from his bench a few feet away.

"What's goin' on?" he demanded.

"That's a 'spot' violation," said Harrell, obviously irritated that Donnelly had come to question him.

"Well," retorted Donnelly, "that's not a violation at the house," referring to the home court at Highlands, but certainly erroneous in his proclamation.

"Well, I guarantee you it's a violation at *this* house," Harrell responded, banishing Donnelly back to his seat.

Later in the game, a Highlands player with the ball in the front court, turned to throw the ball to a trailing guard who was still in the back court. That player jumped toward the center line and caught the ball, landing in the front court.

Highlands was called for a back-court violation—because it's where the player starts from, not where he lands.

Donnelly jumped off the bench and intercepted Harrell Weatherred's co-official, a big, barrel-chested fellow aptly named "Red" Harvick from Tahoka, at the scorer's table.

Donnelly vehemently protested the call, slamming a pudgy fist down on the red wooden one-and-one box on the table. Harvick responded by slamming his hand on the same box, then reaching for his whistle, before releasing the lanyard.

After the game, I asked Harvick about the exchange, and he replied with a huff, "I was gonna whip that sonofabitch!"

Sometimes it's better not to cross a man in a striped shirt—at this house or any other.

*   *   *

Ronnie Peret

A&M's wild and wooly games vs. Baylor and Tech

Ronnie Peret (pronounced like parrot), the tallest player in Plainview High basketball history at almost 6-10, was a three-year starter for Coach Bob Clindaniel in1962-62, 1963-64 and 1964-65 before going on to make All-Southwest Conference twice and SWC Player of the Year in 1968-69 for Texas A&M. He twice led the Aggies in scoring and was the top rebounder all three seasons.

An all-state selection as a PHS senior—once holding the school record with 44 points in a game—and member of the Texas A&M Athletic Hall of Fame, he was drafted by the Los Angeles Lakers but a knee injury curtailed his career. Ronnie also served as a very impressive drum major for the Plainview High School Band.

Ronnie, now an insurance and investments rep in Kemah, near Houston, tells a great story about a major incident with Baylor and a wild finish against Texas Tech. This is his recollection:

In February 1969, we had to go out to Lubbock and play Tech following a brawl during the Baylor game the preceding Saturday night.

We were up by about 26 with about 10 minutes to go in the second half. Baylor was in a full court, man-to-man press, and I was being guarded by my old nemesis, Tom Friedman, a 6-6 senior forward whose butt I had whipped both basketball-wise and literally the past summer during scrimmages with the Dallas Chaparrals. There was no love lost between us.

I was always moved to the point-guard position against a man-to-man press, and had dished off to teammates several times for easy baskets. There was no way Tom could cover me with my speed and quickness advantage over him. This frustrated him greatly.

So, he was over-playing me, trying to keep me from getting the ball, and I saw an opportunity to "fly" on him to the other end. Sonny Benefield saw me, and threw me a "bomb," but it was short, and I had to slow up to make the catch. That allowed Tom to catch up just before I went for an easy layup.

Seeing that he couldn't stop the shot, Tom grabbed for my face with his hands, raked across my eyes with his fingernails, and attempted to throw me to the floor. I still made the shot but lost my balance and hit the floor hard.

When I finished sliding into the bleachers at that end of the court, I started to get up and go clean his clock. But, two of our football finest, tight end Tommy Buchman and offensive tackle Rolf Krueger, grabbed me and held me. Friedman turned to look right into the TV camera and smiled as he held up his hand to signify he had committed a foul.

About that time, Billy Bob Barnett, trailing the play, arrived on a dead run and hit Tom in the mouth with a forearm shot. It lifted him nearly a foot off the ground and sent him, now totally unconscious, flying into the crowd in the bleachers to my right, where the rest of our football team swallowed him up from view. The benches then emptied, and the fight was on, even including several Aggie Corps Seniors, boots and all!

After about five minutes (that seemed like 20), order was restored as the Aggie Band played the Star Spangled Banner. Friedman was loaded on a stretcher and wheeled off the court to a waiting ambulance and we finished the game.

Athletic Director and Head Football Coach Gene Stallings held a press conference and said that it was a miracle that the football team was there to "protect" Tom from further injury.

But the next day a Dallas TV station showed video of our All-American Billy Hobbs from Amarillo Tascosa astride Tom and beating him about the head and face.

Our university president, Gen. Earl Rudder, (U.S. Army, Rt.), asked to speak to us before our chartered plane took off Monday morning for Lubbock. His chauffeur-driven white Lincoln Continental drove up alongside of our Trans-Texas DC-3. He climbed aboard and just stared at us for about two minutes, then began to speak.

He said, "Gentlemen, we have just concluded one of the most embarrassing times in A&M history. You men are now going to play another game at a place where there exists an even more horrendous opportunity for a repeat of what occurred Saturday night.

"You need to know that I fully expect that you, as representatives of Texas A&M University, will conduct yourselves on and off that court as gentlemen and ambassadors of this fine institution, and I do not want a repeat of Saturday night's embarrassment. Do I make myself crystal clear on that?"

We all nodded in the affirmative. Then he went down the aisle of the plane, asking each one of us individually, including the entire coaching staff, if we understood exactly what he meant, and required a verbal answer of "Yes, sir!"

He then wished us luck in our game and a safe trip and walked off the plane and back to his car. Not another word was spoken as we buttoned up the door for takeoff and fastened our seatbelts.

Then, there was a pounding on the back door of the plane. The manager opened it to find President Rudder standing there, motioning for the door to be let down. He reboarded the plane and walked back up the aisle, turned around and stared at us again for about a minute more.

"As I said, I fully expect you men to conduct yourselves as gentlemen and ambassadors of Texas A&M at all times," he said. "However, if a fight gets started anyway out there, you men damn sure as hell better win it!"

After a unanimous standing ovation, he shook all our hands as he slowly made his way back down the aisle a second time and deplaned. He stood by his car, waving, as we started our takeoff.

The Tech Saddle Tramps found out where we were staying in Lubbock that night, and drove through the motel every hour on the hour towing that damn bell and ringing it, all night long, until the motel clerk called some of Lubbock's Finest to block off the parking lot.

At the Lubbock Coliseum, following our introductions and while the house was dark in preparation for the introductions of the Tech players, the crowd threw about three dozen eggs at us. They barely missed us, but totally trashed the floor on our end, causing the entire area to have to be mopped and dried completely before the game could begin, delaying the start of the game by about an hour.

Shorty Lawson and Bob Smith were the officials. We were ahead by one point when a Tech player threw up a falling-down "prayer" of a shot that hit the backboard and went in, but well after the buzzer had gone off.

It took real courage in front of a huge crowd of highly partisan Tech fans to disallow that basket, but both Bob and Shorty made the same call simultaneously.

The crowd went ballistic and we started pushing and shoving our way to the dressing room. I saw some Saddle Tramps grab Shorty and start punching him. I ran over where they had him on the ground and started throwing them off of him. I grabbed him, threw him over my shoulder, and ran for the dressing room with him yelling at me to put him down so he could go back and whip "those snot-nosed little punks!"

I ran into him at the airport in Dallas a few years later and we laughed about that incident. He told me that he boxed in the Navy, and could've held his own with the Saddle Tramps, if I'd only put him down.

Shorty never really forgave me for that!

*   *   *

Rasslin' matches can stir up strong emotions

I guess it's in the nature of most boys to want to box or wrestle.

Despite being warned by our father to not wrestle on the bed, my brother and I engaged in close-quarter contact one evening, and when he tossed me, I stuck my foot through the bedroom window.

My dad whipped off his belt—the sound of leather through pant loops is unmistakable—and began flailing at us, unaware that my ankle was dripping blood.

In high school, the off-season included wrestling (or some variation thereof), as two guys would square off, throw forearms at each other, and try to knock the other to or off the mat.

This activity occasionally got out of hand, like the time one guy got his upper teeth chipped off by an errant elbow and the day the Party of the First Part drove the Party of the Second Part into the lockers and bloodied his nose after PSP insulted PFP's girlfriend.

Lloyd Reese and I both weighed about 140 and weren't much on physical contact, so we paired up and did the "brother-in-law" routine, hoping the coaches wouldn't notice we weren't hitting each other very hard.

Channel 7 in Amarillo used to carry live wrestling matches on Saturday afternoon, and invariably an elderly couple—both toothless—sat on the front row each week.

As a young sportswriter, I interviewed two of the most famous "rasslers" of this region—Dory Funk, Sr., and Ricky Romero—one night at the National Guard Armory.

I asked them the best way to get into the grappling game, and Dory suggested wrestling in college. Ricky, his ears cauliflowered (rolled up) from years in the ring, said emphatically, "Tell them to stay away; this is no kind of life."

Ricky told me he wrestled four times one Fourth of July, starting out in Dalhart and finishing in Littlefield.

Several Saturday nights after finishing sports at *The Herald*, I'd walk over to the arena on Beech where the Kiwanis Club sponsored wrestling. Sometimes the heat wasn't so hot and sponsors Bob Hilburn (also an advisor for the Kiwanis Key Club for young men) and Jack Oswald claimed they wore short-sleeved shirts to convince patrons the building wasn't as cold as they thought it was.

One night Zuni War Cloud had Cyclone Negro's head between the ropes with his foot thereupon, causing the prone opponent considerable consternation.

Not surprisingly, referee Nick Roberts was distracted by the howling crowd, conveniently not noticing ZWC's indiscretion.

Roberts looked out into the audience and spied Orville Harkins, manager of the Levine's Department Store, quite noticeable in a shiny green suit and white Stetson. He looked to Harkins as if to ask, "Did Zuni War Cloud indeed have his foot on the rope?"

Orville took a long drag on his big cigar, blew a puff of smoke, and arrogantly shook his head, "No."

Instantly, an older woman jumped out of her folding chair and raced, Coke cup in hand, toward the haberdasher shouting, "Orville

Harkins, you know he had his foot on the rope! I'm gonna throw this Coke all over you!"

Fortunately, she didn't.

My late Uncle Hack Hackler of Amarillo was absolutely convinced that wrestling was on the up and up until he stopped for coffee one night after the matches and one of the good guys and one of the bad guys came in together all buddy-buddy.

My chiropractor father said he was called to the City Auditorium (located on the site of the present City Hall and police station) because one of the wrestlers had a knee problem.

As the crowd howled, one of the "bad guys" came behind the curtain and said, "Doc, I sure hope you can fix him up. We have to wrestle in Levelland tomorrow night."

Finally, this is a story that's alleged to be true: Someone from the wrestling matches in Lubbock would call the *Avalanche-Journal* each week and report the results for a two-paragraph story.

On July 2, 1969, veteran wrestler "Iron Mike" DiBiase died of a heart attack in the ring. A young sports writer took the call and duly reported: "Veteran wrestler Iron Mike DiBiase died in the ring at the Fair Park Coliseum Wednesday night. In other action . . ."

Hey, he died in Lubbock tonight. He's supposed to die in Amarillo tomorrow night.

*   *   *

Burle Pettit

Rare as booze at a Campbellite dance

One of the great Texas sportswriters of an earlier era was Burle Pettit, who later rose in the managerial ranks of the Lubbock *Avalanche-Journal*. He continues to write a folksy column for the *A-J*.

When I started at Wayland, one of my main tasks was to send stories about upcoming games in the Lubbock and Amarillo papers.

Burle wrote a note to thank me for the stories, adding that "a Wayland mailer is about as rare as booze at a Campbellite dance."

Since I was a member of the Church of Christ at the time, I was certain he was correct.

That sports information job included putting out press guides (and raising the hackles of printer Jack Oswald when I was late submitting copy), running off statistics on a frequently balky spirit-duplicator machine (with purple ink on my fingers to prove it), and calling in reports to the district statistician in Sherman in the days way before computers compiled everything.

Burle claimed he got me several raises at *The Herald* by offering me jobs at the *A-J*. Truth be told, I was only offered the area sports editor's post in 1978, about a month before I was promoted to editor, and Burle had already moved out of sports.

One of my favorite stories about Burle was the time West Texas State was ballyhooing "Mercury" Morris (future star running back for the Miami Dolphins) for All-American in 1968.

Athletic Director Frank Kimbrough, who had coached at Wayland and Plainview High in the late 1920s and early 1930s —coaching Wayland against Texas School of Mines in the first night college game in Texas history in 1929 at El Paso High School—said a team down the road could make quite a bit of money by playing WT every year.

He was speaking, of course, of Texas Tech, which had given up playing the Buffs—sporting such Joe Kerbel-coached stars as "Pistol Pete" Pedro and Jerry Logan—after a 30-27 season-opening loss in Lubbock that launched a 1-9 campaign in 1962.

Burle wrote great prose, though it might take you to the 10th paragraph to find out the score. Which reminds me of the first and maybe only time the late James N. Allison, Sr., then owner of *The Herald*, spoke to me.

A former Associated Press reporter, Mr. Allison approached my desk and said, "May I make a suggestion to the sports desk? Put the score in the lead." He obviously had read a recent baseball account in which I had not reported the score until the fourth paragraph." I lay the blame at Burle Pettit's typewriter.

A legendary Texas sportswriter was Blackie Sherrod, who toiled for the *Fort Worth Press, Dallas Times Herald, and Dallas Morning News.*

Blackie covered a Texas Tech-Texas game at Lubbock in the mid-1970s. I'm pretty sure he slept through most of the game but woke up in time to write a better story than anyone who actually saw it.

A great—if not necessarily true—story is told about a young sportswriter at the *Fort Worth Press* who decided to add a sentence to the story about the passing of the coach for the legendary Red Grange.

As the story goes, the "Galloping Ghost" of Illinois lore was doing color on NFL games at the time and was known to butcher the King's English. So the young scribe added to the obituary, "Contacted at his home, Red Grange said, 'It *are* a great personal loss.'"

Reportedly, Blackie Sherrod ordered the presses stopped and the line expunged from the story.

I don't know if it was buried deep in the story or not.

*   *   *

Game was closer than the score indicates

Bill Davis, athletic director and head football coach at Plainview High School from 1968-71, was a very fine Christian man. But he didn't have the world's greatest sense of humor.

Bill West, a zany assistant coach, showed up one summer morning to help paint or do other chores at the old fieldhouse and declared to the other assistants, "Boy, Davis is mad at me, but I don't know why."

"That's because you parked in his space (closest to the door)," one of the other aides explained.

Jim Pollard, who followed Bill as head coach in 1972-73 and later was superintendent in Canadian, told me after Plainview beat Borger, 10-9 on the road in 1971: "That game was a lot closer than the score indicated."

Despite the great line, Pollard said he was in dutch since Bill didn't think I ought to be quoting the assistant coaches.

Bill was none too happy with me for my admittedly snotty lead after Plainview lost a game in Amarillo en route to a 2-8 season in 1970.

"It was like a nightmare from which you wake up screaming, only Plainview never woke up here Saturday night, losing to Amarillo High, 23-0." I went on to assert that the Bulldogs played like "Ned in the first reader."

True, but snotty.

With three winning seasons and a 23-16-1 record, Bill left after the 1971 season—a gut-wrenching 13-7 loss on a muddy field in a thick soup

("The Bog in the Fog") in Hereford, costing the Bulldogs the first-ever playoff appearance in school history.

A lot of folks had told Bill that Plainview was snakebit and he shouldn't go there. I think he was convinced after that season and went down to Hurst to coach at L. D. Bell High School for several years.

Maybe he didn't have to tolerate any snotty sportswriters.

* * *

Visiting the "Friendly Confines" of Wrigley Field

Carolyn and I have said when we retire we're going to travel across the country (and parts of Canada) to see every Major League baseball park and maybe a few minor league ones as well.

I've seen games in the Astrodome, both Texas Rangers parks, Wrigley Field and U.S. Cellular in Chicago, the new Yankee Stadium, the old and new parks in Baltimore, Kaufman Stadium in Kansas City, the old Busch Stadium in St. Louis, and Coors Field in Denver.

I've also seen pro basketball in Dallas, San Antonio, and Oakland, the Dallas Cowboys at the Cotton Bowl, Cowboy Stadium, and AT&T Stadium (Jerry's World), and National Hockey League games in St. Petersburg, Florida, and Landover, Maryland.

In 1985, we took a family vacation to see my brother in suburban St. Louis and my sister in suburban Chicago. Major league baseball games definitely were on the agenda.

George Ragor, who worked for McGavock Motors at the time, grew up in Chicago, and his mother lived only a couple of blocks up the street from Wrigley Field that sits in the heart of a residential area.

We parked our van behind her house, and she had two neighborhood boys keep an eye on it for us.

Walking to the park on a beautiful sunny afternoon several years before Wrigley finally became the last stadium in the majors to have lights, we were greeted by a friendly man. He wore a cap that said

"Andy Frain." I figured he was a beloved figure at the venerable old stadium and just about as old as it was at the time (71).

Soon, I saw several folks with the same name of their caps. Turns out that's the name of the security company that serviced the park.

We bypassed the food at Wrigley in favor of a Chicago Dog at a nearby eatery. I wished I could ship some home.

We had just walked up to the iconic sign, "Welcome to Wrigley Field—Home of the Chicago Cubs," when Plainview High graduate, the late Walt McAlexander, greeted us. The former Texas Tech and Lubbock Christian sports information guru was on a vacation as well.

In retrospect, I'm sorry I didn't buy one of the prematurely prepared T-shirts that declared the Cubs as National League champions. The year before, they had San Diego down two games to none in the National League Championship Series but then lost three in a row to miss out on their first World Series trip since 1945. They still haven't made it.

During pre-game warm-ups, Steve Garvey, the slugging first baseman of the San Diego Padres, was the target of cat-calling by the left field "Bleacher Bums."

He dropped to one knee behind second base and clasped his hands as if begging the fans not to boo him. As fate would have it, he kind of shut them up with a homerun right in amongst them about the fifth inning.

Also on that trip, we saw the Cardinals play the Padres and also the Giants at the old Busch Stadium in St. Louis.

For a lifelong baseball fan, it was pure Heaven.

*   *   *

You never know what you can get 'til you ask

In 1983, several of us on the Chamber of Commerce Sports Committee decided to organize a "Night with the Pros" to honor three former Bulldogs who were playing in the National Football League.

Lawrence McCutcheon had set all kinds of records at Colorado State and then had four seasons over 1,000 yards rushing and one with more than 900 for the Los Angeles Rams. He played in five Pro Bowls and threw a touchdown pass in the 1980 Super Bowl loss to Pittsburgh.

Sportscaster Howard Cosell was always very complimentary of Lawrence, who told me after a great sophomore season at Colorado State, "I'll try to give you something to write about every week." He just about held true to that over the next 10 years.

Over a career that spanned a decade, including time with Seattle, Denver, and Buffalo, he amassed 6,578 yards and 26 touchdowns plus 1,799 yards and 13 touchdowns receiving.

Jerry Sisemore, a teammate of McCutcheon for the Bulldogs in 1967, was a two-time All-American and three-time All-SWC offensive tackle for the University of Texas, and went on to play 12 seasons in the offensive line with the Philadelphia Eagles. He was twice named All-Pro, was a Pro Bowler twice, played in the 1980 Super Bowl, and is a member of the College Football Hall of Fame.

Arland Thompson, an All-SWC offensive lineman at Baylor, had brief stints with Denver, Green Bay, Baltimore, and Kansas City, and also with San Antonio in the USFL.

Pondering who we might get for a speaker for the banquet, I recalled that Lawrence's backfield coach when he broke in with Los Angeles was Dick Vermeil, who was Jerry's head coach for much of his career with Philadelphia. The Eagles were the biggest division rivals of the Dallas Cowboys in those days.

Through the Eagles' front office, I contacted Vermeil's agent, a fellow named Jerry Gold. He said Vermeil usually got between $5,000 and $7,500 for speaking engagements (that's $12,000 to $18,000 in today's money).

I told him we were just a Chamber of Commerce project and would Vermeil consider coming for less. Gold said he would call me in a week. He called back in 20 minutes and said Vermeil would come for free if we could have the banquet on a certain night. The coach would speak at the banquet on his way to a meeting in San Francisco because "he likes to do things for his players."

Vermeil, who later came out of retirement to coach the St. Louis Rams to a Super Bowl title and then was successful in Kansas City, was very personable and an excellent speaker. He recently was voted the second greatest motivational coach in NFL history behind the legendary Green Bay Packers' Vince Lombardi.

We gave the three players Jimmy Dean pigskin jackets and, with the assistance of banker and avid outdoorsman Joe Don Scott, we gave Dick Vermeil a $450 Browning automatic shotgun.

That story proves you never know until you ask . . . and that free beats $5,000 to $7,500 any day of the week.

*   *   *

Willie Stargell

Willie Stargell threatened in Plainview

The passing Willie Stargell, the Hall of Famer for the Pittsburgh Pirates, in 2001 at age 61 brought to mind one of the most unusual experiences I had in the newspaper business.

One Monday morning in the summer of 1982, the late Owen Egger came into my office and asked if I had seen that "colored boy who plays for the Pittsburgh Pirates on Howard Cosell's show Sunday. He was talking about getting threatened by a guy with a shotgun down here at the baseball park."

Do what?

I decided he was talking about Willie Stargell and after he left, I immediately asked Ron White, who was working in advertising at the time, if he had seen Cosell's show. He said he had and that Mr. Egger was right—Stargell was talking about an incident here about 1960.

Fascinated by this brief bit of information, I decided to investigate further. I checked the National League schedule and found out that the Pirates were playing in San Diego. A call to the Padres' publicity director revealed that the Pittsburgh club was staying at the Bal Harbour Hotel.

I put in a call and left a message for Willie Stargell, never, of course, expecting that he would call back.

But the next morning, about 10 o'clock, the phone rang and a deep voice said, "This is Willie Stargell returning your call."

After I stammered and stuttered a few seconds, I told him why I was calling.

He told me the piece Cosell did on him was about a series of racial incidents that happened to him during his career.

He said he was playing for a team in the Sophomore League—either in San Angelo or Roswell, New Mexico (the team moved during the year)—and when he went to Jaycee Park to take batting practice, two white men were standing near the gate.

"One had a shotgun, and he said, 'Nigger, if you play today, I'm gonna kill you,' and then started laughing. Well, I was just an 18-year-old kid at the time, and that shook me up," he related.

"I don't mean to imply that that was the attitude of all the people in your town—just some at the time," he explained.

(The New York *Times* reported in an obituary that "Stargell would recall the time he approached the entrance to a ballpark at Plainview, Texas, in his first professional season, and two men wearing trench coats approached him. One of them pulled out a revolver, uttered a racial epithet, and said that if he played that day, "I'm gonna blow your brains out." Stargell remembered: "I was real scared. But by the time the rest of the team got there, I decided that if I was gonna die, I was gonna die doing exactly what I wanted to do. I had to play ball.")

Stargell said the white players on the team stayed at a local motel while the black players and a Cuban player stayed in "some apartments down in the flats. All I remember is that the room was so small, it looked like they just built it around the bed."

After our conversation, I immediately called Leanna McCutcheon, mother of former pro football star Lawrence McCutcheon, and asked if she knew who might have housed the players. She surmised it was Strewgon Sanford.

As was his custom, Mr. Sanford, who is now deceased, was sitting in his green Oldsmobile across the street from *The Herald* at Mills Barber Shop. He told me he didn't remember Willie Stargell, but he did recall the Cuban player.

The next year, when Plainview hosted the Southwest Regional Babe Ruth Tournament, I called to see if Stargell might be interested in being the guest speaker at a banquet. I wanted him to see a better side of Plainview than he had seen more than 20 years before.

Unfortunately, he had speaking engagements in Pennsylvania on either side of the night we needed him here.

As he was about to retire later in 1982, Stargell said: "One of the reasons we've gotten along here (Pittsburgh) is because I never felt that I should ever be a judge of someone. Everybody is somebody no matter what their nationality or religion. You have to work together. I could never go to bed at night thinking I misused someone. Before we put titles on anyone, we have to remember we're people."

If that guy who was ugly to Willie Stargell here more than 50 years ago is still alive, I hope he'll ask forgiveness if he hasn't already.

By all accounts, Stargell was a humble and loving man.

One who would be willing to forgive and forget.

*   *   *

Stargell story sequel and a missed homerun

On a mission trip to New York with our church choir in 2010, several of us visited a neat little place called Serendipity, noted for its sandwiches and ice cream.

Gary Lloyd, my friend and across-the-alley neighbor, introduced me to a man he called "Kenny G" (not to be confused with the jazz saxophonist) and told me he formerly played for the Pittsburgh Pirates and Houston Astros and was a scout for the New York Yankees.

A little later, Gary told me his new acquaintance had played minor league baseball with future Hall of Famer Willie Stargell of the Pittsburgh Pirates, and Stargell told him of being threatened by some white men in Plainview.

Astonished, I told Gary that I had written a column about that incident in 1982, but Stargell's story was slightly different than "Mr. G's."

Wondering who this mystery man was, I phoned Kevin Lewis at *The Herald* and asked if he might Google the Houston Astros' all-time roster and see if he could find someone named Kenny G-something. No luck there.

But, as luck would have it, I was sitting in the lobby at the Sheraton Hotel near Times Square the next day and here comes Mr. G walking through.

I hurried over and reintroduced myself and told him, "My friend said your name is Kenny G." Turns out he just used that name as he was waiting for his turn to enter the restaurant.

"My name's Ron Brand," the man said.

"I knew it," I said excitedly, "I almost saw you hit a homerun in the Astrodome in 1965, but my family and I were on the club level and could hear the scoreboard (with snorting bulls and fireworks) going off, but they wouldn't let us in."

Fifty years ago, my aunt was the nurse for the wife of Harry Kalas, who later was the voice of the Philadelphia Phillies for 38 years and also the voice of NFL Films. Kalas was doing two innings with Gene Elston and Loel Passe on Astros' radio. My aunt used her influence to get me into the area where players met their wives so I could get some autographs.

An attendant came out a couple of times and said the game was still going on. I decided to run back in and see if the Astros could pull out a win.

Alas, Ron Brand, who had started the rally with the Astros down 8-1, hit into a double play to end the game as Houston lost, 8-7.

"I think that was the last homerun I ever hit in the majors," Brand told me.

It was. And to think I just missed it.

*   *   *

Frosty Kennedy...60 homers for the Ponies in 1956

"Frosty" Kennedy hits a homer for hype

Anyone who lived in Plainview in the mid-1950s probably knows the name "Frosty" Kennedy, even if they never saw him play a game for the Plainview Ponies.

That was the minor league team that moved here in 1953 when the Lamesa franchise folded in the old West Texas-New Mexico League.

Twenty-seven-year-old outfielder Forrest Kennedy, who hit .403 for Lamesa, came along in the package and was an instant hit—no pun intended.

Many folks enjoyed summer evenings at Jaycee Park, watching the local team, which folded after the 1961 season, briefly having an association with the Kansas City Athletics.

"He was a real character," Plainviewan Luther Bain told me when Kennedy died in 1998 in Covina, California, at the age of 72.

Frosty sported massive arms and showed them off by wearing sleeveless shirts, as did another more famous slugger of the day, Cincinnati Reds first baseman Ted Kluszewski.

He always had a big chaw of tobacco, which liberally stained his uniform. The late Tom Locke recalled Frosty removing his chaw, wadding it up, and rolling it toward the opponents' dugout when he'd hit one out of Jaycee Park.

Discretion being the better part of valor—and arrogance—he probably didn't do that on the road.

Those hometown homers earned him a wad of money stuck in the wire mesh screen by appreciative fans. He said he collected $269 for a game-winning shot against Clovis in the 13th inning of a playoff game.

The late Walt McAlexander, a 1962 PHS grad who served as the Ponies' bat boy one season, says he used to listen to veteran KVOP sports announcer Tut Tawwater do the games—"live" here and by "re-creation" from the Western Union wire for road games.

Walt recalls Frosty rumbling toward the mound after striking out his last time up on a night when he already had three or four hits. Rather than fighting, Frosty wanted to congratulate the pitcher on finally getting him out.

Walt, who was a sportswriter for the Lubbock paper for 14 years, then worked in sports information at Lubbock Christian and Texas Tech, was excited about seeing Frosty's name and picture at the Baseball Hall of Fame in Cooperstown, New York, for being one of the 11 men to ever hit 60 or more homeruns in a season.

Of course, the first to do it was Babe Ruth, the legendary "Sultan of Swat," in 1927, the year after Frosty was born.

Tut Tawwater says the league's pitching in 1953 and again in 1956 when Frosty hit 60 round-trippers in the restructured Southwestern League "was pathetic . . . about like high school."

Former *Herald* Sports Editor Bob Carroll said Frosty took advantage of "invitingly close" fences at Jaycee Park (358 feet to center compared with about 400 now) for a number of "cheap" homeruns.

When I mentioned that to Frosty in a feature story I did in 1985, he snorted, "Hell, I didn't hit no cheap ones."

He claimed he could have hit 120 homeruns in a well-lighted major league stadium.

Frosty recalled that he hit his Babe-matching 60th homer in San Angelo on the last evening of a 144-game season. Trying to help him, the San Angelo catcher was telling him what pitches were coming, but Frosty says he went 1-for-8 in a doubleheader the night before and it really didn't help him.

His history-making homer in the third inning hugged the leftfield foul line and the umpire called it fair on a close decision.

In 1953 Frosty hit .410 with a 40-game hitting streak, with 224 hits, and 169 RBIs. Three years later (he played in Amarillo in 1954 and Yuma, Arizona, in 1955), he batted .327 with 184 RBIs (the major league record is 190) and scored 151 runs.

Playing for 12 different teams, Kennedy averaged .342 during a 10-year minor league career that began in 1948, hit 228 homers with 1,083 runs batted in and 1,572 hits.

Although he signed with the Pittsburgh Pirates organization, he never made it to the majors in an era when there were more than 400 minor league teams in America—soon to greatly dwindle with the popularity of television.

Frosty also said something else pretty brash in that 1985 interview: "I'm the greatest player ever. Babe Ruth hit 60 homers but never batted .400. Ted Williams and a lot of other guys hit .400 but never hit 60 homers. I did both."

Considering that Joe Bauman hit 72 homeruns and batted over .400 for Roswell in 1954, Frosty might have been just a bit, shall we say, off-base about being "the greatest."

But give him a homer for hype—and no cheap shot either.

*   *   *

When did they change the rule?

When I attended Wayland's last football game at Panhandle State in Goodwell, Oklahoma, in 2012, I was reminded that sometimes public address announcers fancy themselves as play-by-play folks.

The P.A. guy was an unabashed "homer" for his team. The home crowd probably loved it, but I found him rather annoying, especially since Wayland got clobbered, 67–14.

It reminds me of the story the late Carlos McLeod told about going to an out-of-town game when he was pastor of First Baptist Church in Silverton.

Carlos, who handled the P.A. duties at Owl games in those days, says the home-team announcer was doing play-by-play and said, "The wide receiver is out to the right." When the home-team defensive back apparently didn't see the man split out, the announcer repeated forcefully, "I said the wide receiver is out to the *right!*"

Willis McCutcheon, president of Happy State Bank, has moonlighted as a high school official for many years. He tells a great story about a woman announcer at a six-man game.

When a player from the home team intercepted a pass on an extra-point play and was running down the sideline, destined to give his team one point, the woman said into the open mike, "No, no, no, you can't do that!"

The interceptor slowed down at midfield and was immediately buried by the pursuing opposition.

After a long pause, the embarrassed announcer meekly asked for all to hear: "When did they change the rule?"

*   *   *

The hoss, he *safe*, but the jockey *out!*

My dad was a good storyteller and loved his military experience. He recounted the time a cavalry unit—wearing caps with a horse on the front—was playing baseball in Japan, and there was a bang-bang play at first.

The black umpire quickly assessed the situation and declared in a loud voice: "The hoss (meaning the player's cap), he *safe* . . . but the jockey (the player wearing the cap) *out!*"

Which reminds me that Roger Horan, an experienced Little League coach, would yell at me from the stands, "Andrews, you're anticipating the play," i.e., determining a runner to be safe or out too quickly.

I remember the first high school game I umpired was between Plainview and Lubbock Estacado. When I called an Estacado runner out on a close play at first, the Matadors' coach protested and said, "You must have been the one I heard about."

I could only think, "No, sir, this is the first high school game I've ever called."

After my first foray into Little League coaching when my oldest son was 10, I confided to Roger Horan, "We were 4-12, but I don't think I'm that bad a coach."

"Yes, you are," Roger declared bluntly. "It just takes you a while to learn how to coach."

Boy, was he ever right.

However, I did manage to coach a Babe Ruth team to the 13-year -old championship in 1987. We went to Mineral Wells for a state tournament and lost both of our games.

But a poignant moment came when Bobby Feaster, who also coached in the Plainview system, said we would all go home if money taken from one of the player's bags was not returned.

All the players marched through our barracks quarters at Fort Wolters, but no money appeared. Bobby then said he was going to give the players one more chance, "and if you took the money and don't return it, I hope you die and go to Hell."

I looked at another one of the coaches, my former Little League teammate David Hipolito, and I think we both were nearly in tears but also trying to stifle a laugh.

I suspect that put the fear of God into the players who apparently pooled their resources and made sure the $20 was returned.

Fear sometimes is a great motivator.

*　　*　　*

Lou Balenton

When the game got late, Lou Balenton got "fidgety"

For several years, longtime Plainview postman Lou Balenton and I umpired Babe Ruth baseball together, two games a night, four nights a week.

Lou, who came from Conway, Arkansas, and had starred in basketball and track for Wayland in the early1960s and played on a short-lived baseball team, was one of the college's first black athletes. He was a 6-6, 180-pound drink of water.

Lou has pastored the Trinity Baptist Church in Morton for 38 years, making that long trek every Sunday morning. His wife, Eva, was a teacher at Thunderbird Elementary for many years.

A goodhearted guy with a sometimes crusty exterior, Lou got more and more fidgety—shoulders hunching, head shaking—as the games dragged on, especially if he was working the plate.

Any "delaying" tactics by a team leading with the two-hour time limit approaching made Lou that much more testy.

One night, Don Vinson, co-owner of Don and Shorty's Garage downtown, called "time" late in the game. Don had a crippled leg, so it took him a little while to walk from the first-base coaching box to home plate to counsel with his batter.

When Don's trek resulted in a three-word admonition that could have been rendered from the coaching box—"Hit the ball!"—I thought Lou was going to have a fit.

At the very least he was mumbling under his mask.

*   *   *

Floydada coaching legend L.G. Wilson

Stud buzzards, wrong grammar, & suspicious minds

Easily my favorite of all coaches whose teams I covered while sports editor of *The Herald* from 1970-78 was the very successful L.G. Wilson at Floydada and later Tulia.

One of the most memorable pictures I ever took was L.G. and legendary official James "Curly" Hays of Abilene (who also worked Southwest Conference games for many years) conferring on the sidelines at Dick Bivins Stadium in Amarillo during a Floydada-Childress bi-district game. It was 1976, the wind chill had to be about zero, and both men were wearing hoodies. It was two great veterans of the game.

Floydada met Charlie Johnson's great Childress teams several times in the playoffs, including once in Plainview's Bulldog Stadium.

An old Childress grocer, Hoot Voyles, came up to the press box at the end of every quarter to report the score. When Floydada's John Cagle led a late drive to upset the Bobcats, Hoot called the store one last time to sadly report, "Well, Evelyn, they beat us."

As I was getting set to do the annual pre-season football preview for the newspaper, L.G. colorfully described a particularly talented linebacker for his Whirlwinds as a "stud buzzard."

L.G. told me that when he was an assistant at Temple, an excitable young coach would come in nearly every Monday morning telling the head coach some tale like, "I saw the quarterback out drinking Saturday night."

L.G. said, "When I got to be a head coach, I told my assistants, 'Don't be comin' in here gettin' me all upset with that kind of information.'"

Another colorful guy was Earl Miller at Tulia. When I called him for his pre-season assessment of the Hornets, he declared, "I think we will have a real *well* team." I didn't know for sure if he was talking about the relative health of his club or just trying to avoid the ire of an English teacher on the use of "good" and "well." Sorry, he got an "F" that time.

Earl went on to coach at Midland Lee and was portrayed in the famous movie *Friday Night Lights*, since Lee tied with Odessa Permian and Abilene Cooper for the district title and lost the coin flip to Permian.

One of my stranger recollections was the time I went to Olton to secure information from Don Beck on his Mustangs. First, he had one of the assistants usher me out of the dressing room, perhaps fearing I might glean some information to pass on to rival L.G. Wilson at Floydada.

When the Lubbock *Avalanche-Journal* reporter asked Beck why he hadn't listed the classifications of his players on the roster, Beck furrowed his brow and said, "I hate to put their classes on there because people look at how many seniors you have and they pick you to win district and put all that pressure on you."

To which the *A-J* reporter said, "Hell, coach, nobody cares. Just put their classification on there."

Don Beck reluctantly complied.

I thought it was very well of him to do that.

*   *   *

Just put Bob Hayes's name on there

When Carlos McLeod came to First Baptist Church-Plainview in 1969, he liked to bring celebrities and talented folks to town to speak to the church or community outreach events.

One such notable was Tom Landry, coach of the Dallas Cowboys. After Landry finished giving his testimony one Sunday night, he exited the church just as a youngster rushed up with a football in hand.

Thrusting the ball toward Landry, the boy said, "Put Bob Hayes's name on there," referring to the fleet Cowboys wide receiver and former Olympic sprinter.

The coach smiled and said, "But my name is Tom Landry."

"That's OK," the kid responded, "put Bob Hayes's name on there."

I think Landry dutifully did as asked.

*   *   *

Dapper sports editor in 1975

Fashionable attire wasn't always appropriate

As all fashionable young men of the 1970s, I wore some pretty flashy clothes. Actually, they were pretty awful.

A Christmas tree-green suit with black patent leather shoes, a peach-and-white sport coat with peach-colored pants, and a maroon suit with large white checks and maroon patent leather shoes come immediately to mind.

Shortly after being hired as athletic director and head football coach at PHS in 1974, the late George Kirk walked into *The Herald*. Noting my royal blue leisure suit with red and white piping, white polo, and white patent leather belt and shoes, George announced, "That looks like something I'd wear to recruit in South Oak Cliff," alluding to African-Americans players who surely would have dug my style.

I was incensed several years later when a guy wouldn't even pony up a quarter for my baby blue leisure suit at a garage sale.

By the way, George Kirk, father of current Plainview Superintendent Rocky Kirk, coached the Bulldogs to a record of 23-15-2 from 1974-77, got a large fieldhouse built and a second deck added to the press box. He told me one night after a tough loss to Monterey, "Danny, one of these days you're going to get to cover a district champion."

As it turned out, I got promoted to editor after he left for Klein High School in the Houston area and PHS finally won its first-ever championship in 1978.

A year before Baylor won its first Southwest Conference title in 50 years, George came to Plainview from Waco where he had been offensive coordinator under Grant Teaff.

Carolyn and I attended the 1975 Cotton Bowl in Dallas. Dr. Robert Mitchell, longtime cardiologist here, had offered me a bottle of J&B Scotch if I could find a buyer for his tickets. I ran a sports blurb and editor Jim Servatius claimed the booze.

I wore a flimsy top coat, a green leisure suit, and the aforementioned white patent leather belt and shoes. My feet nearly froze off in 20-degree temperatures.

While such attire was fashionable, it wasn't appropriate for all occasions.

*   *   *

Not exactly a sportsmanlike gesture

Margie Hunt McDonald, a former Wayland Flying Queen, was women's coach at the University of Wyoming from 1975–83, then became the first Executive Director of the High Country Athletic Conference, which later merged with the Western Athletic Conference.

She served as the Deputy Commissioner of the WAC and then went on to work as the Coordinator of Women's Basketball Officials for the Mountain West Conference. Since 2005, she has done the color commentary for UW women's basketball radio broadcasts.

At the 2003 National Women's Hall of Fame ceremonies in Knoxville, Tennessee, Margie told a great story about legendary Nera White, who led Nashville Business College to 10 national AAU championships, earning All-America honors 15 times. Nera was an inaugural member of the Hall of Fame in 1999.

When she was a freshman in 1960-61, Margie set up in the lane and took a charge from Nera. "She put her knees right in my chest," Margie recalled.

"When Nera reached out her hand to help me up, I thought that was a nice gesture, but she pulled me up close and said, 'You little s---, you ever do that again I'll kill you.'"

I thought former Wayland President Roy McClung was going to fall out of the stands laughing.

*   *   *

Chris LeFevre

Handling those worst basketball calls

Tom Hall, who has coached many of the Plainview Lady Bulldogs in summer league basketball for 18 years, and Xcel Energy community rep Chris LeFevre, who moonlights as a striped-shirt, tell great stories of bad calls in basketball.

Tom, who has been assisted in recent years by retired DPS Sergeant Gordon Miller (he also has been a spotter for PHS and Wayland football games on radio), was coaching a game in Lubbock several years ago and a young official was working that day.

It appeared a ball was going out of bounds off a Plainview player when a Lady Air player made a near-miraculous save. Alas, the young ref blew his whistle a bit too soon and gave the ball to the opponent.

Tom, a former basketball official himself, stood up and said calmly to the ref. "Young man, I want to congratulate you. If you officiate for the rest of your life, you've already got the worst call you'll ever make behind you."

The ref stared at Tom for a moment, then burst out laughing as Gordon restrained himself from falling off the bench.

Chris LeFevre, honored as Plainview's Man of the Year for 2013, was the subject of an April Fool's story by Kevin Lewis in *The Herald* in 2012, alleging he was going to play for the new Wayland football team to fulfill a lifetime dream at age 51.

He was working a game a couple of years ago when a coach jumped up to protest a call across the court, shouting, "You're terrible!" Chris mouthed something and ran on as play continued.

Less than a minute later, the flow of the game put Chris near the unhappy coach and a timeout was called. The coach stormed toward him, demanding to know what Chris had said.

Feigning ignorance at first, Chris said, "Oh, now I remember. You said I was terrible. That makes sense. They *always* put the worst officials with the worst coaches."

The coach blinked, then broke up laughing.

I told him, "Chris, God had to put that in your head. You would have never been able to think that up on your own."

Since I reffed basketball for about 15 years, I know something about bad calls, because I made my fair share of them, and other mistakes.

One particularly stands out.

I was working a girls' game in a tournament at Abernathy the same year the college game switched from six-player to full court. High school still played the divided-court game for another year or two.

Just as I started to hand a player the ball for an inbounds play, I counted six players on the court, dropped the ball and got about halfway toward calling a technical foul.

Then it dawned on me: Dummy, this is not a college game. Six players are legal.

I handed the player the ball and she promptly threw it the length of the court and out of bounds.

Her coach called timeout and demanded, "Danny, what's going on out there?"

When I told him I had a brain lock, he cut loose a forceful profanity.

The result: A technical foul.

*   *   *

Bill Phillips

"We always lose when we eat at Underwood's"

Bill Phillips was my sophomore football coach and junior varsity baseball coach. He served as head basketball coach at Plainview High from 1968-75, taking the 1970-71 team to the state semifinals.

On my 16th birthday, Bill called me over during practice and said, "Andrews, you're loafing. I hear you're pretty bad about that."

Well, first, he ruined my birthday (and I reminded him of that frequently in later years) and, besides, I thought, "Who would have told you I'm bad about loafing because that ain't true." Maybe he mistook my being slow of foot for laziness.

Which reminds me of what Dallas Cowboy wide receiver Pete Gent (author of *North Dallas Forty* and speaker at the 1966 PHS All-Sports Banquet) once said: "What I lack in speed, I make up in cowardice."

Bill, who had several nervous ticks, would pick at his face and say often, "This is gonna be the toughest team you've ever played."

Bill also was famously superstitious, wearing the same outfit (and allegedly the same underwear) as long as the Bulldogs were on a winning streak.

They were on one at Bulldog Gym one night when Doyle Edmiston, a bear of a man who coached Lubbock High, decided to vacate his seat on the Westerner bench and sit down next to Bill.

When referee Bobby Randolph turned around and asked Doyle what he was doing on the Bulldog bench, Edmiston responded, "I just wanted to come down here and sit next to a winner."

Bill was just as picky about where the team ate back in the days when it was common to have a meal at a restaurant following a game.

He told assistant Rollie Rinker, "I don't like to eat at Underwood's (a famous barbecue buffet) because we always get beat when we eat there."

Rollie politely reminded him: "Bill, we don't eat there until *after* the game."

Bill about stroked out in old Gregory Gym during Plainview's state semifinal game with Houston Cypress-Fairbanks when the Bulldogs, down 18-6, finally appeared to score on a long jumper by Curtis Thompson. However, it had rained hard before the game and a puddle of water had formed not far from where Curtis launched his shot, and an official waved off the bucket.

Plainview rallied but lost 58-55. I'll always think that if they had won, the Bulldogs—with David McAlister, LeRoy Buckner, Curtis Thompson, Charlie Bassett, and Willie Carreathers starting—would have slowed the ball down and would have frustrated Houston Wheatley in the finals just as Cy-Fair did.

Bill always coached first base for the varsity baseball games for Harold Green and later Jim Sears. My junior year, Baxter McAllister, who went on to play briefly in the Houston Astros organization, was tossing pebbles at Bill from the Mackenzie Park dugout.

Finally, Bill turned and said, "Baxter, if we had seniors who had a better attitude, we'd have a better team."

Since that was the last game of the season, the admonition was a little late coming.

One day at Lazbuddie, in a JV baseball game, Phil Mitchell was on first but paying no attention to "Bubba" (as he was affectionately known) giving the "steal" signal at third.

Finally, Bill yelled out, "Mitchell!" and swiped his hand across his chest with a flourish—an obvious instruction for Mitchell to head for second on the next pitch.

Mitchell, who was known to sleep with his bat when he was on a hitting streak, was called on in Pampa by Coach Jim Sears to pray before the post-game meal.

Mitchell solemnly intoned, "Dear Lord, let us live such a good life that when we die, even the undertaker'll be sorry."

Despite his basketball success in Plainview, I always maintained Bill was "run off" by a couple of administrators. It probably was a factor that Bill didn't seem to encourage some very gifted athletes to play football and not just concentrate on basketball.

After one year at Carrollton High School, he went to the Southwestern Oklahoma Junior College at Altus. He coached there for 28 years, doing double duty with the men and women during most of that time. No telling how many times he told to his Pioneer players, "This is gonna be the toughest team you've ever played."

I'm not sure if the undertaker was sorry when Bill Phillips died, but I sure was, and Tom Hall and I were honored to give a eulogy at his funeral.

*   *   *

Tom Locke watches a pop up

Tom Locke: Victim of a long-distance beaning

One of the more colorful characters with whom I played high school baseball in 1966 and 1967 was Tom Locke, beset by acne and possessed of a gait that made you wonder if he might just fall apart.

My first "introduction" to Tom was when he made an error on the first ground ball I hit in my only year in Babe Ruth baseball in the summer of 1964.

I should have been so lucky, making four errors at third base for Barry McMennamy and Kenneth Griffith against the Harvest Queen Mill Braves, coached by Tom's dad, Tom, Sr., and Angus Ott—two of the best men I have ever known.

During our senior year at PHS, we played in Pampa in the days when the railroad tracks ran just beyond the outfield fence. As we sat on the bench, Tom pondered this question: "If someone hit a homerun and it hit the engineer and killed him and derailed all the cars, would it be considered a freak accident?"

Tom convinced freshman Oliver Thompson that he could impress Coach Jim Sears if he took a "bunting bat" to the plate during batting practice. Sears nearly fell off the mound when he saw Oliver with a skinny fungo bat in his hands.

Tom was not happy with me in a game against Amarillo Caprock when Sears put on the suicide squeeze and I failed to get down a bunt because the pitch broke way outside.

"Blankety-blank, get the ball down, Andrews," growled Tom, a sitting duck, literally, as his legs seemed to turn to rubber about three feet from the plate.

We went to Amarillo to play Palo Duro one afternoon and, late in the game, Coach Sears asked if I thought I could hit fireballing lefthander Pat McKean (who went on to play at Texas Tech) since lefty-batting Tom Hall was having no luck with him.

"Sure," I said with mock bravado, then began to tremble at the thought of facing McKean.

As luck—and I mean that in the truest since of the word—had it, I closed my eyes, stepped "in the bucket," and doubled down the right field line, sliding into second with a dramatic flourish. The next time up, McKean walked me on a 3-2 count. I honestly do not remember seeing any of his pitches.

Well, we lost 11-5, but grizzled old Bill McElduff apparently wasn't pleased with the way his Dons had played, so he lined them up on the left field line and began hitting fly balls toward center. The players had to catch the ball or chase it down and run it back to home plate.

Jim Sears thought that would be a great drill for us, so he did the same thing the next afternoon.

Unfortunately, as he was running out to right field, Tom Locke was struck in the back of the head by a ball batted by Sears.

"Ticked off would be the operative—and polite—term here. Tom Locke summarily quit the team . . . at least for about four days. Bad for us, providential for me—a sometimes third baseman-right fielder who was more valuable as a scorekeeper since I also was covering our games for *The Herald*.

Plainview had its annual weekend stint that Friday in Borger and Saturday at Amarillo High after a night at the Plainsmen Hotel on Route 66 where assistant coach Bill Phillips's sister worked.

I figured to play some against Borger, but Sears put freshman Danny Davis, who was to become an outstanding high school player, into the game in right. Danny staggered around under a fly ball and it fell for a hit, allowing two runs to score.

In those days, you couldn't stand up in the Borger dugout because the roof was only about five feet high. Angry at Sears, who was well out of earshot in the third base coaching box, I wheeled and threw my scorebook toward the dugout entrance and yelled, "That's what you get for playing a damn freshman ahead of a senior!" That would be me.

The next day, I got to start at third against Amarillo High at the Sandies' park next to the minor league stadium. Tony Soliz, the regular third sacker who had beaten Pampa earlier in the year with a leadoff homerun in the first for the only baserunner we had in an otherwise perfect game by the Harvester hurler, had moved to short.

I drove in a run in the first inning with one of the few hits I had all year.

The first Sandie to the plate in the bottom of the first hit a "Baltimore Chop" to me. When the ball finally settled in my glove, it appeared the batter must have fallen down because he was barely down the line.

So, I took a couple of deliberate hops and fired toward first. The ball took off like a jet leaving an aircraft carrier. If first baseman Tom Hall had been 17 feet tall, he could have caught that ball.

I had one other error and ended the game by virtually shot-putting a ball to second for a force out to end the game. I also went 0-for-3 my next trips to the plate and, to save further embarrassment, encouraged Sears to pinch-hit freshman Dennis Martin my last scheduled at-bat.

I was sure glad Tom Locke had second thoughts, and Sears was smart enough to let him come back to the team on Monday.

*   *   *

Bill Cunningham

Bill Cunningham: House of the Rising Soap Bar

Another athletic character during my high school days was Bill Cunningham, a catcher on the baseball team and tackle on the football squad.

He frequently would grab a soap bar in the shower at the old fieldhouse just south of the end zone at Bulldog Stadium and sing a popular song by "The Animals."

> *There is a house in New Orleans*
> *They call the Rising Sun.*
> *It's been the ruin of many a poor boy*
> *And, God, I know I'm one.*

After belting out a verse or two, Bill would wiggle fiercely and fire the soap bar against a wall—similar to several guitarists of the day smashing their instruments.

During a baseball game in Pampa, I chastised Bill for using a pocketknife to "whittle" on the bench or perhaps leave his initials for posterity.

I also had to protect his good character by yelling, "Hey, guys, Coach Phillips is here!" when assistant baseball coach Bill Phillips unexpectedly appeared at the door as Bill and a teammate were perusing a *Playboy* magazine in the adjacent bedroom of our Amarillo motel. Paper slapping against the wall has a distinctive sound.

Bill was catching one night in an American Legion game at Mackenzie Park in Lubbock when I fired a strike to the plate from left field and cut down a runner by a good five feet.

If video were available, it probably would reveal that I was only 50 feet behind the shortstop, but it seemed like a bullet from 300 feet. Bill smartly applied the tag for the third out.

As the Lubbock team exited the field, the stunned victim of my accurate missile said to his coach, "That must have been a lucky throw."

My teammate Ron Roberts, a longtime plumber here, challenged that remark: "We don't have any luck on this team."

To be honest, it was probably like those guys sang on *Hee Haw*: "If it weren't for bad luck, we'd have no luck at all . . ."

I discovered in another Legion game that summer that I was no coach, sending a runner home from third on a 3–2 pitch when he was the only man on base. Ever heard the term "easy out"?

Bill Cunningham went about 6–2, 240 as a senior—a man among boys.

But, three years earlier and quite a few pounds smaller, it was a collision with a boy who looked very much like a man that brought him both pain and notoriety.

In the summer of 1965, Bill was on a Babe Ruth All-Star team coached by the late Guy Wingrove.

At Jaycee Park, Plainview was playing a practice game against a Tulia team that included future Texas Tech All-American tackle Phil Tucker, who must have been 6-3, 250. The word was that Tulia had a man playing for them.

Earlier in the game, Tommy McBee, a solid athlete who went on to play wide receiver at the University of New Mexico and son of Chicken Inn restaurant owner Louis McBee, launched a fly ball that hit the top of the fence in right.

Joe Don Martin—speedy like McBee—was racing toward third when he thought Guy Wingrove yelled, "Go back, go back!" Guy was saying, "Go in, go in!"

Confused, Martin headed back toward second, then cut across toward first and was tagged out to end the inning.

Shortly afterwards, Phil Tucker had made his way to third for Tulia. A batter bounced to McBee at first and Tommy cut loose a perfect throw home to Bill Cunningham. The ball and Tucker arrived at the same time and Tucker plowed over Bill.

Although there were no "protection" rules at the time forcing a runner to give himself up at the plate, the umpire called Phil out for "roughing the catcher."

The Tulia coach and players were incensed and so were a bunch of Plainview fans—still under the false impression that a grown man had just run down a kid—and they stormed the field.

Order eventually was restored when the visiting team decided to forfeit and high-tail it back to Tulia.

Bill Cunningham probably went home, showered and slammed a bar of soap against the wall.

* * *

Frugality slows American Legion games

The American Legion baseball program was overseen for a couple of years by ginner Sam Langford, a former Texas Leaguer who played 114 games in the outfield for the Cleveland Indians in 1928.

He's still in the major league record books as the last man to throw out four runners from the outfield in one game when he did it against the Chicago White Sox.

Tom Wheeler, a crusty old advertising salesman for *The Plainview Daily Herald*, took over for Sam and ran the program for several seasons.

Ford car dealer Jack Morris sponsored three teams in the program—appropriately named the Thunderbirds, Falcons, and Mustangs. Jack also sponsored the local Punt, Pass and Kick competition for years.

With his bald head and thick mustache, Tom Wheeler looked like a walrus who happened to be wearing a white, short-sleeved shirt with a pocket full of ballpoint pens.

If nothing else, Tom was frugal, usually providing only two or three baseballs per game. If a batter happened to foul a couple of pitches out of the park, we'd sometimes have to wait until they were retrieved and returned to the umpire before play could resume.

One of those "men in blue" was Bill McNeill, who worked in the medical supplies field.

One night Bill didn't have anything to sweep off the plate so Tom dispatched a youngster to run up Broadway to Furr's Supermarket and purchase a whisk broom.

Apparently unable to find such an item, the kid returned with a big green feather duster. Bill snapped part of the long handle off and stuck the duster in his back pocket.

I have not seen such an unusual sight in my life. It looked like a strange bird had landed at Jaycee Park.

*   *   *

James Bentley

A basketball event never seen before . . . or since

Forty years ago, the late James Bentley and I were officiating a sophomore basketball game at Plainview High School when something happened I had never seen before or since.

A Clovis player shot a free throw so softly that it "took English" and died on the flange of the basket.

While I have often seen a ball stick between the goal and backboard, this was a brand-new occurrence.

The Clovis coach—and I have claimed it was Eric Roanhaus, who later became head football coach and has led the Wildcats to 10 state championships and nine runners-up in 36 seasons—jumped up and yelled, "That's our ball!"

Amazed as was everybody else in the gym, I had no clue what to call, but James Bentley, a veteran ref, decisively informed everyone: "That's a jump ball at center court!"

I'm sure glad he knew . . . or at least acted like he did.

One afternoon, James and I called a JV game at Bulldog Gym, and when I stopped by the coach's office where officials "dressed out," someone said Jimmy Pope at New Deal was trying to track me down. Jimmy said I was scheduled to work both varsity games there, and they were wondering where I and my partner were.

Rather panicked at the news—obviously I had forgotten to put the games on my schedule—I spied James Bentley sitting in the stands, still attired in his uniform. "Can you go with me to ref at New Deal?" I pleaded.

We loaded into my car, and I called the sheriff's office to say a 1972 black-over-yellow Mercury might be headed to New Deal at a higher-than-usual rate of speed.

We got there at the half and finished the girls' game and worked the boys. Not surprisingly, I was not invited back to New Deal again.

James and I worked a twin bill at Nazareth right before Christmas of 1981. He had announced to our chapter he was going to hang up his whistle after the break. He told me that night, "I've called 1,003 games and don't have a penny to show for it."

James also was a baseball umpire, and he and I were working a Plainview game with Snyder one afternoon at Jaycee Park. James was the base ump and, racing toward third to make a call, he pulled to a stop and peered toward the bag, hands on his knees. Everyone waited for a call as to whether the Plainview runner was safe or out, but James never made one.

Albert Lewis, assistant to veteran head coach Speedy Moffatt and later head coach at Snyder, yelled at James, "What did you call him?"

"I called him *safe!*" James yelled back.

"You haven't called him anything yet," Lewis insisted.

I'm certain if there was photographic evidence, Lewis would be right.

James, who coached at Kress and then Estacado Junior High, where he had a reputation for swinging a mean paddle for disciplinary measures, also officiated football.

He tells about a coach who didn't like a call he made and verbally let it be known. James tossed a flag and said that would be 15 yards for unsportsmanlike conduct.

Whereupon the coach let out another barrage, and James yelled back at the coach as he continued to march down the field, "That's 30 . . . want to go for 45?"

*　　*　　*

Eddie Owens

Conscripted out of the stands to umpire

One of my dearest friends—and the guy who succeeded me as sports editor of *The Herald*—is Eddie Owens, who recently joined the Wayland Advancement staff after working in public relations for United Supermarkets and Covenant Hospital. He formerly was Wayland's sports information director.

In the late 1970s, Plainview was playing doubleheader baseball games on Tuesdays. One afternoon, I discovered my partner had been called out of town, so I phoned every other umpire I knew and not one of them could get off work to help call the first game that started at 2:30.

Desperate, I told Eddie—then-sports editor of the twice-weekly *Plainview Reporter-News*—that I needed him to work the bases.

"I'll help you and, don't worry, most games you won't have one close call," I assured him, no doubt reminding him of the enticing $10 he would be paid for his assistance.

Wanting to be perfectly above board, I told the Lubbock High coach my predicament and, as I recall, he was not thrilled, though understanding.

Well, there must have been four close plays in the first two innings, and Eddie missed every one of them. On the last one, I looked down at the Lubbock High coach in the third base box and he was white as a sheet.

Fortunately, a "qualified" ump showed up for the second game—much to the relief of a coach, myself, and a conscripted umpire.

*   *   *

Long and exciting roads to the end zone

Not long ago, I passed a guy in the hallway at the YMCA. He spoke and I said, as I am wont to do to people I don't know or whose name I can't recall, "Howya doin', Buddy?"

He said, "You don't recognize me, do you?"

I backtracked, looked him over and admitted, "Sorry, I don't."

"Bobby Reyes," he said, instantly turning on my memory bank.

In 1979 at Lubbock's Lowrey Field, it looked like Monterey would score and go into the locker room with a two-touchdown lead against the Bulldogs.

But Bobby intercepted a pass *eight* yards deep in the end zone and set sail down the east sideline, headed due south. About the Monterey 20, he cut back toward the middle of the field to avoid a tackler and dived into the end zone to complete the longest play in Bulldog history.

It was three yards longer than Stan Rigler's 105-yard return of a missed field goal against Tascosa at Dick Bivins Stadium in Amarillo in 1965 and six yards longer than Taber Minner's 102-yard kickoff return in 2001 at Bulldog Stadium as Plainview outlasted Andrews, 46-42 in the most exciting game I've ever seen.

Another thrilling play in 1979 came against Hereford. On the last snap of the game, Ervin Davis took a pitch and ran toward the home stands, hotly pursued by the Whitefaces.

Ervin, who went on to play for the University of Texas, suddenly spun and threw back across the field to quarterback Jeff Gould, who caught the pass and went 58 yards for a touchdown for a Bulldog victory.

I got to call that Andrews game with Tom Hall and still keep a tape of the second half. Look me up sometime and we'll listen together.

And maybe we can find the video of Bobby Reyes' record-setter.

*   *   *

Tom Hall   Danny Andrews

Tobacco ventures: Have you spit yet?

My forays into the use of tobacco have, thankfully, been few and far between.

In the eighth grade, my neighborhood pal Charles Crownover pried open the bathroom window of his locked house and swiped some of his dad's Marlboros.

We walked a short distance to the old dairy barns (where the baseball parks are located on Beech) and puffed away. However, every time a pigeon took flight, we'd get scared, thinking someone was coming, and quickly snuff out the cigs.

Which reminds me that for probably 50 years, every time I saw another boyhood pal, the late Larry McDonald, he'd remind me: "Never light a cesegar in the barn."

He was alluding to the poster created by one of our second-grade classmates at Hillcrest Elementary for Fire Prevention Week. Obviously, the youngster meant to write "cigar" but we got the message.

Years later, I would smoke an occasional TV Crook, which only cost about 50 cents and had a pleasing aroma, or indulge in a cigar handed out by a proud new father.

Again, not being a regular smoker, I didn't realize how much cigars could cost until Rollie Hyde, publisher of *The Plainview Herald* from 1990-2005, and I were in San Francisco for a Hearst meeting and noticed a smoke shop.

"I think I'd like to smoke a cigar," I told Rollie, an occasional indulger in stogies himself. But when I saw that the cheapest smoke was $6.50, I quickly decided I'd rather spend my money on Ghirardelli chocolate at another nearby establishment.

Of course, a rite of passage for a baseball player is trying out a "chaw" of tobacco.

One day after practice in high school, my buddy Tom Hall pulled a package of Red Man out of his back pocket and asked if I'd like to try it.

"Sure," I said bravely, pinching a sizable portion between thumb and index finger.

After a few minutes, Tom, working on a much larger portion, asked, "Andrews, you spit yet?"

"Un-huh," I replied in the negative.

"You goin' to?" Tom inquired.

"Uh-huh," I moaned as my eyes watered and my mouth burned.

Sick? Man was I sick. I never tried that kind of tobaky again, nor snuff, politely known as "smokeless tobacco," either.

If tobacco is a real man's vice, I know where I stand.

*   *   *

God definitely looks after children and idiots

Like most people who tend to talk a lot, I have opened mouth and inserted foot any number of times.

But God was sure looking out for me one Sunday morning in 1975 in Harrisburg, Virginia.

I was covering the Wayland Flying Queens in the AIAW National Tournament at James Madison College for *The Herald* and also broadcasting the games for KFLP Radio, based in Floydada but which had a studio in the Gabriel-Wayland Shopping Center at the time.

KFLP gave me a green metal box to carry the telephone and other equipment in. I probably couldn't have gotten through security with it these days.

The Queens were looking forward to a match with tiny Immaculata College, a Catholic school in Frazer, Pennsylvania, not far from Philadelphia. The Mighty Macs—later featured in the 2009 movie of the same name—had won three national titles in a row.

Immaculata's cheering section, led by a cadre of nuns, was not happy that tournament officials requested they quit beating on metal buckets, claiming it was Wayland that manufactured a protest.

After two games—including a disappointing Wayland loss to Immaculata—my wife Carolyn, as well as Wayland Vice President Joe Wood and his wife, Dot, asked if I had seen the large lady in the tight T-shirt gyrating around and leading cheers for the Mighty Macs.

Broadcasting the games with former coach Harley Redin, I hadn't seen a thing.

On Sunday morning, the Kodak All-American Team was recognized at a breakfast at a local hotel. It wasn't a huge affair in those days before the national media took much notice of women's basketball.

I sat at a table across from Dr. Francis Breen, director of hematology and oncology for Mercy Catholic Medical Center in Philadelphia, and his wife Judith. They were big fans of Immaculata, and Dr. Breen shot 8-millimeter film of the games in those days when video was just becoming popular.

At least three times during the very pleasant conversation over breakfast, I started to ask the Breens about the "big lady who leads cheers in the stands," thinking she must be a beloved fan. For some reason—providential, in retrospect—I never asked.

When I related the breakfast conversation, Carolyn, Joe, and Dot howled, "That cheerleader is the doctor's *wife!*"

I can only imagine the embarrassing moment:

"So, who is that big fat woman who leads cheers for your team?"

"Uh, that would be *me?*"

"Well, I hear you do an *excellent* job."

Like I've always said, "God takes care of children and idiots."

*   *   *

Nancy Lieberman: Can a girl do that?

One of the greatest female basketball players ever was Nancy Lieberman, who starred at Old Dominion in Virginia And is an inaugural member of the Women's Basketball Hall of Fame.

She was an Olympian in 1976, No. 1 draft choice of the Dallas Diamonds of the Women's Pro Basketball League—whose first coach was former Wayland Flying Queens mentor Dean Weese—played in a men's league called the United States Basketball League, later coached the Dallas Fury of another women's league, and also played for the Washington Generals, who served as the regular opponent of the Harlem Globetrotters.

Nancy, who is a commentator on national telecasts of women's basketball, was the speaker for the 25th anniversary of the Plainview Queens Classic tournament in 2001.

The Queens played Old Dominion in a tournament in Norfolk, Virginia, in 1978. She raced down the floor on a fast-break, planted her left foot at the free throw line, spun about 45 degrees, and bounced the ball between her legs to a teammate—all in one blur.

The teammate sank her shot but, unfortunately, was called for traveling.

The only thing I could think of was, "Wow, Pete Maravich (the magical point guard at LSU of an earlier time) couldn't have done that any better."

*   *   *

Boy, that looks like the Flying Queens

I have had a number of "Twilight Zone" experiences in my life, but none quite like something that happened at the National AIAW Tournament at Penn State in 1976.

Carolyn and I flew to State College, Pennsylvania, with Rusty and Yvonne Savage of Kress in their four-seat, single-engine plane.

On Saturday, we decided to take a drive out into the Amish Country of Lancaster, Pennsylvania. That was an eye-opener as we topped a hill and a man in black coat and black hat was driving a horse-drawn plow. Another fellow was steering a plow behind a huge horse. A little woman in a buggy was not impressed when I took her picture.

That's where we also learned at Arby's that if you order "tea," at an eatery back East you'll probably get hot tea unless you specify "iced."

Anyway, after a pleasant afternoon, we headed back for the Queens' game that I was to broadcast.

As we walked into the gym, I looked out onto the court and thought, "Those uniforms look just like the ones the Queens wear." As I walked a few feet farther, I couldn't believe my eyes: "What is (Queens point guard) Leann Shieldknight doing out there?"

I hustled upstairs to the broadcast area and asked why the Queens were already playing.

The Penn State sports information director apologized that the game had been moved up an hour and no one had thought to personally inform me since it was announced on the P.A. (surprisingly,

I must have been talking and missed it) and it was in the paper (the last paragraph . . . missed that, too).

I said some things for which I later apologized and rang up KVOP to tell board op Dennis Noblett (a Wayland student) to get me on the air as quickly as possible.

The Queens won that game over Mississippi College but, sadly, lost to eventual champion Delta State, Mississippi, 61-60 in the semifinals on Monday night. The Lady Statesmen, led by All-American Lusia Harris, went on to win the first of their three straight national crowns.

Lusia was never mistaken for anything but a superstar.

*   *   *

Gerald Myers and "home cooking"

In 1965, when Gerald Myers—later the men's basketball coach and then longtime athletic director at Texas Tech—was coaching at Lubbock Monterey, he figured his goose was cooked one night at Bulldog Gym.

Only one official showed up for the game—the other apparently went to Lamesa to call that night—and just before the game, I reached over the wall behind the scorer's table and got only one prong in the outlet, blowing out the scoreboard.

Gerald was white as a sheet, figuring PHS Coach Bob Clindaniel was doing all he could to try and get the generally uptight Borgerite in a fizz.

As it turned out, we got the scoreboard in operation, the ref worked the game solo, and Monterey won with ease.

*   *   *

Speaking foreign name and profanity, too

My wife of more than 45 years is normally fairly calm. But she nearly went into apoplectic fits in the early 1970s when Plainview was sporting some pretty hot basketball teams and Monterey was known for "The Stall."

The Plainsmen—first under future Texas Tech coach Gerald Myers and later under Joe Michalka (Muh-hall-kuh)—would invariably go into a four-corner offense if leading late in the game . . . sometimes even earlier than the fourth quarter.

Pass the ball, pass the ball, dribble the ball, dribble the ball, pass the ball.

Good tactics, most of the time, but it drove Carolyn batty. She'd stand up and scream in disgust, elbow me in the ribs, and fume mightily.

To this day, whenever a team slows the ball down—especially if they're playing well but trying to protect the lead—Carolyn predicts disaster.

Probably Joe Michalka—a nervous sort—was right when I called him for comments in advance of a Plainview-Monterey game and he said, "You know, mine is the only name they can say in Lubbock and cuss at the same time."

That was true of at least one Plainview woman as well.

*   *   *

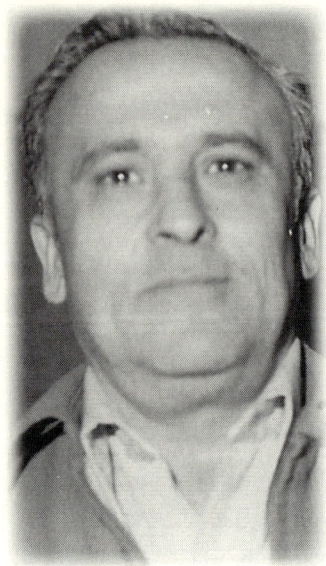

Mario Trevino   John Anderson

Flying popcorn and hallucinations

Two of Plainview's most vocal basketball fans in the early 1970s when Bill Phillips' Bulldogs were pretty doggone good were Mario Trevino and John Anderson.

Mario was manager of Walker Bros. Produce, and you never had to guess what he was thinking. He also was a big University of Texas fan and claimed to frequently call up the head football coach—whoever that might at any given year—and offer his advice.

John had been manager of Baker Castor Oil before getting into the banking business and, of course, eventually serving as mayor.

His eldest son, Mike, was a solid sub on the 1970-71 team that advanced to the state semifinals and a starter on the next year's team that lost in bi-district.

One night in Hereford, Mario was sitting in the upper deck at LaPlata Junior High—home of the Whitefaces –when a ref's call didn't suit him.

Out of nowhere came a bag of popcorn that landed just about center court, scattering kernels everywhere. No one seemed to know—or at least admit—where the Jiffy came from. But Mario, by now sitting quietly, eventually was identified as the culprit.

John was so demonstrative—just the ringleader of a bunch of folks who got a bit overwrought—that I wrote in my sports column, without mentioning names, that some folks needed to act better.

John got the message and alleged to have repented, but I think he was soon back to his old ways.

I know he was one hot afternoon several years later when Plainview was playing Monterey and John's younger son, Jeff, was a member of the Bulldogs.

I was umpiring the plate and, with sweat dripping into my eyes, called a pitch about a foot outside a strike on a Plainview batter.

John, seated directly behind home plate where he could better critique my umpiring, called out in a loud and theatrical voice, "Oh, oh, he's *hallucinatin'*!"

I had to back up and take a second to get my composure.

The sad thing is, I'm pretty sure he was right.

*　　*　　*

Bob Clindaniel

**Bob Clindaniel leans on Charlie Thomas as
assistant Bill Phillips shows his dismay**

Watching Bob Clindaniel was better than the game

Bob Clindaniel came out of Ostrander, Ohio, to play basketball at Howard Payne in Brownwood and eventually migrated to Plainview after coaching at Olney.

Over the next 17 years, he had several playoff squads, including two state semifinalist teams in 1954 and 1955 in the days when only one team out of a district advanced to the playoffs.

Bob was built like a fireplug, had played professional basketball, and had a deadly two-hand set shot. He was a good math teacher and also was a fine golfer and coached the PHS team.

A very amiable individual, Bob followed football coach Don Williams at a Bulldog Booster Club meeting at which Don predicted his team would probably expect some poor officiating. Bob predicted with a chuckle that his team would likely suffer from poor coaching.

Though an emotional individual, the closest he came to profanity was "Gosh O'Friday!"

One night, in a pique over the officiating in Hobbs, he stormed out of the gym and ran out a door. It locked behind him so he had to re-enter through the foyer/concession area.

At a couple of games in Bulldog Gym he jumped up on the bench, put his arm on the rail, banged his head several times, and then turned to slide spread-eagle down the wall.

A former player swears "Bullet" walked down the row of chairs on the sideline in a fit of displeasure with the officiating.

At other times, dismayed at the play of his team, "Clin" would lean over to put his head on the shoulder of a player and groan aloud.

When he went to Wayland for a 12-year stint starting in 1968-69, he would—upon experiencing a call he didn't like—turn and plead with friends Garland and Kathryn Lott and Joe and Patsy Payne in the stands or feel his way along the pullout bleachers like a blind man.

Not known for his sartorial splendor, Bob showed up at a playoff game with Dallas Baptist in the following attire: A black "cowboy cut" leisure suit, a blue Banlon pullover shirt, and black and white patent leather shoes. Not so bad.

But when he leaned forward on the bench, as he was accustomed to doing, his coat and shirt rode up and revealed bright green underwear that—contrasted with the dark colors—looked like a blinking neon sign.

At least it was more interesting than what was going on out on the court.

*　　*　　*

O.T. Ryan

No love loss with Pampa basketball coach

Plainview always had a big basketball rivalry with Pampa, very successfully coached by Clifton McNeely and then by his understudy, Terry Culley.

The Harvesters had some great players, including future world champion and Olympic shot putter Randy Matson and a hot-shooting guard named Wayne Kriese, who later got kicked out of TCU for "playing cards." I don't think it was Old Maid.

One night in 1966, Bob Clindaniel decided the best way his Bulldogs could beat the Harvesters on the road was to just stall the ball. They did, but eventually lost, 18-17.

I imagine that tactic frosted Terry Culley's Cheerios.

He didn't like the fact that O. T. Ryan, fairly new as head band director at PHS, would have his pep band (later "disbanded") play loudly behind the Pampa bench during timeouts. Culley could barely hear himself think.

One night after a game in Bulldog Gym, he was standing on the court, brandishing a menacing index finger at Mr. Ryan. Oscar Truitt (that was his real name but nobody ever called him that—even the band kids called him O. T.) was plumb red in the face and wagging his finger right back.

Basketball usually has a winner. I think that confrontation ended in a draw.

*   *   *

Don't fool with a former pro football player

When former Hale Center and University of Texas star Monte Lee left pro football after stints with St. Louis, Detroit and Baltimore, he wound up coaching tennis at Plainview High School in the spring of 1967.

I don't know if Monte had ever picked up a racket in his life.

Of course, the following fall he was added to the regular coaching staff.

Normally a very humble, mild-mannered fellow, Monte had a highly competitive and even volatile side from time to time.

The story is told that he almost jerked the door of a Tulia dressing room off its hinges when he found it locked at halftime.

When Bill Brown, the assistant basketball coach at Pampa, came into the Plainview dressing room to insist that then-junior varsity coach Bill Phillips shake hands with him, Brown decided that gesture was not as important as he thought when Monte intervened and told him to take a hike.

The story is legendary about the time two young men decided to wear Black Power arm bands in Monte's classroom. When they refused to take off the arm bands, Monte reportedly literally threw one boy, still seated in his chair, across the hall and into the wall.

When he returned to the classroom, the second fellow decided discretion was the better part of messing with a mad Monte Lee and had quickly removed the armband.

*   *   *

Need a football referee? Gimme a whistle!

Although I umpired baseball for about 20 years and officiated basketball for about 15, I never called many football games after a stint with the intramural flag variety in college.

I managed to make some of my fellow students mad by forfeiting a game one night at the Wayland Bowl when a trackster from California on a dorm team insisted on tackling despite my warnings.

On the second offense, I told him he had 30 seconds to get off the field or I would forfeit the game. His very loud response was to "Forfeit this blankety-blank," using a word I'm not sure had ever been heard theretofore on the Wayland campus.

So I did.

About 1992, my youngest son and I went to the Tiger League All-Star game for fifth and sixth graders at Bulldog Stadium, knowing the game would be into the first quarter by the time we arrived.

But when we walked in, it was obvious the game hadn't started. I asked someone, "What's the matter?" and he replied, "The referees didn't show up."

"Gimme a whistle," I said, figuring I had seen enough games on television that I knew most of the signals.

Three guys who had called some Tiger League games but had no experience as a referee volunteered to help, so here were my simple instructions: "You guys carrying the chain, don't move until I tell you, and the rest of us, let's keep our flags in our pockets as much as possible."

The game went off pretty much without incident although I did have to sternly remind one overly demonstrative coach that the game was for the kids and that he should get his panties out of wad. Or words to that effect.

We did have one play where a wide receiver seemed to "hide out" near the sideline before he caught a pass on what was to be a trick play.

One of the officials threw a flag and explained to me that he thought the receiver had to be at least 10 yards away from the sideline. Unfortunately, he didn't know the signal for such an infraction.

So I decided, "How about this?" rubbing my stomach in a circular motion while patting my head at the same time.

Probably just as well I didn't demonstrate that to the crowd.

*　　*　　*

Pressed into football play-by-play service

I did color and statistics for Plainview High football for a couple of seasons with the baritoned Mike Fox (recently named head of the Plainview-Hale County Industrial Foundation) on KKYN in the early 1990s but decided to "retire" after the Bulldogs' second straight trip to the quarterfinals in 1993 under Steve Parr.

Steve, by the way, coached the Bulldogs to a record of 63-53-1 in 11 seasons with trips to the quarterfinals in 1992 and 1993 and within one game of state in 1998 before moving on to Amarillo Palo Duro in 1999.

In a game at Lubbock, my oldest son, Brandon, wearing the same No. 44 I wore for the Bulldogs 24 years earlier, set a new Andrews family varsity record with this third catch of the year and was hauled down one yard shy of a touchdown.

I did continue to help Mike Fox—who worked state playoff football games with the late Warren Hasse of Pampa on the Diamond Shamrock Network for several years—and Mark Finkner do PHS basketball broadcasts. I had to jump in and report that the Bulldogs had lost in overtime to Port Arthur Lincoln in the 1993 state semifinals when both were momentarily left speechless by the buzzer-beating shot.

Similar fate had befallen Plainview against Fort Worth Dunbar in the regional finals several years before in Midland. The Lincoln game was, as Yogi Berra used to say, "déjà vu all over again."

Happily, in Carl Irlbeck's final game coaching the Bulldogs, Plainview beat Austin Anderson, 52-50 in 1994 for the 4A championship as Rob Bass made a layup on an inbounds play just before the buzzer.

I've told Rob for years that by the time he's 50, the story will be that he made the shot from midcourt.

Anyway, I got pressed back into football service in the first game of 1994. Just after the kickoff to start the second half with Plainview trailing Estacado 14-0, press box attendant Bob Magallanes, a coach and fellow basketball ref partner, came into the stands and said, "Danny, can you come up the press box? The Lubbock radio announcer is sick."

I walked into the visiting radio booth and an ashen-faced young fellow was sitting in the floor with a wet paper towel on his head.

He asked if I could do play-by-play. While that wasn't my usual job, I sat down beside former Texas Tech and Kansas City Chiefs player Thomas Howard who was doing color.

I put on the headset and told the announcer of a small station in Lubbock to give me a couple of minutes to look at a program and we'd resume the broadcast.

Well, as it turned out, Plainview rallied to win, 18-14, and I always claim some credit for the victory.

The next week, KJAK radio station owner Woody Van Dyke called and asked if I could do the Lubbock High-Canyon game. But I told him I thought I'd stay on the sidelines, thanks just the same.

I didn't want to press my luck and make future audiences sick.

*   *   *

Bobby Moegle

Legendary coach and a near heart attack

Back in 1976, *The Herald* ran a survey of what readers liked and didn't like about the paper's content.

There was a space for other comments and someone wrote: "Do you think *The Herald* should let the sports editor umpire high school baseball games? In his attempt to show how fair he is, he misses many calls. Many of us disagree with this."

Editor Jim Servatius showed me the comment, and I pondered who might have made that observation. Determining correctly, I called a player's mother and asked her about it. Her response was, "Danny, I don't think you can win. If you call for us, the other team says, 'Why not, he's the local sports editor.' If you make a call against us, the Bulldogs think you're just trying not to show favoritism."

I told her I understood her remarks but "that doesn't say much for my integrity. And, besides, it's also pretty hard to find umpires who can work 2:30 doubleheaders on weekdays."

Anyway, I decided to call veteran Monterey coach Bobby Moegle, never afraid to express is opinion about umpires, to see what he thought. I asked, "When you come to Plainview do you already think you're down a couple of runs because the umpires are calling against you?"

"Heck no," Bobby said, "as long as you and (Buddy) Dodson and (Jimmie) Chennault at calling, we don't have any problems."

Good enough.

Monterey came to town not long after, and the Lubbock paper reported that Moegle would get his 500th career win if the Plainsmen won the first game of the doubleheader.

However, Lubbock sports writer Tom Halliburton told me before the game that Bobby had miscalculated his victories and had actually won No. 500 about three games before. But because the paper had been reporting each win as closing in on 500, the *A-J* didn't announce the mistake.

In the top of the seventh, leading 7-0, Bobby insisted the Plainview pitcher balked. Neither plate umpire Buddy Dodson nor I saw a balk.

As Moegle walked across the diamond by the mound, he hollered at me, "Now I know why those mothers are calling you up."

I thought, "You sorry so-and-so."

When he hollered it again, I waved my right arm and said, "You're outta here," and walked toward the dugout. He came out and stuck his cap right on mine and said, "You're a hot dog. You're the biggest hot dog I've ever seen. Why are you runnin' me out?"

Surprisingly calm, I looked him right in the eye and said, "You know why I'm running you, so get outta here."

"Where am I gonna go?" Moegle asked.

"I don't care where you go, just get outta the park."

He strode out of Jaycee but circled back around behind the dugout, peering through the chain link fence.

In the bottom of the inning, Bill Westbrook of Plainview led off with a grounder to short, and I called him out on a close play as he dove headfirst to try and beat the throw.

Bill expressed his disgust with a profanity, and I ejected him from the game. By now, I'm good and mad.

In the second game, Ron Reeves, later to become the starting quarterback at Texas Tech (and now a colleague in Coaches Outreach Bible Study which he leads at Monterey and I lead at Wayland), drilled a shot to left with a runner or two on base.

Left fielder Jamie McAlister, later a very talented quarterback at New Mexico State, tried to field the ball but tripped and slid into the fence. The chain link had come loose from the ground and was protruding slightly. Jamie got his head caught and was trying to get up without seriously injuring himself.

Meanwhile, with Monterey runners scoring, Plainview fans were screaming, "He's hurt. He's hurt. You gotta stop the game!"

"No," I thought, standing near home plate, "he could be dead but I can't stop the game."

Among those yelling loudest was Bill Westbrook's brother, Steve. I determined I would take my mask off and clobber Steve with it if he approached me after the game, which Monterey won, 3-2.

The Wayland All-Sports Banquet happened to be scheduled that night so I raced home to take a shower and get on to that event.

After I got dressed, I couldn't find my car keys. I frantically searched the house and then remembered I had dropped them into the ball bag I was wearing and then tossed the bag into the closet.

Seriously frustrated—owing to the lost keys and the events at the baseball field—I decided, "I'm gonna have a heart attack, and it's all Bobby Moegle's fault."

*   *   *

Danny Andrews umpiring a Plainview High School game

Bobby Moegle: Another opinion about umpires

Jimmie Chennault was scheduled to work a Texas Tech-Texas A&M doubleheader in Lubbock in 1974 with Gib Weaver of Lubbock. But Gib had something come up, so Jimmie took Buddy Dodson with him.

Texas Tech—which included pitcher Clint Wall and infielder Tommy McMillan of Plainview—won on Friday 15-13, and Jimmie had to overturn a call by Buddy, working his first college game ever.

The Saturday game was weathered out, and Gib Weaver had another conflict and couldn't work the Easter Sunday doubleheader.

Buddy umped the first game behind the plate, and when veteran A&M manager Tom Chandler came down the third base line in the first inning, barking at Buddy about a call, Mr. Dodson gave him the old heave-ho.

Bobby Moegle was watching the game and remarked to Lubbock sportswriter Walt McAlexander, "I don't know why Kal (Segrist, the Tech manager) uses these guys. They're not even good high school umpires." (Guess Bobby must have changed his mind two years later, but Walt reported that comment in his column the next week.)

When Monterey came to Plainview, Moegle sent a runner home on an infield grounder, hoping to catch the Bulldogs napping. But

Plainview was able to make a throw to the plate with catcher Bert Wall holding onto the ball despite being bowled over by the runner.

I was working the plate and made a demonstrative "Out!" call.

Buddy Dodson, observing the game from the third base seating area yelled out at Moegle, "That's some of your blankety-blank high school *coaching!*"

Good thing I didn't hear that or I might have died of a heart attack laughing.

After Bobby retired with three state championships to his credit, I wrote him a congratulatory note and received a very nice hand-written response from the future Texas Sports Hall of Fame inductee, saying he always got a fair shake when I was umpiring.

Sure made it hard to hold any grudges.

*　　*　　*

Regional tournaments: It ain't over til it's over

Plainview has been privileged to host a good number of Southwest Regional Babe Ruth and Cal Ripken Tournaments since the first one was held here in 1977.

Two years earlier, Joe Jacobs and I, representing the Chamber of Commerce, made Plainview's bid for a tournament while our 14-15-year-old all-stars were playing in Paragould, Arkansas.

Players and a bunch of fans loaded up on a Greyhound about 4 p.m. on a Saturday and rode all night to get to Paragould, not far from the Missouri border.

Long distance bus riding is bad enough for adults and not too hot for a 2 1/2-year-old like our oldest son was at the time.

We stopped at a Baptist church not far from Paragould and heard some of the best, albeit maybe the fastest, singing I've ever experienced.

Although Plainview lost 1-0 to Albuquerque and 9-8 to the host team, we had a good time then and a better one two years later, although we got off to a bit of a rocky start.

I went to Babe Ruth Park on Sunday evening to make sure the VIP tent to provide shade for tournament dignitaries was in place and found the water spigot between first and second base running wide open.

I figured someone would be back soon to turn it off. Wrong . . . it ran almost all night.

Tom Hall called me the next morning and said, "You better get down here. Gebo is out here with his helicopter drying off the field. (Unnamed friend) went off and left the water running."

Sure enough, H.M. Gebo, the farm and ranch store owner, had his copter hovering over the infield that supposedly was to be spray-painted green to enhance its look.

God provided more water in a couple of days, forcing tournament officials to buy up all the cat litter in town and some farmers to provide flame cultivators to try to dry the infield.

In the championship game, Jefferson Parish, Louisiana, defeated a team from Austin, led by future Toronto Blue Jay Kelly Gruber and future New York Mets, Boston, and Cleveland pitcher Calvin Schiraldi. First, they were teammates at the University of Texas before playing for World Series champions.

We loved the team from Jefferson Parish and their coach, who took his players to Mass every day; Houma, Louisiana, barber Ralph Sellers, who prepared an authentic Cajun meal for tournament officials; and state directors Bob Milburn of Oklahoma whose son, Jack, had starred at quarterback for OU; Henry Higgins, head of Boys Club work in Arkansas; and Southwest Regional Director Bill Smith, a vice president of the University of Science and Arts of Oklahoma.

In 1983, we held the press at *The Herald* until Plainview finished a tournament game at nearly 2 in the morning. I told former Press Superintendent Ben Thompson he should have shot me. I'm sure the press crew back then had that in mind.

Thirteen years later, Mike Parker and I were co-chairmen of the 14-15-year-old tournament.

When I told Mike and *Herald* Publisher Rollie Hyde, both natives of the Sooner State, that a team from Southeastern Oklahoma would be in the tournament, they said something like, "That's where your wife might also be your sister."

When the team's representative called me, his first question was, "What time zone are y'all in down there?" I wanted to say, "Pacific, we're right near San Diego."

When the team's fans got off the bus, most of the women could have counted their teeth on one hand.

Several years later, when we hosted another tournament, Ron Warren, former Plainview school administrator and now Minister of Spiritual Development and Leadership at First Baptist Church, claimed Southeastern Oklahoma kids who stayed in his home were fascinated by flush toilets and his lawn sprinkler system.

On the last day of the 1996 tournament, Mike Parker, Donnie Brumley, and I had the championship trophy and other hardware ready to present to Pine Bluff, Arkansas, which appeared ready to close out a victory against Nederland.

We had stepped just inside the field, next to the first base dugout. But Donnie said, "Do you think we ought to be on the field yet?" We decided maybe our appearance was premature so we retreated to the stands.

The team from near Beaumont had come through the loser's bracket and defeated Pine Bluff earlier in the day to force a second game.

The Arkansas team needed just one out—just one strike—to win the game. I remember the pitcher walking in front of the mound, squatting down, and taking a deep breath.

A Nederland batter hit a tapper toward third, and the pitcher fielded it but threw high to first and the ball sailed down the right field line toward a bench that served as seating in the "bullpen."

Umpires had made it clear that a ball getting under the bench would be a ground-rule double if the fielder did not try to retrieve it.

Unfortunately for Pine Bluff, one of the fielders, instead of leaving the ball alone, fished under the bench as the runner raced around the base paths to tie the game.

Nederland went on to win in nine innings and then advanced to Dickinson, North Dakota, and won the World Series.

It was a reminder that the game ain't over 'til it's over.

And for tournament officials to stay off the field until it is.

*   *   *

That bad ol' Bulldog "Streak" finally ends

On a nice September night in 1963, you would have thought the Plainview Bulldogs had just won the Super Bowl—four years before that game was even invented, the Cotton Bowl, and the state championship rolled into one.

By holding off the Littlefield Wildcats, 20-18 before 4,500 fans in Bulldog Stadium, Plainview ended one of the state's longest losing streaks—24 games in a row.

It began the last game of 1960 when Herman Smith was head coach, continued unabated for two seasons with Don Williams at the helm, and continued three games deep into 1963.

The last time Plainview had won was a 13-6 victory over Pampa when Dwight Eisenhower was still in the White House. A late interception return for six points ended an 11-game winless streak, otherwise the skid would have reached 35 games.

To illustrate the futility of the losing streak, the Bulldogs had been outscored 1,145-75, an average outcome of 48-3. They were held scoreless seven times in 1961 and again in 1962.

After being clobbered 86–6 by Big Spring in Bulldog Stadium in the 1962 opener, they didn't score again until a 40-6 loss to Pampa in the next-to-last game of the year.

Three times in 1961 they gave up 65 or 66 points and closed 1962 with a 74-8 loss to Amarillo Tascosa.

The 1963 Bulldogs, who had opened with promise of improvement in a 22-15 loss to Albuquerque Highlands, didn't score the next two weeks, losing to Amarillo High, 13-0 and Borger, 55–0.

Littlefield, where Williams had coached before coming to Plainview, was 2-2, and the 3A Wildcats, certainly not wanting to lose to their former coach, were coming off a 7-6 loss to Denver City, the No. 1 team in 2A.

The big news in Plainview that week was that "Sugar Shack," written by Keith McCormack of the local String-A-Longs band and his aunt, Faye Voss, around the coffee table two years before, was the No. 1 hit in the nation for Jimmy Gilmer and the Fireballs.

Also, the school board was planning a $465,000 addition to Plainview High School on the west side of the present building.

At the Granada, Doris Day and James Garner were starring in *The Thrill of It All*, an appropriate caption for what would happen at Bulldog Stadium on Friday night.

In national news, singer Eddie Fisher said he was ready to end his marriage to actress Elizabeth Taylor. No more ready than Plainview was to end its losing streak.

The Dogs broke on top 7-0 when Tom Sawyer tossed a 23-yard touchdown pass to Jerry Wright, and Trent Jordan kicked the extra point. Sawyer and Jordan would go on to play at Texas Tech.

Littlefield came right back on an 83-yard touchdown run by Grover Pigrum. Early in the second quarter, Harold Scroggins tossed a 35-yard touchdown pass to Sawyer, who alternated between halfback and quarterback, and Jordan was true on the kick again.

John Dick Carl's one-yard run with 8:01 to play brought Littlefield within two points, but Joe Don Ford's 42-yard scamper set up a 3-yard run by Sawyer and though two attempts at the PAT failed, the Dogs led 20-12.

Pigrum's 8-yard touchdown run with 2:50 to play made it 20-18, but a 5-yard delay penalty proved disastrous for Littlefield as Pigrum was stopped two yards short of the goal line on the extra point try.

The Dogs held on despite an onside kick try by Littlefield, and a fumble with 14 seconds left had PHS fans holding their collective breath.

"When you've lost for so long, you expect stuff to go wrong," said Tom Sawyer, who is a lawyer and rancher in Lexington, between Austin and Bryan. "It was sweet to beat Littlefield; all our coaches (Don Williams, Deverelle Lewis, and Gerald Ritchey) were pleased. They were good guys."

Herald Sports Editor Bob Hilburn, a dyed-in-the-wool Bulldog fan, wrote a glowing column praising the 32-member team's determination to win the game. In a Sunday advertisement, Gabriel's Department Store saluted the entire team as Players of the Week.

"When Friday's final gun sounded, the stands broke into an uproar of excitement. Some laughed. Others stood in their tracks for minutes after the game had ended, apparently not knowing what to do next. Some wept guardedly and others openly," Hilburn wrote.

"We dare anyone to say today that Plainview is the only 4A team in Texas that doesn't play football," he penned, alluding to a comment attributed to veteran Amarillo sports writer Putt Powell.

After that eventful game, car horns blared well into the night as the celebration continued.

The infamous Streak had ended.

The thrill of it all!

*   *   *

Warren Hasse

Warren Hasse: Man of a thousand programs

Warren Hasse was the longtime voice of the Harvesters in Pampa where he started out as a sports writer in the late 1940s and later owned radio station KPDN.

He also broadcast West Texas State football for more than 30 years and did playoff football games for the Diamond Shamrock Network.

Warren apparently kept every scorebook he used and every game program he could get his hands on.

In 1974, Plainview hosted the West Texas Babe Ruth Tournament, and Warren came to broadcast the Pampa games.

I told him the first curve ball I ever saw was off a Pampa pitcher in a 1966 game where the home plate umpire, whom I had visited with when he officiated the Plainview Invitational Basketball Tournament a few months earlier, told me to "Hit one out" when I came to bat.

I was out in front of that pitch at least a foot but the ump, who apparently liked me, called "Ball!" That elicited a squawk from the catcher who begged the arbiter to check with his partner at first.

"Nope, it was a ball," he said, sticking to a very bad call.

I told Warren I fouled out to first base on the second pitch. The next day, he showed up with the scorebook from that game, opened it and pointed to my name with the symbol "FO-3."

"Yeah, you sure did," Warren said with a smile.

Almost 20 years later, I was covering the Bulldogs' football game in Pampa when Warren asked if I needed a program and laid one in front of me. I glanced at the Plainview roster and did a double-take after seeing some familiar names like star running back Jesse McGuire.

It was the 1958 Plainview-Pampa program.

I stopped in Pampa a couple of years ago to meet Warren for coffee at Braum's. We had a great visit and, figuring in his late 80s that he didn't have many years left, I asked: "How are you with the Lord?"

"Fine," he said with his familiar smile, "and when I get up there, I'll put in a good word for you."

I'd sure like it if it was Warren who put the "Lamb's Book of Life" in front of me with my name in it.

*   *   *

Free baseball tickets, but not for Sooner fans

When Plainview's Lady Bulldogs won the state 5A basketball championship in 1987, I took off to watch the games—something I was never able to do when PHS won three straight 4A state titles from 2001-2003, because I was at home helping put out special Sunday sections saluting the teams.

The best part of that trip was meeting Lori Wells, future wife of Brent Wells and now my down-the-street neighbor. She's about the sweetest person I know. And Brent's not a bad guy either.

I also recall sharing an ice cream cone with Tyler Cooper—son of new Wayland Athletic Director Rick Cooper. Tyler's mom, Janie, was assistant to Kathy Harston. Both Janie and Kathy were former Flying Queens.

Tyler, who is orthopedic residency, was about 18 months old. He'd take a bite of ice cream, then give me a kiss on the cheek. The last time I saw him was several years ago when he was playing for his dad at West Texas A&M. Walked on the balls of his feet, just like his father.

I digress.

On Saturday afternoon before the Lady Bulldogs beat Austin Lanier, 59-47 in the championship game, Sports Editor John Walker and I walked over to Disch–Falk Field to watch Texas play Oklahoma in baseball.

We were both wearing red jackets and a woman standing near the entrance asked if we wanted free tickets to the game. But first she inquired, "You're not from Oklahoma, are you?"

"No, ma'am," we almost simultaneously assured her. "We're from Plainview, Texas."

She smiled and handed over tickets to great seats down the first base line.

We sure were glad we weren't OU fans that day.

Charity, you know, only goes so far.

* * *

"Now you chunkin' in there, Turk!"

I really don't have any hobbies. I tried golf for a week in 1973 and couldn't figure it out so I gave it up and saved myself a lot of money and heartache.

Here is an example of my game: The last time I played 20 years ago at Plainview Country Club, I launched a shot about 150 yards out on No. 15 to within six feet of the pin, then walked up and left my putt five feet short.

Watching the Texas Rangers on TV or listening to them on radio is about as close as I can get to a hobby. It was quite painful this past season due to the Rangers' injury-plagued demise.

I did get to see the fifth game of the 2010 World Series in Arlington—a 5-1 Rangers loss to the San Francisco Giants. Earlier in the day, my son Brad paid $100 a ticket for us to sit in front of the giant scoreboard at Cowboy Stadium to see the home team lose to Jacksonville. Considering I paid $825 for the two baseball tickets, I wanted to stand up about the fifth inning and holler, "Somebody owes me a refund!"

Years before the Washington Senators moved to Texas, I spent many a night lying in bed listening to Gene Elston and Loel Passe broadcast Houston Astros games.

That pastime had no appeal to my neighborhood pal Mike Wadzeck who said, "Andrews, you'd rather make up an all-star team than have a date." Mike also didn't care for my questions when we studied for tests: "Blank did blank in blank?"

Gene Elston was the smooth lead play-by-play man for the Astros while Loel Passe was the consummate "homer" for the team that abandoned the name Colt .45s when they moved into the Astrodome in 1965.

"Now you chunkin' in there, Turk!" Loel would praise a fastball by Dick Ferrell to retire an opposing batter. He assured fans that Bob Watson would hit 30 homeruns in a season (he never hit more than 22). "Hot ziggity dog and sassafras tea" was an exclamation for a spectacular play.

I did a phone interview with Loel from his home in Houston not long before he died in 1997. When I asked about Gene Elston, he said something like, "Some announcers give too many statistics." Elston's quote after Passe died was something like, "Of all the people I've ever known, Loel was one of them."

I sensed no love loss between two guys who worked together for 15 years. They may not have liked each other but I sure liked them.

"Hot ziggity dog and sassafras tea!"

*　　*　　*

Sure glad that jacket wasn't on fire

For many years, John Copeland was the men's basketball coach at Lubbock Christian University, a big rival of Wayland until going NCAA Division II in 2013-14.

John also is a former national team-roping champion.

One night at Hutcherson Center, he went nuts on a no-call against the Pioneers. He leaped off the bench and began racing down court, all the while trying to get his coat off. It hung up on his shoulders.

I told him later, "John, if that coat had been on fire, you'd have been a dead man."

* * *

Texas Tech fan's face as red as his cap

One of my favorite Hearst newspapers colleagues was Jack Loftis, editor of the state's largest paper, *The Houston Chronicle.*

About 10 years ago, Jack, a Baylor graduate, was on his way home from a Bears football game when he struck up a conversation in the Dallas airport with a Texas Tech supporter who began to rail about how *The Chronicle* was always "digging up dirt" on the Tech athletic program.

Eventually, the man introduced himself and asked Jack, "What do you do?"

"I'm editor of *The Houston Chronicle,*" Jack said with a chuckle.

The Tech fan's face turned about as red as his cap.

* * *

Basketball, barbecue, and chocolate pie

I refereed quite a bit at the small Lamb County school in Spade, including one night with Tom Hall.

"What time does the first game start?" I tentatively asked Tom as we were on the road but running a bit late. "I can't remember if it's 6 or 6:30."

"Doesn't matter," Tom insisted, "they can't start without us."

We soon found out they could. The girls' game started at 6, and two coaches were enlisted to ref until we got there.

Spade had no football team, so the first game of the year was designated as Homecoming. A nice meal always was provided. On one occasion, it happened to be barbecue with all the trimmings, and chocolate pie.

I told my ref partner David Frizzell of Lockney that I thought I'd have some supper before our work began. "You're gonna eat *before* the game?" David said with astonishment in his voice.

I did, then went out and called one of the best doubleheaders I've ever worked.

That's my story and I'm stickin' with it.

SCHOOL DAYS STORIES

Journey through yearbook brings great memories

Out of a class of 335 graduates, I suspect only two or three of us could tell you 47 years after leaving Plainview High School what the class motto was. I love it: "When duty whispers low, 'Thou must,' the youth replies, 'I can.'"

I took a quick journey through the 1967 Plain View yearbook, for which I served as sports editor, and was reminded of some outstanding people and some fun times.

* Our graduation was held at First Baptist Church when that was about the biggest indoor venue in town. The Rev. James A. Mock, rector of St. Mark's Episcopal Church, was the baccalaureate speaker on Sunday before graduation. For the uninitiated, baccalaureate was a time for a minister to give words of wisdom, admonition, and encouragement to the graduates.
* The yearbook was dedicated to Foy Dodson, who taught physics, and his wife Jewell, the typing instructor. Fortunately, I never was good enough in math to have Mr. Dodson's class so I never learned to work a slide rule – the equivalent of a calculator in those days.

* A photo proves we certainly had the prettiest cheerleaders as a group in PHS history: Rhonda Lewis, Carol Buchanan, Patti Purcell, Nancy Douglass, Cindy Greer, and Mary Beth Beane.

* Karen King was valedictorian and Gloria Clanton, with whom I went to grade school at Hillcrest, was salutatorian. Obviously, none of Gloria's "smarts" rubbed off on me.

* Mack Walker and Mary Beth Beane were voted Best All-Around with Billy Rogers and Cindi Smith runners-up; Colin Coe and Mary Beth were named Most Friendly; Ronald Kersh and Marjan Heck were Senior Favorites with Pat Buchanan and Carol Buchanan (no relation) runners-up.

* I escorted Glenda Fuller at Coronation in the PHS Auditorium. Lords and Ladies dressed formally and bowed and curtsied, respectively, as we were introduced in the Court of Queen Rhonda Lewis.

* It was the first year for a girls' drill team dubbed the Royal-Scarlets. Their instructor was Joyce Kite, a former Wayland Flying Queen now enjoying life in Hawaii.

* Vincent Barron, an all-district outfielder teammate of mine on the baseball team, was recipient of the Battling Bulldog award in basketball. Guard-linebacker Gary Covey won Most Valuable Player in football. He played in the Texas High School All-Star Game in San Antonio. As it turned out, he was in for only three snaps and I was at the concession stand for two of them.

* Sadly, only 22 of the 107 businesses advertising in the Plain View are still operating.

* I was never in the A Cappella Choir but still love their "anthem" to close each program, graduation, etc. In abbreviated form, it says:

The Lord bless you and keep you
The Lord lift his countenance upon you
And give you peace
The Lord make his face to shine upon you
And be gracious unto you
Amen.

The Lord was very gracious in allowing me to grow up in Plainview and be a proud Bulldog for life.

*   *   *

Vernon Stokes

First Wayland "dancer" lights up a seventh grader

Dancing was declared legal on the Wayland campus about five years ago, although I suspect some kids have participated in "foot functions" since the university was founded in 1908.

As I circulated around Plainview Country Club, it struck me that the main thing wrong with dancing that night was that no one thought to bring some air freshener to counteract the smell of sweaty bodies.

I contend the first person to dance on campus was a slender, crewcut lad from Sundown by the name of Vernon Stokes. Picking up some extra bucks as an umpire in the summer baseball program—then located about where Wilder Field now sits—Vernon was hit on the foot by a foul ball. He reacted by hopping up and down on one foot, doing a jig and other gyrations until the pain subsided.

Vernon was my seventh-grade basketball coach and a wonderful history teacher as well. He also had an extra job, leading music at Seth Ward Baptist Church, to help support himself and wife, Belva, a former Flying Queen.

He has served Wayland faithfully as a trustee and donor, including a scholarship in memory of two adult daughters he lost to cancer within a couple of years. He has received two major awards from Wayland for leadership.

My first "licks" came courtesy of Vernon because I was so weak I couldn't do chin-ups. I guess he decided lighting up my bottom (I was wearing gym shorts) might serve as incentive.

I wrote a couple of columns about this child abuse. Vernon told me several years ago as I was relating the story to State Rep. Pete Laney at the groundbreaking of the Laney Student Activities Center that "you never tell the whole story. I gave you a week to do 40 chin-ups."

"Vernon, I couldn't have done 40 chin-ups if you gave me the whole year," I assured him.

About 10 years ago my brother was the community relations manager for AT&T in Midland where Vernon had been Director of the District 18 Service Center before a stint as superintendent of schools in Odessa.

Vernon was speaking to a large teacher group, and Guy presented him the paddle that classmate Thomas Waldrep had purloined from his coach nearly 40 years before.

Vernon's face turned a bright shade of red.

About the same color as he made my hind parts back in 1961.

*   *   *

Jim Sears

"Licks": Cruel and usual punishment

Although I was generally well-behaved in school, I was on the receiving end of what we called "licks" on several occasions.

From what I hear, I was lucky to come along well after Larry McBee was assistant principal at Plainview High. Though small in stature, they said Larry could lift you off the floor with one swing of the hardwood.

As related in the previous story, I got a couple for not being able to do 40 chin-ups in a week. I also got one from Coach Deverelle Lewis for throwing a cup of cold water on someone in the shower, and one from Coach Bill Mayfield. Bill liked me, and I think he "broke his wrist" at the last instant to lessen the impact.

But I was not so lucky with new baseball coach Jim Sears, who had been drafted out of the University of Houston by the Cincinnati Reds.

While I was pretty proud of it, Sears was disdainful of the "D" I had made in math. The grade between "C" and "F had been declared a passing grade only a year or two before.

"Andrews, a 'D' is not even passing in most schools," Sears huffed.

While most paddles I had seen that came in contact with what Forrest Gump called the "but-tocks" were fairly wide, Sears used a baseball bat with half the barrel sawed off.

I took the wallet out of my back pocket and dutifully bent over, teeth clenched and eyes closed tight awaiting impact.

I can't adequately describe what a lick feels like, but suffice it to say your body temperature goes up about 20 degrees and the pain is quite excruciating.

I think an old baseball term "going for the downs" would apply here. When that board met my rear end, I stood straight up and dropped the wallet.

Assistant coach Bill Phillips, witnessing the punishment with a mixture of sympathy for me and admiration for Sears' swing, declared: "That's the hardest lick I've ever seen anybody take."

If my butt wasn't on fire, I might have appreciated that compliment more.

*   *   *

John Blaine

Math problems before the Civil War

As chronicled elsewhere in this book, mathematics and I had only a passing acquaintance. In fact, I didn't like it and it didn't like me.

Consequently, after failing in the first few weeks of geometry as a sophomore, I was assigned to Fred Joachim's "regular" math class.

But "Daddy Fred," as some students called him, had a well-earned reputation of being very hard.

When I reported to his class, he said flatly, "You're about a month behind, get a notebook and get caught up."

I immediately retreated to the counselor's office and begged for mercy. Happily, I was dispatched to the "basic" math class taught by John Blaine.

Mr. Blaine had come to Plainview in the late 1950s as athletic director and math teacher after a stellar coaching career at Dimmitt and Sundown.

It was in his class that I learned how to remember the Pythagorean Theorem: The square of the hypotenuse is equal to the squares of the other two sides, or A squared plus B square equals C squared.

Three Indian braves' squaws were pregnant. Each decided to kill an animal to provide a hide on which their squaw could lie when she had the baby. The first killed an elk, the second a bear and the third a hippopotamus.

The first two had sons but the third had twin sons, proving the sons of the squaw on the hippopotamus are equal to the sons of the squaws of the other two hides.

It was Mr. Blaine's practice to have six students working on a particular problem at the board while the rest of the class pondered over the problem at their desks.

One day Mr. Blaine asked, "Does anyone have the correct answer?" As was frequently the case, no one did.

"My, my," Mr. Blaine lamented, "I wish they had easy problems like that when I was in school."

I couldn't resist leaning out of my desk and whispering in a stage voice to Dwight Yarbrough, "They didn't have problems like that before the Civil War."

When I turned around, Mr. Blaine was looking directly at me and invited me to repeat to the class what I had said. "I'd rather not," I moaned, not feeling nearly so clever now. But Mr. Blaine insisted, so I meekly repeated the smart remark.

He invited me to remain after class and when the other students dispersed, Mr. Blaine said, "Danny, what you said was really pretty funny. But we have a lot of students in here who need to learn."

He might well have added, "You included."

John Blaine and I became fast friends from that day until his passing a decade later.

Mike Wadzeck   Patti Purcell

One-punch fights and a real donnybrook

I've always said I'm a lover, not a fighter. My lone serious boyhood fisticuffs was a one-punch affair, and I was the punchee.

Across-the-street pal Mike Wadzeck and I were trying to impress Dale Davitte—a year older and far more talented than either of us with our basketball skills on her driveway up the street.

Dale and Patti Purcell, who insisted she could outrun sprinter Joe Don Martin, would have been great PHS athletes if anything more than tennis had been offered for girls at the time.

Memory escapes me as to what triggered a verbal exchange between myself and Mike, but I do remember saying something real intelligent like, "If you don't like it, why don't you do something about it?"

Whereupon he socked me in the kisser. My eyes watered as my lip started to puff up. I suggested he go home. Fortunately, he did without firing off another blow.

Actually, Mike was lucky to be alive at that point because I had threatened to kill him sometime earlier when he found a salamander and said he was going to put it on my face.

In junior high, it seemed nearly every boy at both Coronado and Estacado junior high schools loved Donice Noel, who happened to go to Coronado.

One day it was rumored that a bunch of Estacado guys were going to load up in Mike Bailey's pickup and come over to Coronado for a big noon-hour row, reportedly because Donice's present boyfriend from CJHS had "done her wrong."

Ashamed to say, I hid out in the boys' bathroom. I thought, "I love Donice, too, but she ain't worth dyin' for."

The first day of school of my seventh and eighth-grade years at Coronado—then located at 12th and Galveston—were *punch-uated* by fights in the front yard.

In the first, one fellow banged another's head on the curb, and in the second, a seasoned boxer bloodied his would-be opponent's nose with a straight-smash and a right cross. End of fight.

One afternoon, Stanley Earl Beasley—we just called him Stan—squared off on the tennis court adjacent to the building. I don't think there was much fighting, but Lanny Savage certainly showed which side he was on despite getting his tang tonguled: "Come on, Stanley, give him a *jodo chap!*"

But the dangedest fight I ever saw happened in 1968 at Bulldog Gym with Plainview playing Amarillo Palo Duro.

I was covering the game for *The Herald* but sitting in the stands with my future wife. Tommy Baker broke away for a layup to end the game and, as I looked up after writing down the play, a bunch of guys were piling *over* the railing and onto the floor.

"What in the world . . .?" I thought.

It was a real six-alarm, no-holds-barred, hit-'em-before-they-can-hit-you slobber-knocker.

There already had been bad blood between the two teams because Kenny Redin had "stomped" a prone Palo Duro player a few weeks earlier in the game at Amarillo.

Anyway, future pro football stars Lawrence McCutcheon and Jerry Sisemore were right in the middle of the fracas. Jerry had a Don's head cradled in his huge right arm and was banging on his noggin' kind of like Nolan Ryan did to Robin Ventura in that famous brawl in Arlington 20 years ago.

Now this is the same Jerry Sisemore (future University of Texas All-America lineman and future Pro Bowler with the Philadelphia Eagles) who came out second in a one-punch fight with senior quarterback Ronald Kersh when Jerry was a sophomore on the varsity in 1966.

When that set-to began, I thought, "Ah-oh, Kersh, you've had it now." Kersh might have thought the same, but sometimes he who hits first, hits best. One punch—let's shake and make up.

In the big donnybrook, Principal Lamont Veatch was vainly trying to restrain McCutcheon (future Colorado State and Los Angeles Rams record-setting running back), who looked like a racehorse trying to bolt the gate.

Nick Barron had jumped out of the stands and was threatening to coldcock one of the Amarillo players who was squared off with the aforementioned Tommy Baker.

Thankfully, order was restored after several scary minutes. Most players probably went to school the next day, bragging as to how they beat the snot out of somebody the night before.

*　　*　　*

"Greasy spoons" and profound language

When I started Coronado Junior High in the fall of 1961, we had two "greasy spoon" eateries.

Actually, Pearl "Babe" Couch and Geneva Kersh who were neighbors out in Hillcrest, might resent their establishment just north of the school and cheek-to-jowl with a railroad track being labeled a "greasy spoon."

Ginny's son Ronald and I chose to dine there the first day of school but were solemnly instructed by a freshman girl that we should, under no circumstances, eat at the Sandwich Bar east of Coronado lest we get a "bad reputation."

Now, the last thing a seventh-grader wants is a bad reputation. But the lure of a boat of 15-cent French fries (which, by the way, were swimming in grease) was too much to resist.

Aptly-named "Shorty" Marshall and his wife Ella ran the snack bar south of Estacado Junior High, a big draw for students who might otherwise walk several blocks to the bowling alley for lunch.

The Marshalls posted a sign that admonished "No Profound Language," obviously meaning to discourage "profane" talk.

Since their clientele consisted of seventh, eighth, and ninth-graders, the chances of profound language was pretty slim.

* * *

Discretionarily expedited to homeroom

Jack Lamb, a very formal man who I never recall wearing anything but a suit, rimless glasses, and hair combed straight back, succeeded Charlie White as principal of the old Coronado Junior High in the fall of 1963.

Mr. Lamb had a big vocabulary but disdained articles such as "a," "an," and "the."

The man who wrote a script for me for the ninth-grade banquet and identified himself as "titular head of Coronado Junior High," would announce over the P.A. system: "Students, at discretion of homeroom teacher, you will be expedited to gymnasium for pep rally."

"Discretion" and "expedited" were not regularly used by anyone I knew, but we dutifully marched to the gym as instructed.

*   *   *

Playing hooky from school . . . just one time

I played "hooky" from school just once.

By the way, that term was first recorded around 1848. Bartlett's Dictionary of Americanisms give this example: "He moped to school gloomy and sad, and took his flogging, along with Joe Harper, for playing hooky the day before." (Mark Twain writing in *Tom Sawyer*.)

When I was in the third grade in 1957, it snowed, and my teacher, Hazel Hale, warned us not to throw snowballs.

Never admonish a third-grader to not do something that's fun. I flung one during morning recess, she saw me and said I had to come in after lunch and write on the board, "I will not throw snowballs again."

We lived close enough to walk home for lunch and, for some strange reason, the barbecue my mother served that day just did not sit well with my stomach. Mother believed my story, and I stayed home that afternoon.

I compounded my fib by repeating it to Mrs. Hale the next day in explaining my absence.

She never disputed it and didn't make me write on the board either.

*   *   *

Nov. 22, 1963: A sad and unforgettable day

Just as almost anyone 50 and up can vividly remember, I will never forget where I was on a cold, sunny Friday in November 1963.

I had just finished lunch at Coronado Junior High and was walking out of the cafeteria when Bobby Johnson, whose folks ran a jewelry store, said, "President Kennedy's been shot."

I'm sure my initial reaction was "Yeah, right" or "That's a joke," but I took off running to Owen Grocery right across the street east of the school.

There I found, the proprietors, Condie and Anna Owen, hovered over a white table-model radio listening to the awful news from Dallas.

I got a few details and ran back to the cafeteria. Several teachers were seated at one table, and I reported, "President Kennedy has been shot."

As I recall, they didn't say a word. They just got up and filed out of the cafeteria. It was like they were thinking, "Danny, that's not funny," but they never responded verbally, never said, "We already know," or anything else.

Soon the bell rang for our first afternoon class. Mine happened to be study hall, and we students sat in dead silence, listening to the reports over the intercom.

Finally, the announcer said, "President John F. Kennedy died today in Dallas at 1 p.m. Central Standard Time."

I'll never forget bursting into tears . . . and recovering just as quickly.

We were glued to the television most of the weekend, but some of us football players gathered on the practice grounds north of Coronado and, I guess, tried to divert our attention to other things on Saturday.

We had just left church on Sunday when we heard the report that alleged assassin Lee Harvey Oswald had been killed by Jack Ruby as he was being transferred from the police station in Dallas.

Of course, we all watched the funeral on Monday—black-and-white coverage on all networks. There was Jackie in her black veil, 3-year-old John-John saluting his father's casket, the large entourage of dignitaries marching to Arlington Cemetery, and the howitzers firing off a booming salute.

Our young, energetic, visionary President who had encouraged us to not ask what our country could do for us, but to ask what we could do for our country; who had challenged America to put a man on the moon before the end of the 1960s; who stared down the Russians during the Cuban missile crisis; who seemed to live an idyllic life in the White House, was suddenly, horribly cut down in the prime of life.

It was—and remains—a very sad and confusing time.

And an event none of us who experienced it will ever forget.

WAYLAND STORIES

Paul Armes

Glad to be mistaken for the president

It's almost certainly because of the white hair that I have been mistaken by several students for Wayland President Dr. Paul Armes.

It has to be the hair, since he stands 6-7 and I'm only 5-11.

For the past eight years, it has been my privilege to work with Paul Armes. I emphasize *with*, because he is a true servant leader and would never say someone works *for* him.

That includes my wife who has been his executive assistant since he came to Wayland.

It's sometimes a little hard to call him "Doctor Armes" since I knew him as "Paul" from denominational meetings when he was pastoring in Lubbock and Corpus Christi or serving as president of San Marcos Baptist Academy immediately before coming to Wayland 14 years ago as the university's 12th president.

Maybe he has a hard time calling me "Danny," since it's usually, "Hi, Mr. Andrews."

Sometimes we enjoy just talking about pastors and denominational folks we know and have known. He definitely has a compassionate pastor's heart.

He and his lovely wife Duanea and the Andrewses have enjoyed getting to be grandparents over the past seven years. Sarah Thompson of Lubbock has three children and Ashley Cox of San Antonio has one.

Duanea and I say we "robbed the cradle" since our spouses are a year younger than we are.

Although Paul Armes, an El Paso Coronado High School graduate who played freshman basketball at Baylor and has a degree from "Jerusalem on the Brazos," he bleeds Blue and Gold.

During special events, he proudly wears the Wayland ring-inscribed with "Prez"--the Association of Former Students gave him several years ago.

So, I'm flattered to be mistaken occasionally for a good and godly man.

*   *   *

Roy McClung

There was no one like Roy C. McClung

A man I really came to love was Dr. Roy Cornelius McClung, pastor of First Baptist Church-Plainview from 1958-63, then president of Wayland Baptist College from 1963-80.

Dr. McClung, who died at age 95 in 2013, recalled that the tears of Dr. A. Hope Owen "wet the platform" as his venerable predecessor prayed at his inauguration at First Baptist Church, which Owen also had pastored before moving to Wayland.

Though small in stature, Roy McClung had big goals and big visions. During his tenure at Wayland, such buildings as Harral Memorial Auditorium, Moody Science Center, Caprock Dormitory, Hutcherson Center, and the Museum of the Llano Estacado were constructed. Many other campus improvements were made and extension education was launched in other cities.

The Roy C. and Genelle McClung University Center, which has been the site of so many community events, is named for him and his gracious wife.

He weathered the storms of a denominational report that said Wayland and several other small Baptist schools should close and of a quiet but disconcerting insurrection by several professors.

Dr. McClung loved sports, and it wasn't beneath his dignity—I guess nothing was since he was a "chicken sexer" while attending Southern Seminary in Louisville, Kentucky—to put on a pair of knee-length shorts and act like a cheerleader.

One year the Flying Queens won the national AAU championship. At chapel, Dr. McClung enlisted several students to join him to form a "train" and lead the student body in a cheer.

At the head of the train, Dr. McClung led the group around the stage, pulling his right arm up and down like a conductor tugging on a whistle while encouraging the crowd to repeat: "The Queens are No. 1 *now*; the Queens are No. 1 *wow!*"

My favorite memory of Dr. McClung was during check-in at the Hyatt Regency Hotel in Houston prior to the Baptist General Convention of Texas' annual meeting in 1980.

When Dr. McClung saw Dr. James Basden, head of the Christian Education Coordinating Board, come into the lobby, he immediately fell to his knees and began bowing to his "boss."

I thought, "Only Roy McClung."

*   *   *

Mike Melcher

Mike Melcher: I'm certain about this guy

When Joe Provence, an icon at Wayland for nearly 50 years (almost half as alumni director) decided to retire in 2006, a guy I had never met also applied for the job.

Although the committee was nice enough to recommend me for the position, they thought the very personable Mike Melcher would be a good addition to the Advancement staff as Director of Corporate Giving.

My first thought was, "Wayland must be hard up hiring an old newspaper hack and a longtime car salesman."

My second thought was, "I hope this Melcher guy's not a know-it-all. If he is, there will be two of us in the same building."

Mike, who moved up to Executive Director of University Advancement several years ago, worked hard to earn his Master of Management from Wayland and has taught business classes online.

Together, we claim to know nearly everybody in Texas (and quite a few beyond). He'd start talking about someone and I'd say, "I served on a committee with that guy," and I'd mention somebody and Mike would say, "I sold him several cars when I was in Littlefield."

It's a running contest to see who's the first to see somebody he knows when we go into Sam's Club or some other large establishment. A couple of years ago, I followed Lubbock TV weatherman John Robison into a restroom at Sam's and asked if he'd come out and meet Mike and act like he knew me. One step ahead, Mike had already asked a checker to do the same.

Mike has had major issues with snoring. I've been able to room with him by bringing along ear plugs. Jon Petty, our Director of Public Relations, Mike, and I laugh every time we think about the time on a retreat in Ruidoso that Jon had to vacate the room he shared with Mike and crawl into the bed with me because the snoring was so loud.

Well, Mike Melcher, a Slaton native and proud former member of the "Goin' Band from Raiderland" at Texas Tech, has become one of the best friends I've ever had.

Mike has a boisterous laugh but a tender heart, and I've seen his eyes leak numerous times as we talk about emotional issues. They also light up when he discusses his vivacious wife Deb, sales coordinator for the Wayland University Store, his three kids and six grandchildren.

He's survived two heart attacks and a very serious head-on collision, so he's grateful for every day of life.

Mike likes a curious observation I made in a meeting several years ago: "You don't know what you don't know 'til you don't know it."

I don't know a lot of things. But I do know this: I love Mike Melcher like a brother.

*   *   *

Hope English

Where there's Hope, there's hope

I owe an incalculable debt to Hope Ott English for two keystone events in my life.

First, she introduced me to my future wife in the fall of 1965 when we were all in what we called "Dummies Geometry" at Plainview High.

When the alumni director's job came open at Wayland in 2006, Hope encouraged over dinner with Carolyn and me, "Danny, why don't you apply for that job at Wayland."

I first dismissed the idea, figuring I would drop dead at my desk at *The Herald* when I was about 80—if they kept me around that long. The more I thought, "You know, if I'm ever going to make a career move, age 58 might be it," the more I decided I should follow Hope's advice.

Forty-five years with one great woman and more than eight years at a very satisfying second career are great blessings from God.

A former classroom teacher and then Coordinator of Advanced Academic Services for the Plainview school district, Hope was Director of Leadership at Wayland before joining the Advancement staff seven years ago.

As Director of Donor Relations, she has done an excellent job in every area of responsibility, especially stewarding the individuals, families, and organizations that have endowed scholarships that will continue to benefit Wayland students until the Lord's return.

Full of enthusiasm, passion, energy and ideas, Hope is a gifted organizer, especially for Wayland's Centennial Gala in 2008 and, for *the* past three years, the Power of the Purse, a women-in-philanthropy project that has raised more than $100,000 for an endowed scholarship, refurbishing the lobbies of two women's dorms and other university improvements.

The 2002 recipient of Plainview's Woman of the Year award from the Chamber of Commerce and former co-teacher of a singles Sunday School class at First Baptist, she loves her two sons, Chad and Brent, both former PHS golfers, and is a proud "Deucy" to her twin grandsons as well as a granddaughter.

Like all of us, Hope has had her ups and downs. But she is a woman of strong faith and made a comment I will never forget: "God never wastes a hurt if we use it for His glory."

If anybody was ever well-named, it's Hope English.

*   *   *

Jimmy and Donna Dean at home at Christmastime

Donna Dean stands by the statute of her late husband in Jimmy Dean Hall at Wayland Baptist University

Phone calls from Virginia originated in Heaven

I have had some exciting phone calls in my professional career, but none quite like the one I received in May of 2008.

That it came on the National Day of Prayer made it even more special.

When I came to Wayland, I wrote letters to a number of folks I believed had the financial wherewithal to endow a scholarship for $25,000. That money is invested with the Baptist Foundation of Texas and only the interest is used to fund scholarships.

We call it the "Forever Gift" because you never have to put another cent into the scholarship, and it will continue to bless several students each year until the Lord returns.

Because I had met him several times and did a feature for *The Herald* about his autobiography, *30 Years of Sausage, 50 Years of Ham*, written with his wife, Donna Meade Dean, in 2004, I thought entertainer-sausage king Jimmy Dean might have an interest in endowing a scholarship in honor of his mother.

Ruth Dean had cut hair in her home in Seth Ward to help provide for Jimmy and his younger brother Don. She had taught Jimmy how to play the piano.

Jimmy called me in September 2007 and said he might have an interest in a scholarship and would let me know. When I received no response, I emailed Donna since Jimmy didn't mess with this new-fangled communication mode.

"I assume the decision wasn't positive," I said, trying to be as positive as I could via email. She responded, "No, Jimmy is still thinking about it."

While his CPA later told us, "A 10-minute meeting is too long for Jimmy," it was another seven months before the phone call came—first from Donna asking me to return a call to Jimmy.

When I called back, he said, "I want to do something substantial for Wayland. I want to give you a million dollars." It took me a minute to catch my breath.

Now, when you ask for $25,000 and a man says he'll give you a million, you know God is at work.

That phone call came on a Thursday just before lunch. By Tuesday morning the stock had been sold and was in the bank. Jimmy didn't let any moss grow under his cowboy boots.

It was the largest individual gift ever received by Wayland and only ranks behind the $2 million Flores Estate of the early 1960s as the largest gift ever to the university.

When we had a luncheon in Jimmy and Donna's honor in September 2008, Robert Black of the Wayland music faculty was playing hymns. Before the program began, Jimmy looked at me and said, "I wish I could remember Mother's favorite song." In a moment he said, "'Our Best.'"

I knew Robert, who plays by ear, would know the song and as he struck up the tune, Jimmy and I quietly sang part of the refrain:

Our talents may be few, these may be small
But unto Him is due our best, our all.

It was a sweet moment as was his "demand" for a hug after the luncheon. My face was red as a beet.

Sadly, Jimmy passed away in June of 2011 at the age of 81.

The second great call was received from Donna Dean a couple of years ago by Mike Melcher, Executive Director of University Advancement.

Donna had hoped to build a museum to Jimmy and to the Civil War on their property. Their beautiful home, called Chaffin Bluff in the Richmond suburb of Varina, Virginia, sits on a Civil War battleground.

But Donna said she ran into one governmental roadblock after another.

When Mike suggested that the museum in Jimmy's honor be built in his hometown, Donna cried and said it was an answer to prayer.

Subsequently, she gave $5 million for the project. Ground was broken last June and completion is due in the summer of 2015.

Those calls to Plainview may have been made from Virginia, but we believe they were initiated in Heaven.

* * *

Bill and Sue Coward

Tacos and *Hee Haw* on Monday night

One of my fondest memories during college days was Monday nights at Collier Hall, one of three married-student housing complexes built in the early 1960s near 10th and Vernon.

On many Monday nights, upstairs neighbors Bill and Sue Coward would get together with Carolyn and me to eat homemade tacos and watch a new TV program of country music and cornfed comedy called *Hee Haw.*

Sue Perrin and I graduated from Plainview High in 1967, Bill was a year ahead in Seagraves, and Carolyn was a year behind at PHS in 1968.

Sue will never forgive me for mouthing, "We have the worst twirlers in the world," during a pep rally. That she could read my lips as I was standing at the top of the gym while she twirled a baton on the floor is beyond me.

We all piled into their Camaro and went to Six Flags one weekend. The clerk at the motel made Bill and me show our rings to prove we were married.

Hee Haw gave corny an absolutely new connotation, not to mention a different spelling as the setting was Kornfield Kounty with broadcasts on radio station KORN.

It was hosted by country music stars Buck Owens and Roy Clark (who once was part of Jimmy Dean's band) and featured celebrity guests who also participated in the silly one-liners as they popped up in a make-believe cornfield.

Q: What do they call *Hee Haw* in Arkansas?
A: *Lifestyles of the Rich and Famous.*

A regular on that show was Grandpa Jones, brother of former Wayland sociology professor Eugene Jones.

Jones would wash imaginary windows, and voices off camera would ask, "Hey, Grandpa, what's for supper?"

Jones might reply: "Venison rolls with onions an' taters, with a good bowl of okra and t'maters, and a homemade light bread a-golden brown, and the strongest coffee there is around."

The voices would reply, "Yum, yum!"

My favorite character was used car salesman Junior Samples, who could be reached at BR-549. He allegedly couldn't read and frequently muffed his lines.

Two memorable songs came from that show. The first had two people singing four lines to the camera with one turning and half-spitting on the other at the end:

> *Where, oh where, are you tonight?*
> *Why did you leave me here all alone?*
> *I searched the world over and I thought I'd found true love.*
> *You met another and PTHHP! you was gone.*

The other usually had three or four of the regulars, and maybe a big ol' hound, lying near or on the front porch of a shack singing:

> *Gloom, despair, and agony on me-e!*
> *Deep dark depression, excessive misery-y!*
> *If it weren't for bad luck I'd have no luck at all!*
> *Gloom, despair, and agony on me-e-e!*

That aside, there was no gloom or despair on Taco and *Hee Haw* Monday nights.

*   *   *

David Nall

'Ratting' on a college neighbor to his coach

David Nail, now a paint contractor in Justin, Texas, after years of operating a pharmacy there, was running track while I was a student at Wayland.

We both tied the knot in 1969 and lived in the married students apartments.

One night, I stepped out of my front door just in time to see the former Tulia standout taking receipt of a six-pack of adult beverage from fellow trackster Jim Clark, not to be confused with the inventor of Internet browser Netscape from Plainview by the same name.

They didn't see me, but my self-righteousness was indignated so I informed Coach Bill Hardage of this indiscretion. In 45 years of retrospect, I don't think it was something Bill really wanted to know, and I don't know if any punishment was ever meted out.

But, shortly after I began work at Wayland in 2006, David sent a nice contribution. A couple of months later, I went by to see him and we had a great "catching up" visit.

I asked him, gingerly, if he knew about me ratting on him to Bill Hardage many years before.

"Yeah," David acknowledged with a straight face, "and I've never forgiven you for it." Then he broke up laughing.

He went on to tell me he had sent money to a former teammate from whom he had stolen $10 off an ironing board in the dorm when nobody was looking and to the owner of a gas station in Tulia from which he had swiped money, candy, and other items.

The former teammate needed a medical procedure but didn't have the money until David's gift—many times the pilfered amount—arrived unexpectedly.

The gas station owner said he knew David had taken items "under the table" but said he couldn't accept the rather large amount of money Mr. Nall sent as repayment with a repentant spirit. David insisted.

I told him if it had been me, I probably would have sent an unsigned note but certainly no money.

David had just recorded a great CD of gospel and pop music and, long story short, his new career just exploded. He got air play all over the world and won numerous awards.

Maybe that was God's way of saying, "You did the right thing, son, now I'm going to bless you."

At least, that's what I'd like to think.

*   *   *

Dick and Connie Helms

Folding clothes for our best college friends

Our best married-couple friends in college and to this day are Dick and Connie Helms.

Dick came to Wayland in 1965 from Broomfield, Colorado, and was the first Pioneer Pete mascot. He wore a big papier-mache head that featured a coonskin cap.

For at least the first year, Dick also carried a shotgun filled with blanks. When he fired off a round one night, unsuspecting veteran referee Bobby Scott said it scared him enough he thought he was going to have to change his underwear.

Connie Moore and her twin sister, Cathy, came to Wayland from Hobbs, New Mexico, in 1969. Connie, a Wayland cheerleader, later ran a gymnastics studio on the north side of the courthouse square while Dick worked at Plainview Athletics on the west side.

We all went to church together, attended the same Sunday School class, were in a "share group" of young couples on Sunday nights, and enjoyed each other's company frequently.

Their three sons – Jason, Jared and James – all fairly well paralleled the ages of our three children, and their proud of their six grandchildren.

We still laugh when I remind Connie that I would sit in her living room floor and fold clothing straight out of the dryer.

In the mid-70s, the Helmses moved south where he owned Big Spring Athletics for many years, and Connie taught and later was a technology director for the school district.

Several years ago they moved to Seguin, but we see each other here or there, usually once or twice a year.

The distance has never dampened the affection we share one bit.

Greater love hath no one than to fold the clothes of a friend. If that's not in the Bible, it should be.

*   *   *

Collier Hall Apartments at 10ᵗʰ and Vernon

Functional Wayland married student apartments

Though certainly not built for beauty, the Wayland married-student apartments at 10ᵗʰ and Vernon were functional.

Carolyn and I were charged $62.50—all bills paid—for a one-bedroom apartment that included stove and refrigerator.

She bought a champagne-colored French provincial couch when Bain Furniture downtown went out of business, but it seemed a bit out of place for an abode constructed of concrete block.

When we moved a year later, I suspect the maintenance staff had to secure the cabinet screws because Carolyn could slam them with such ferocity when she was mad at her husband, which seemed to be often . . . as well as justified.

The walls were pretty thick but if you opened the medicine cabinet and pressed your ear close, you could detect activity next door.

One morning, shortly after his wife departed for work, one of our neighbors welcomed a female classmate. We soon heard squeaking noises coming from the bathroom and—not wanting to jump too quickly to judgment—assumed they were working on a biology experiment.

Another neighbor used embossed letters to stick on his door declaring himself "Richard Rogers, E."

When a former Marine inquired as to the meaning of "E," Richard said it stood for "Evangelist."

"Well, just because I'm a karate expert, I don't put 'Dale Trimble K,' for Killer, on my door," he sniffed.

Benny Gresham drew the ire of housing director Clyde Herring for posting a butcher-paper sign on the east outside wall that said, "These apartments have cockroaches and Wayland won't spray for them."

I drew similar irritation from Mr. Herring when I came out of my downstairs apartment and declared loudly that basketball player Ted Welch was mad because Mr. Herring wouldn't give him his $50 deposit back.

As I walked out into the parking lot, whom should I see standing outside an apartment upstairs but Clyde Herring.

I guess I should have posted on my door "Danny Andrews, B."

For Blabbermouth.

*　　*　　*

Danny Murphree

Danny Murphree: There's none better

There are good guys in this world, and then there's Danny Murphree.

When I first met the Friona Flash, he was slender, speedy, and very dark-haired. Well, 47 years can cause anybody to go 0-for-3, even if Danny's sport was track.

But when you convert meters to yards, he's still the fastest quarter-miler in Wayland history, noting that 400 meters is three yards shorter than 440 yards.

I came to appreciate this more when I signed up for the Fat Man's 440 at Wayland Bowl one night, running out of gas at the 330-mark and barely wobbling home.

Danny coached at Floydada a while, then returned as interim head coach when Bill Hardage went to East Texas State to work on his doctorate. Danny also coached the Queen Bees basketball team to the state championship in 1971.

After farming in his hometown for 12 years, "Murph" returned to Wayland as Director of Property Management in 1988.

He and the former Linda Allen of Kress got hitched two weeks after we did in 1969. Danny and I have been church friends, deacon brothers, and choir pals for a lot of that time. He received Wayland's Distinguished Service Alumni Award at Homecoming this year. Linda is retired after many years in teaching and administration for PISD and now teaches in the School of Education for Wayland.

Danny's also a good grandpa to the five offspring of sons David, who directs Wayland's maintenance department, and Trent of Corpus Christi, both former PHS Bulldog footballers.

Oh, yeah, and he's Executive Vice President of the Danny Club for which there are no dues, no meetings, and no benefits. Veteran PHS girls' basketball coach Danny Wrenn, a fellow Wayland graduate who guided his team to three straight state championships in 2001–2002–2003, is secretary-treasurer, a largely ceremonial non-job.

I have moved several times over the past 45 years, and I think Danny was a volunteer every time except the last one. You know, friendship only goes so far.

He also "sat up" with me at the hospital after I was in an auto accident nearly 40 years ago. He still flashes a pained expression, followed by a big laugh, when he recalls, "They had you plugged up from both ends."

When you want a definition of "dependable," look in the dictionary and you'll find Danny Murphree's picture there.

*　　*　　*

Gary Abercrombie

Aber: Crown him with many crowns

Another fellow who is the same great guy I met at Wayland nearly a half century ago is Dr. Gary Abercrombie.

Gary was a handsome rascal (well, he still is), a fellow member of Alpha Phi Omega men's national service organization, and generally Mr. Campus. He was recipient of the Citizenship Award in 1973, the highest honor for a Wayland senior.

Janice Hudgins of Hale Center eventually wooed him away from all the other girls who were chasing him, and they have three great kids—Cody, Lauren, and Todd—and welcomed their first grandbaby this summer.

"Aber" went off to dental school in Houston and returned to establish a thriving practice here. He loves it when he has my mouth propped open. "It's the only time he can't talk," Gary tells his assistants.

I can still utter "shmart-alec" well enough to be understood.

In recent years, he has taken to singing the old hymn "Crown Him with Many Crowns" when I venture into his office for him to make another repair.

The only time I have ever seen Gary remotely out of sorts was the day my indoor soccer team was clobbering his with Tanner Terrell scoring one goal after another. Gary sidled up to me and said, "Danny, I put in some of my subs," with direct implication that I should do the same.

Gary is a pretty good golfer, a generous financial supporter of Wayland where he is a trustee and Distinguished Alumni honoree of 1999, and a backer of positive things in his community.

I love him because he's a fellow church member, choir participant, and deacon brother. The thing I admire most about him is that he's been teaching third-graders in Sunday School for more than 30 years.

No telling how many youngsters he has influenced to make their personal commitment to Christ.

He may not have but a crown or two himself, but he'll sure have some big ones when he gets to Heaven.

*   *   *

Wayland gets unexpected extra publicity

Wayland received some unexpected extra exposure in May of 2010 when Carolyn and I attended a Texas Rangers-Kansas City Royals game in Kansas City.

Making contact with almost 30 Wayland alums on a combination business-vacation trip through the Texas Panhandle, Oklahoma, and Kansas, I sent a note to the broadcast booths of Rangers radio announcers Eric Nadel and Dave Barnett and TV announcers Josh Lewin and Tom Grieve, noting that we were attending the game and celebrating our 41st wedding anniversary.

Grieve mentioned the Andrewses being from Wayland, our respective positions, and the anniversary in the fourth inning on TV (FOX Sports Southwest reaches 6.5 million homes in 34 TV markets in Texas, Louisiana, Arkansas, Oklahoma, and New Mexico), while

Nadel gave a similar "special shout-out" in the fifth inning, then added: "Wayland Baptist University. They used to have the best women's basketball team in the country."

"Yes, they did," Barnett responded.

"The Flyin' Queens . . . under Coach Dean Weese," Nadel continued, adding, "In fact, the Dallas Diamonds for whom I broadcast had Coach Weese running the show. That's about the time women's basketball was changing . . . becoming a much more athletic game."

"Thanks to our friend Nancy Lieberman," Barnett added.

After leading the Flying Queens from 1973-79, Weese coached Dallas in the new professional league but was fired by the financially struggling franchise owners at midseason.

Dean went on to coach seven state championships at Levelland High to add to the three he won in Spearman. With a record of 1,207-197, Weese was inducted into the Women's Basketball Hall of Fame in Knoxville, Tennessee, in 2000.

Lieberman, a former college All-American at Old Dominion in Virginia, Olympian, and pro basketball player (including Dallas after Weese departed) now runs a big basketball camp in the Metroplex.

* * *

KHBL Radio and "technical difficulties"

When I started Wayland, I migrated to a small cubbyhole on the second floor of Gates Hall, the stately administration building.

That small enclosure was the home of KHBL Radio—named for World War II veteran H. B. Lambert after his mother gave money for the equipment in his memory.

The station only had 100 watts of power so listeners were basically confined to about a four-block radius. That did not bode well for a big audience for Wayland basketball games aired from the Plainview High School Gym.

Some wag said, "I can pee farther than KHBL gets out."

The station was mostly run by student volunteers. My shift was usually in late evening and, because we only had one 45 turntable to play the latest singles, you had to talk while cueing up the second record if you wanted to play them back to back. Otherwise, you could intersperse the 45s with the big 78 vinyls or play multiple selections from the latter.

One guy wrote to record distributors and had a great classical music collection for more refined listeners who wanted to stay up late. A black basketball player from Indiana hosted "Mellow Fellow's Soul Kitchen" in the days long before rap music was invented.

A staple for evening "Vespers" was Billy Graham's *Hour of Decision*, played on reel-to-reel tape.

One evening a disc jockey failed to properly thread the tape in the receiving reel and when he hit the button, the tape spewed out into the floor.

Thinking quickly, the announcer flipped on the mike and said solemnly, "Due to technical difficulties, *Hour of Decision* will not be heard tonight only."

On Oct. 19, 1967, the lovely Carolyn Fuson kept me out for my 19th birthday until a few minutes before my show (if it had a name, I don't recall it) was to begin at 10 p.m.

Unfortunately, the doors to Gates Hall were locked and I couldn't remember the station's phone number. Carter Frey, an upperclassman at McDonald Hall dorm, said we could pry the screen off Dean Bryan Clemens' office window and possibly gain entrance. But the mission was aborted when the lone campus security officer made his rounds at a most inopportune time.

The next morning I sheepishly apologized to station manager Sammy Norman for failing to show up. He said, "That's OK, I just said, 'KHBL will sign off two hours early tonight only.'"

He might have added "due to technical difficulties."

*   *   *

A bawdy scheme at Wayland? I don't think so

I served as editor of *The Trailblazer*, student newspaper at Wayland, my sophomore and junior years.

Some "firsts" in my tenure included a 12-page (tabloid size) edition and paid advertising ($1 a column inch).

Another first was drawing the considerable irritation of Dean of Students Paul Butler (my junior-high speech instructor) for an editorial that said Wayland should join the 19th century and stop prohibiting coeds from wearing pants to the library and dining hall.

Also, girls playing tennis had to wear a wrap-around until they got to the court, no parading past hormonally juiced males.

Paul, who later wrote an informative and often witty outdoors column when I was at *The Herald*, told me I was impeding his efforts to liberalize the dress code.

Roger Posey, father of current Wayland women's soccer coach Shiloh Posey, wrote a forthright letter to the editor decrying the lack of Christian civility on the part of a bunch of "preacher boys," who walked out on a chapel performance by Efton Smith and his band. OK, they did play some rather worldly music.

Which reminds me that the offertory music at College Heights Baptist Church one Sunday in 1970 was "One Toke Over the Line." Hey, it was OK, because even though a "toke" is a marijuana joint, the song mentioned "sweet Jesus," so it had to be legitimate, right?

Coincidentally, Lawrence Welk thought it was a "modern spiritual" when a young couple sang it on his show. But, I digress.

I'll never forget receiving a letter in response to a picture we ran of a couple holding hands in front of a box to promote "Penny a Minute," which allowed men to keep their date a minute past the 10 p.m. weeknights and 11 p.m. weekends curfew for each penny donated. All proceeds would benefit summer missions.

A letter arrived at the newspaper's office. It was signed by a Clay Miller, Universal Life Church, decrying "this scheme to take advantage of unsuspecting coeds, no doubt dreamed up by some of your more ribald students who have visited the bawdy Mexican border towns."

Let me assure you that in no way was that young woman coerced into having her picture made.

"I always thought Wayland would take its place in Heaven's Top Ten Conference, right alongside Bob Jones University. I hope the brothers at Wayland will return to the business of saving souls," Mr. Miller continued.

After his signature, another line caught my attention. CC: Dr. Roy C. McClung (president of the college).

I called up to the president's suite and the Voice of God answered. Dr. Neil Record, Dr. McClung's assistant, said he had not seen the letter but offered some sage advice: "Danny, I wouldn't worry too much about that letter. Universal Life Church has been known to ordain dogs for a price, and Bob Jones University has 10-foot gates up to keep the sin out."

Wayland had no gates. And though I'm sure there was some sin on campus, we were not guilty of this salacious charge.

As far as the idea being dreamed up by "ribald students who had visited bawdy Mexican border towns," I didn't know anybody who had enough money to travel past Tahoka.

*　　*　　*

Danny and Carolyn pull taffy at a Wayland party in 1968

Memories of fun and folks at Wayland

I still don't know all the strings that were pulled to get me to go to Wayland instead of my intended destination of West Texas State University in Canyon.

I do know that Dr. Neil Record, assistant to President Roy McClung, came to Anthony's in the Gabriel-Wayland Shopping Center in the early summer of 1967 and encouraged me enroll at WBU. I suspect *Herald* Sports Editor Bob Hilburn wanted me to assist him and used his influence.

The plan was for me to attend Wayland a year or two and then transfer to the University of Texas and major in journalism as Bob had done. A "D" in history and strong interest in a local gal named Carolyn Fuson sort of quashed that plan.

I guess Dr. Record stayed too long because Anthony's manager Fred Harrell told me, "Hey, he's not paying your salary."

Anyway, I had four great years at Wayland even though I didn't have some of the typical college experiences since I only lived in McDonald Hall dorm for one semester.

Here are some fond memories:

* The first day of school, outside the Slaughter Hall cafeteria (and don't think that name didn't foster some jokes), two gentlemen introduced themselves to each other in very formal tones: "I am Mahesh Chavda," said the first. "And I am Gerald Askew," said the other. Mahesh went on to become an international evangelist and Gerald was the first African-American newscaster on Lubbock TV, doing the Sunday night news on Channel 13.

* Upperclassmen took advantage of us beanie-wearing "Slime" by yelling "air raid" for a jaunt around campus and dousing us with fire extinguisher foam from atop a women's dorm. This was done by basketball star Chet Sample, recipient this fall of Wayland's Distinguished Alumni honor for his long tenure in sports and the education department at Sul Ross State University in Alpine. It was not his finest moment.

* Mike Ballew of Gainesville was the most unpretentious person I have ever known, even though he did drive a new Cadillac to school his senior year. We were in Alpha Phi Omega, men's national service fraternity, and he still calls me "Scratcher" to this day.

* Irish shot putter Gerard Downes, who ate peas off a knife and sometimes had to be manhandled into the shower to eliminate his "manly odor," was my weightlifting coach at the old Wayland "crackerbox" gym. I could squat 240 pounds, I just couldn't get back up despite Big G's loud encouragement, "Up, Andrews, up!"

* Kenny Wood, son of Vice President Joe Wood, is one of the most talented guys I have ever known. His imitation of Johnny Carson and Karnack the Magnificent on the *Tonight Show* talent presentation is legendary.

* Dr. Estelle Owens from Jasper, Texas, started school the same year I did. She has gone on to become an esteemed Professor of History, University Historian, and recipient of the Distinguished Alumni Award in 2013. She said on the university's Centennial video that teachers who don't love students should "go do something else, like sell shoes."

* Dorothy Jamar, a demanding English teacher, told basketballer Charles Hardin of McAdoo and me that we had a "character flaw" when we failed to turn in a paper on time. She might have had one for having her English class write a paper about what they saw in class and half of them said, "The boy by the window in the football jacket (that would be me) is asleep."

* Financial officer Charles Bassett insulted me the first time I met him—probably "Andrews, you knothead"— and has continued unabated for 47 years. Charles coached Summer Baseball for several years and drew the ire of the mother of homerun-hitting Billy Jett by intentionally walking him several times in the city playoffs. "You're hurting his feelings when you walk him like that," Mrs. Jett protested to Charles, who responded, "He hurts our feelings when he hits it out of the park."

* Melba Jo Willis, the secretary in Public Relations, remains one of the sweetest people I have ever known.

* And I think Guy Woods was inspired when he wrote the alma mater in 1950.

On the Plains of Texas
Where the wind sings loud her name
Gateway to a world resplendent
Far and wide her fame
Where the Caprock's firm foundation
Meets a sky of blue
Stands our Alma Mater... Wayland true!

Wayland for thy understanding
Love and gracious care
For thy hopes, thy faith in youth
So kind and deep and rare
May we ever keep thy spirit strong
Thy courage bold
Pioneering Wayland
Hail thy Blue and Gold!

MISCELLANEOUS STORIES

Twilight Zone experience: Lost in America

Directions and I have never been fast friends.

I only recently learned left from right. Seriously, when I broadcast baseball and a ball goes toward the outfield, I have to think "left field" or "right field"? New York's east and California's west . . . right?

My Wayland boss, Mike Melcher, loves to tell about the time I got lost coming home from Artesia, New Mexico, from a Baptist meeting several years ago.

When I got to Roswell at 7 p.m., I called my wife and told her I'd be home about 10. As I drove along, listening to the Dallas Cowboys postgame show, I rolled down the window a time or two and thought, "Gee, it's a lot cooler than it was in Artesia." A little later, I thought, "I should be seeing the lights of Kenna and Elida."

The next time I saw lights the sign said "Encino."

Suddenly, I thought I was in an episode of the *Twilight Zone*, pondering with furrowed brow, "How in the world did I get to Encino?"

After a while, it hit me: I had forgotten to make the turn back east coming out of Roswell and, instead, was headed due north.

Luckily, I had plenty of gas because between Encino and Clines Corner, electricity seems nonexistent.

When I finally pulled into Clines Corner and filled up with ridiculously high (for the time) $3.29-a-gallon gas, I called Carolyn and told her, "I don't think I'm gonna make it home by 10."

The next logical move—by a frequently illogical individual—was to head for Santa Rosa to spend the night and drive home on Monday.

When I called Mike Melcher to tell him what I had done, he couldn't quit laughing.

I did spend the night in Santa Rosa and, thanks to having my Wayland directory, made a couple of visits on the way home to salvage something good out of a mistake.

The next time I left town, headed for Albuquerque, my colleagues Martha Robison and Hope English made sure I had the new GPS they had recently purchased.

I have to brag a bit that I have driven on the Los Angeles freeway and right into downtown Manhattan without incident, though I was relieved that a bellman offered to drive our rental car to the local agency.

Sadly, "getting lost" stories are all too common for me. I can't tell you how many times I've heard the voice on my GPS saying, "Make a U turn; make a U turn." This, of course, was after my wife discovered the unfamiliar language we were hearing was Turkish and the appropriate adjustment was made.

In 1985, our family took an excursion to see my brother in suburban St. Louis and my sister in suburban Chicago. Running into a dead-end in Webster's Grove, Missouri, we headed into East St. Louis, not exactly the safest place in the world, we had heard.

My wife, ever the practical one, suggested I "get us out of here."

I, ever the clever one, asked, "What do you want me to do, turn this thing into a helicopter?"

Finally, we see a guy in a van, flag him down and ask directions to Chicago. "Go up here about a mile and turn right." We do . . . and drive what seems like 50 miles until I, ever the intelligent one, determined that we were going the wrong way.

I pulled into a gas station and out walks a guy with a red rag in his pocket. "I'm about as lost as anyone can get," I moaned.

"No, there's always someone more lost than you are," he said with a reassuring tone.

A couple days later, I nearly caused my brother-in-law to have a heart attack when I turned onto a one-way street in downtown Chicago.

Trying to find Old Alexandria, Virginia, a touristy spot not far from Washington, D.C., I walked into a convenience store. Just as I started to ask the Korean clerk for directions, he said, "You go down here to the red light, take a left . . ."

Apparently, he had many equally lost-looking people come into the store asking for directions to Old Alexandria.

Driving in Chicago one evening, I thought an Egyptian clothing store looked familiar. It did. I had made a full circle and was passing it for a second time.

In the summer of 2013, Carolyn and I hosted Wayland events in Nashville and Knoxville, Tennessee. We got lost trying to get out of Nashville, having left our GPS in our car back in Dallas and finding the gizmo on our phone less than accurate.

We also got lost trying to find a floral shop in Knoxville and saw half the city trying to get back to a luncheon at a restaurant near the University of Tennessee.

And our GPS took us to the Alamo Rental Car *storage lot* at the Nashville airport on the return trip. Once in, you can't back out without tearing up your tires. By the time a manager came to rescue us and we got through security, they were calling our name to board our connecting flight to New Orleans.

Sometimes traveling ain't no Mardi Gras.

*   *   *

Where did I park that darn car?

I'm notorious for having a poor sense of direction and getting lost. As I just told you, only recently have I been able to tell right from left, but I have friends who say I still don't know down from straight up.

Until one night in 2002, at least I could say I had never lost my own car.

Leaving Covenant Hospital in Lubbock where my father-in-law was a patient, I headed for the east parking garage where I had parked early that morning.

Here, I must admit I had driven in circles for a while, making sure I didn't park in some doctor's spot and risk having my car towed.

That old song by the Kingston Trio, "M.T.A.," kept playing in my head. You know, the one about the guy who gets on the Metropolitan Transit Authority subway in Boston but can never get off. His wife comes down to the station every day and "through the open window she hands Charley his sandwich as the train comes rumblin' through."

When I arrived at the place where I thought I had parked, I couldn't find the 1995 Harvest Gold Chrysler LHS I knew I had driven to Lubbock.

"I did drive that car down here and not the Olds, didn't I?" I began to second-guess myself.

I got back on the elevator at least twice, riding up, then down, walking, looking, and—worst of all—talking to myself.

"Andrews, where is that car? I know I parked it diagonally facing southwest."

Each time, I found no car and just stood there with hands on hips, wondering if I was in some kind of time warp. Or had I, indeed, parked illegally and hospital security had my vehicle hauled off to the city car pound?

Several times I walked to the north edge of the garage, peering down the street, assuring myself that though I had entered the west garage first, I had finally parked in the east structure.

Finally, Jana Bennett and her mother, Nova Sherman—good friends from Plainview—came walking through the garage and asked if I had a problem.

I always have a problem, but the present one was most perplexing, I admitted.

They chuckled and told me to hop in their car and they would help me find the car.

Jana drove slowly—first up, then down the two-lane driveways—as I looked back and forth, insisting the car was parked diagonally facing southwest.

While I'm sitting in the back having this awful senior moment, Nova and Jana question my general sanity.

"Just take me back down to the main entrance. I know I can find it from there," I finally advised, the car growing warmer by the minute to match my red-faced embarrassment.

As we headed to the final turn to exit, there sat the Famous Vanishing Car, facing diagonally *southeast* on the *opposite* side I would have sworn in a court of law I had parked.

Thankfully, I managed to exit the garage without incident, making quite sure I knew exactly where I parked when I returned early Wednesday morning.

After running an errand, I returned to find every single parking space filled on all six floors, figuring I should have either been in the hospital business or the parking garage business or both.

Finding several lots either filled or marked "Physician Parking Only," I settled for a spot in an uncovered lot. Then I headed for the elevator, hoping to find the sky bridge and eventually make the right *left* turn to connect to the main building.

"Next Christmas," I thought, "I'm asking for a compass. And do we have anyone in town who can tattoo (L) and (R) on my hands?"

*   *   *

Taxi! These rides lead to interesting moments

I have had some of my most interesting moments—and most of them fodder for columns—in taxi cabs.

In 1980, Jim Servatius of Midland I wanted to check out Times Square in New York. However, it was a pretty seedy place in those days—totally unlike the splashy billboards and bright lights of today.

I asked an elderly black cabbie, "Can you get in trouble down there?"

"You lookin' for trouble?" he asked.

"No, sir," I assured him.

"Man's lookin' for trouble, he can find it," he said with wisdom dripping from his voice.

On that same trip, Jim, a Catholic, suggested we attend Mass at St. Patrick's Cathedral.

When we tried to hail a cab in front of the Essex House hotel on Central Park, the cabbie first in line turned his back. He saw we had no bags and figured we weren't headed to the airport for a rather expensive ride (about $20).

A Korean cabbie about fourth in line shouted in anger, "He has to take you! Make him take you!" Finally, the man turned around and waved us into the cab. Jim told him, "St. Patrick's Cathedral," and he said, "Where's that?"

Jim was incensed, partly because he assumed the Italian-looking fellow was Catholic and surely would take us straight to the Gothic structure on Fifth Avenue between 50th and 51st streets.

"The national church, and he doesn't even know where it is," Jim said, his voice dripping with acrimony.

Another time in New York, we rode not in a yellow cab—and I understand there are more than 13,000 taxis and 40,000 other vehicles for hire in the five boroughs—but in a Ford Galaxy 500 with a guy who favored Frank Sinatra music on the radio.

A 1992 trip to Chicago included instructions on which taxi service to use from the airport to our hotel and the price: $22.

Advertising Director Jeff Noble and I shared the cab, but when we arrived at the hotel, the driver I judged to be of Middle Eastern descent said the fare would be $28.

Acting as though I had just graduated from an assertiveness training course, I flatly told the driver, "No, the price is $22."

"No, it's $28," he insisted, fumbling for his car radio to get confirmation from the dispatcher whose voice was garbled.

"I'll tell you what," I countered. "I'm going to give you $25, and that includes a tip.

"You must talk to my supervisor," the cabbie said excitedly.

"No, I'm talking to you. You're gonna take the $25, or I'm going to report you to the cab commission," I said, my wool properly steeled.

Apparently intimidated by that remark, the cabbie said, "It is all right. I will take the $25."

"You're darn right you will," I said, picking up my bags as Jeff Noble smiled approvingly.

Actually, I was a bit relieved that the cabbie didn't pull out a gun and drop me on the street.

I was afraid that might happen one afternoon as Dr. Glenn Barnett, Wayland's interim president from 1987-89, and I shared a cab in Dallas.

At an intersection, two hacks got into it over something, stopped the cars, and were standing in the street yelling at each other.

Dr. Barnett and I didn't know whether to bolt and run or just hope the men settled their dispute without gunfire. Fortunately, they did.

It wasn't in a cab but in a shuttle that the driver got mad at another motorist as we came out of Love Field one night. I thought he was going to try to ram the other car as he muttered angrily.

Another time, trying to get from Love to the *Baptist Standard* building in west Dallas, the driver obviously was lost. He finally had to call the cab company and ask for directions. I told him I was sympathetic but was cutting a few dollars off the fare since it wasn't my fault he didn't know where he was going.

But my favorite cab story comes from 1984 when Jesse Jackson was running for president.

Carolyn and I got into a cab in Dallas, heading downtown, when the black cabbie began to rail on Jackson as a philanderer, dishonest, and owner of several mansions.

"I read in the paper he was in town last night. I wish I'd known that. I woulda went up there to that meetin' and told 'em what a crook he is," the driver boasted.

I knew pretty soon he was taking us a rather circuitous route to the hotel but figured, "That's OK, this will be worth a column."

He continued to spew his criticism of Jackson until we arrived at our hotel where I paid several dollars more than normal.

All I could think of was, "Jesse Jackson's a crook, huh? Well, it takes one to know one."

* * *

Danny plays Santa Claus for Mallory Rosetta

Playing Santa was a great Christmas present
(I wrote this column in 2004.)

I have played Santa Claus for schools and other occasions for several years and loved every minute of it.

I love it because I get to dress up in a red suit, white hair and beard, and put a pillow under the coat for padding—not that I need a whole lot.

Of course, I'm not near as authentic looking as my friend Rodney Watson who can grow a full white beard in about a week. His mother made him a very nice suit that puts all others to shame.

This year, I hit every elementary campus—where "my two (or more) front teeth" would seem a logical request for many—as well as Calico Caboose at First United Methodist Church and the Senior Citizens Center. It's the most fun I've ever had playing the Jolly One.

At most places, I just took a walking tour of the rooms, greeted the youngsters (many of whom had to jump out of their seats and hug me), and told them Santa would see them next Friday. Thankfully, few seemed wary of Ol' St. Nick.

I loved the responses of two boys. One turned just in time to see me walk into the room and let out a loud gasp, his eyes wide with amazement that such a legendary person would visit his class.

Another tow-haired fellow with big ears and a deer-in-the-headlights look asked timidly, "Am I on the good list?"

I assured him, "You're on the *very* good list." The look of relief on his face was priceless.

I also got a chuckle out of a darling little girl who took a good look at my attire and said admiringly, "I like your red suit," as though Santa wore any other color.

What I enjoy most is seeing kids I know and watching their expressions when I call them by name or mention a relative of theirs.

The 4-year-old granddaughter of my good friend, Tom Hall, was most impressed, she told her "Dee-Dad," because "Santa didn't just say Mallory, he said Mallory Rosetta."

Several others I knew responded with a puzzled look when I called their name. But this pseudo-Santa didn't fool Kelly Bishop, a tiny 6-year-old at La Mesa, one bit. When I started out of the room, she told a classmate confidently: "That's Mister Danny. He goes to my church."

"You're not the real Santa Claus," one boy insisted, while another punctuated the same declaration with a cautious question mark, "Are you?"

"I don't believe in Santa Claus," said another with a smirk.

My pat response, "Well, if you don't believe, Santa won't come to your house," wiped the bravado right off some faces and elicited immediate loud testimonials from other children in the room: "I believe in Santa!" and "I believe in you!"

Many youngsters wanted to know where the reindeer were. "Back at the North Pole getting in their exercise to be ready for next week," I offered.

Others wanted to know where Mrs. Santa was. "She has to take care of the elves." A precious second-grade boy handed me a little gold ring with a purple stone set in a heart and said, "This is for Mrs. Santa." I wore it on my pinky all day Friday.

"Why aren't you at the North Pole working?" one sharp youngster inquired.

"I'm only in a supervisory capacity. My job is public relations," I said. That seemed to satisfy him.

In most classrooms, I told the youngsters that I used to visit their teacher when she was a little girl, and "she always wanted a dolly or a puppy."

Either that was a very safe guess or the teachers played right along because most responded with a nod of the head and big smile, though one politely chastised, "I never did get that puppy."

The requests this year ran the usual gamut with Gameboys, X-Boxes, computers, pets (including rabbits and hamsters—one boy wanted a penguin; another, maybe the kid with the Rudolph nose that lit up, wanted a reindeer with lights), Barbies, Dora the Explorer, remote-control cars (or "mote control" said one tongue-tied lad), motorcycles, and even clothing leading the way.

But there were the old standbys such as trampoline, marbles, an old Western gun set, and a Pogo stick or things as modest as new crayons or a notebook.

Some of the more surprising responses included five cell phones, a swimming pool, a new room, a jet plane, a fishing rod, karaoke machine, a million bucks, and—every parent's nightmare—a drum set.

Some kids rolled their eyes when Santa asked what they wanted and mulled and hummed a while before deciding, "This is hard," as though they would be stuck with something if they made a bum request.

One animated boy decided he wanted his school to have every grade—even college—so he'd never have to leave. Another said he wanted to be "a little nicer" (maybe nicer than the two little girls who tattled that "my sister isn't being very nice"). A sharp little cookie decided to hedge her bets and said, "Ten thousand wishes."

But the ones that always get you are the kids who respond to the question, "What do you want Santa to bring you this Christmas?" with, "I don't want anything. I just want my mom to be happy. She lives in Chicago and really misses me," or, "My mother is sad because we're moving to Minnesota."

It's hard for Santa to do much about those requests and absolutely impossible when a child requests "a new baby."

My stock reply is, "Have you talked to your mother about this?" and the look usually says, "What does she have to do with it?"

Well, I could go on and on, but I'll close with the delightful parting words of a two-year-old, "Bye, Ho-Ho!"

Hope this job's open again next year.

*   *   *

Danny plays Uncle Sam in fourth grade

Star of stage and but not of screen

I've had a little acting experience in my life.

My first big role came as Uncle Sam in a play at Hillcrest Elementary. My mother made my red, white, and blue costume, complete with top hat, and also helped me dress up as Hans Brinker, he of the Silver Skates, the next year. Unfortunately, I didn't know anybody in Plainview who owned ice skates, so I toted a pair of roller skates.

In an eighth-grade play at Coronado Junior High when Paul Butler, later Dean of Students at Wayland Baptist University, was my teacher, I played a cowboy. My signature line was, "Shoot a mile oatmeal." I have no idea what that meant.

In 2003-2004, I had a part in three productions, playing the Kevin Pollak role (third banana to Tom Cruise) in *A Few Good Men*, a collaboration of the Wayland Theater Department and the Plainview Civic Theater; a dorky guy in a church Christmas presentation; and some scenes in the Civic Theater's production of *Laugh-In*.

I was supposed to play the judge in *Miracle on 42nd Street* but several issues kept that play from ever making the stage. I also played country comedian Jerry Clower in one of the *Hee Haw* shows at The Fair.

Despite the call for extras when Paramount shot scenes for *Leap of Faith* here in 1992, I never "auditioned" nor trekked up to Groom to be in scenes there as many Plainview folks did.

However, I was involved in the filming of *Rookie of the Year* a little later that year—well, sort of.

Carolyn and I made a trip to Chicago and decided to take in a Sunday afternoon baseball game at Comiskey Park when the White Sox played the Cleveland Indians.

We stopped by the organist's booth and I asked if she would play "Deep in the Heart of Texas" but she politely declined.

As I waited in line to purchase tickets, the young woman ahead of me told the woman at the window that she was with 20th Century Fox and was there to film scenes for *Rookie of the Year*.

I tapped the woman from the studio on the shoulder and said confidently, "I have acting experience."

Actually, I didn't, but I quickly told her that scenes from *Leap of Faith* had been shot in Plainview back in early summer.

"Hang around after the game. We'll be shooting scenes," she suggested.

Throughout the game, the scoreboard reminded the crowd of the filming and that some nice prizes would be awarded.

As it turned out, the game went 13 innings so there were only 3,000 or so folks still around at the end. But most of them dutifully filed down close to the field and heard instructions from director Daniel Stern, the tall, skinny, goofy guy in the *Home Alone* movies and *City Slickers*.

Fans were asked to "get into" the scenes and boo the main actor, who was a kid playing for the Chicago Cubs. Since White Sox fans despise their cross-town rivals, we heard words not suitable for public print.

Carolyn and I tried to be enthusiastic about this make-believe game without saying any bad words.

Former major league pitcher Tim Stoddard—wearing a Dodgers uniform—was on the mound. He'd toss a ball toward the plate and the kid would take a mighty swing. Then a guy out of camera range would hit a long fly ball to right field. The kid would take off in this dorky run around the bases to a chorus of catcalls from the stands.

They shot the scene three times before we decided it was time to leave. From watching *Leap of Faith* filming, I realized movie making's not nearly as glamorous or exciting as it would appear, especially if you don't blow up any cars.

A month later, I happened to be back in Chicago for another meeting, and drove past Wrigley Field (home of the Cubs) late on Saturday afternoon. They were winding up filming.

Of course, when *Rookie of the Year* came out, Carolyn and I couldn't wait to see if we made the cut.

Let me just say this. If we did, they would have had to stop the projector and blow the frames up about a thousand times to see if we remotely showed up.

All I could think of in regard to the film makers was "What a bunch of bums!"

Or worse.

*   *   *

Beanie Andrews

That man is the preacher of my church

My dad's youngest brother, Ardeen "Beanie" Andrews, was the great storyteller in a family full of windy recollections—not all of them true and the true ones liberally embellished.

My brother has done some genealogy and says our 17th great-grandfather was a French Huguenot who fled France because of religious persecution and wound up in England, taking up with folks who built the Mayflower.

I told Guy that if Uncle Beanie had gotten hold of that story, that grandfather would have *single-handedly* built the Mayflower.

Beanie told how in the mid-1960s, he walked into the post office in Dumas, where he owned Andrews Furniture Store, and one man said, "Hey, how you doin', Reverend?"

Not thinking much about it, Beanie got his mail, and as he started out the door, another guy called out, "Whadda ya know, Preacher?"

Beanie asked what was up and one of the men asked, "Didn't Ivan Boxwell tell you?" He was referring to a local funeral director.

Sometime earlier, Beanie and Uncle Ross Andrews, a former postmaster in Lockhart, were headed to Eagles Nest, New Mexico, to fish, when a Buick passed them at a high rate of speed.

Shortly after, they saw the lights of a highway patrol unit flashing behind them.

Beanie says he explained to the officer that a car had passed them and must have turned off.

Unimpressed, the officer said he had three days to plead his case before the justice of the peace in the next town.

Beanie claims he told the same story to the judge who said he would check with the officer, but if he felt the ticket was justified, he would send him notice of the fine.

At that point, Beanie is **alleged**—and I underscore, boldface and italicize that word—to have said, "That's fine. You send it and I'll bring every lawyer in Moore County, and we'll burn this courthouse down."

A couple of weeks later, Ivan Boxwell got caught in the same speed trap, and when he went to see the same judge, noticing Ivan was from Dumas, he pulled Beanie's ticket from his lap drawer and asked, "Do you know this Ardeen Andrews fellow?"

"Yes, sir," Ivan said with a straight face, "he's a good man. He's the preacher of my church." Actually, they had only ushered together at First Christian Church in Dumas.

I believe the judge tore up the ticket. But Ivan had to pay—be sure your sins will find you out.

Beanie told another story on Ivan Boxwell. Seems he and an assistant were transporting a body to a northern Panhandle community when they stopped for a restroom break.

While Ivan was gone, a man walked up to the hearse and asked the attendant if he might hop a ride since his car had broken down and he was trying to reach the home of his brother who was quite ill.

"Sure," said the assistant, "but you'll have to ride back there with the casket." The man thanked him and crawled in.

A few minutes later the trip resumed. The passenger scooted up near the front and said, "Dang, it's kinda cold back here."

Ivan Boxwell almost had a heart attack since the assistant had failed to tell him there was an extra "body" in the car.

*　　*　　*

Heading to the "fraidy hole" when storms arise

When I think about storms and tornadoes, I'm reminded of how we used to go to the "fraidy hole" when bad weather came up.

And it seemed to come up pretty often between the mid-1960s to mid-1970s, including the deadly tornadoes that hit Plainview in 1970 and again in 1973.

The basement of College Heights Baptist Church was our place of choice back when they had "neighborhood shelters." Those were later discontinued when idiots began to damage the building. The fact that quite a few folks brought their pets (nothing against animals, you understand) probably also figured into the eventual closure of the shelters.

Another thing, people potentially endangered themselves and others by waiting until the last minute and then driving like bats out of Hell to get to the shelter.

Carolyn and I were at College Heights the night both tornadoes hit. We listened to the radio when the late Jerry Huddleston, news director for KVOP, reported on the 1970 damage as he drove along Columbia in the station's red mobile unit.

Typically, people would sit and visit, some playing games, and wait out the storm. Menfolk would hang around the entrance, watching and waiting, many hating to be cooped up in close quarters, especially with strangers.

One of my earliest and scariest memories was our family finding shelter in a musty old dirt cellar with other folks as a tornado menaced Paducah one summer evening as we returned from visiting relatives in Childress. Thankfully, the storm cleared quickly.

I never think of tornadoes without recalling the night the big twister hit Lubbock in1970. It killed 26, injured more than 1,500 and did $250 million damage. It came less than a month after a tornado cut through the central part of Plainview. We had to write our stories by lantern light and run the press by generator at *The Herald*.

Carolyn and I had been married less than a year and lived in Collier Hall near the Wayland campus.

The Friday evening the tornado hit Plainview, some of our neighbors, Benny and Sharon Gresham, stopped by our apartment and said they had just been out to the Congress Inn (now Days Inn) where they were having all-you-can-eat fish buffet for $1 a person.

That Friday night fish fry became a big event in this town for several years.

About 10 o'clock, the sirens went off. They were later discontinued because officials contended many people couldn't hear them when the winds were high and home-alert technology was coming on the scene.

It looked like a Chinese fire drill with people spewing gravel as they peeled out of the apartment parking lot trying to get to shelter.

We found out the next day that Bennie and Sharon slept through the storm. I would have felt terrible if they had been blown away because somebody didn't wake them up.

Speaking of gravel, a few loose pebbles put me on my keister one summer night three years earlier. I was at the home of my mentor, *Herald* Sports Editor Bob Hilburn, when a tornado warning was sounded.

We piled into Bob's Olds convertible and raced several blocks to First United Methodist Church. As I was getting his wheelchair out of the car and hurrying to get to the driver's side as the clouds seemed to be diving down on us, my feet went out from under me and I hit the deck with the wheelchair on top of me.

Scared and in pain, I managed to get back on my feet and get myself and the handicapped Hilburn to safety.

Carolyn and I were never too nervous about bad weather, but my friend, Janie Hart, was especially fearful when her two children were small.

Janie, who lived across the alley from our home in Hillcrest, would put Harrison and Ellen in our basement (to which we did not retreat due to weather more than twice in 19 years) and sit up way late watching weather reports on TV.

"We're going to bed. Just lock the door behind you when you leave," I'd tell Janie before heading off to the other end of the house.

I didn't particularly cotton to being down in ours or anyone else's basement in bad weather, but at least that "fraidy hole" didn't reek of musty dirt I can still smell from almost 60 years ago in Paducah.

*   *   *

Order . . . order . . . order in the court!

I've watched enough episodes for *Law & Order* and *Law & Order SVU* and even *Matlock* that I could probably hold my own as a lawyer.

OK, just kidding.

When I think of lawyers, Bill LaFont, who has practiced in Plainview for more than 50 years, comes to mind. Bill and his wife, Peggy, have been major contributors to Wayland's project to become an All-Steinway piano school.

Bill, who grew up in First Methodist Church and has taught Sunday School there for many years, went on an outing with an Episcopal youth group to Palo Duro Canyon and a rattlesnake bit him on the knee.

Obviously, Bill recovered, but I told him had the rattlesnake known Bill would one day become a lawyer, he wouldn't have bitten him out of professional courtesy.

I love the story Bill tells about a rather arrogant attorney who jumped up to make an objection during a trial presided over by 64th District Judge John Thomas Boyd, who later served as Chief Justice of the 7th Court of Appeals in Amarillo.

Just as the man stood up and said, "I object, your honor," his pants fell down around his ankles, revealing a pair of green polka-dot underwear.

The embarrassed barrister assessed the situation and said, "My God, do I object!"

The courtroom was so overcome with laughter that Judge Boyd had to declare a recess.

I also love the story about gravelly-voiced Joe Cox grilling a woman on the stand: "Miz Smith, didn't you realize that man you were living with wadn't ya husband?"

Cox also had Police Chief H. P. Pelphrey on the stand and asked what "HP" stood for on bullets.

"High-Powered," the chief answered.

"Does it always mean that?" Joe quizzed.

"Yes, sir," the chief replied.

"That mean your name's High-Powered Pelphrey?" Joe asked to instant laughter in the courtroom.

Unlike a lot of folks who say they get called for jury duty often, I think I've only been summoned half a dozen times in more than 40 years of being eligible and have only served on one municipal jury and one county court case.

In the municipal case, a young man was charged with public intoxication, but most of us on the jury didn't feel the police proved their case.

However, one woman said she felt if the police had arrested the man, he must be guilty of something.

Reminds me of what humorist Lewis Grizzard said about the difference between "naked" and "nekkid": "Naked is without clothing; nekkid is without clothing and *up to something*."

Let's have some order here!

*   *   *

Sometimes they just don't know my music

I'll never forget going into the old Plainview Savings and Loan years ago when Blaine Smith, a partner with Coleman Williams and George Meriwether in a local accounting firm now known as Davis Kinard and Co., was a teller.

"How's it goin?" Blaine asked.

"Oh, kind of like ol' Tennessee Ernie Ford said," I replied, not elaborating further.

Blaine looked blank, and I said to a fellow teller, "Guess he's never heard 'Sixteen Tons,'" Ford's signature song that said, ". . . another day older and deeper in debt."

Frame of reference is a moving target, depending on your age, background, education, cultural interests, etc.

That reminds me of what humorist Lewis Grizzard said: "The worst part about dating younger women is they don't know your music."

Perry Dorrell, an advertising salesman for *The Herald* two decades ago, said he saw two teenage girls in a record shop in Beaumont looking at cassette tapes when one remarked to the other, "I didn't know Paul McCartney (part of arguably the most famous musicians of all time, The Beatles) was in another group before Wings."

Another group?

Sometimes younger folks don't know my music.

*   *   *

East Texas and West Texas difference

Some folks say a trademark of West Texans is how friendly they are.

Maybe to a fault.

But I love how Phil Kenley, a former employee of Garrison Texaco from Sulpur Springs, explained the difference between East Texas and West Texas folks.

"Here I can go into United and see 10 people I don't know and they all speak to me. I go back home and go into the supermarket and see 10 people I do know and none of them speak to me."

*   *   *

Can you describe the snowman?

My daughter's father-in-law, Tom Peltoma of San Angelo, said he used to really go all out decorating the yard for Christmas.

One year, he discovered a certain decoration stolen and reported the theft to police.

A black officer arrived and asked what had been stolen. Tom told him, "My snowman."

Very seriously, the cop inquired, "Can you give me a description?"

"Yes," Tom began, serious himself, "he's a little white guy, about four feet tall, with two black eyes, a carrot for a nose, a scarf, and a top hat."

The cop busted up laughing and said, "Guess I asked for that, didn't I?"

*　　*　　*

Norman Wright

Flying those usually friendly skies

Because of being associated with a Hearst newspaper, going on mission trips, taking sports-related ventures, and personal travel, I have flown into 70 airports in this country and abroad.

That runs the gamut from most major cities in Texas to Los Angeles, Denver, Detroit, and New York, to Moscow, Russia, to Helsinki, Finland, and Recife, Brazil, site of many of the World Cup soccer games last summer.

Most of my journeys through the "friendly skies" have been pleasant and reasonably uneventful, though I have had some bumpy excursions.

The first time I ever flew commercially was on a Trans-Texas from Austin to Houston to watch a Houston Astros game after my senior year in high school. Years later I flew Southwest and co-founder Herb Kelleher was passing out peanuts.

On a Dallas-to-Waco flight on Rio Airlines—dubbed by some as "Tree Top Airlines" due to the low altitudes at which they flew—the passenger manifest included me and one other guy. I arrived safely; my bag had been left behind in Big D.

In 1969, I flew in an Aerocommander with Delbert Howell to the National AAU Tournament in Gallup, New Mexico. Delbert let me take the controls for a few minutes but reminded me as I gently pulled back on the wheel that the mountains were still a long distance away.

Before the flight began, Delbert asked the rather large Bob Hooper to move to the other side of the plane to give it balance. Bob was a huge sports fan, barking, "White, white, white!" from his mid-court perch at Bulldog Gym any time a ball went out of bounds, trying to help the officials rule for the home team.

He also would command, "Hup, two, three, four!" when a visiting manager went to the mound in a Plainview Ponies minor league game. He had pledged to symbolically "bury the hatchet" behind home plate at Jaycee Park with Grover Sikes, who had been hired away from Pampa to manage the Ponies in 1957. Sadly, Sikes and his wife were killed when their car collided with a train.

When Plainview played El Paso Andress in the 1978 football playoffs, a group of us took a Southwest Flight that was just $25 each. I recall that trip because Phil Carpenter said he liked to sit at the rear since he'd never heard of a plane backing into a mountain.

Speaking of mountains, the previous spring Flying Queens fans heading to Los Angeles for the national tournament were waylaid in El Paso by a faulty engine. "We could fly with three engines," the pilot said, "but that might not be a good idea over the desert." I wholeheartedly agreed.

In 1982, Norman Wright and I were scheduled to fly into Jacksonville, Texas, to hear a preacher. The skies were very soupy but, since I couldn't help Norman, I read Chrysler chairman Lee Iaccoca's book all the way. We didn't see land until we were about 500 feet from the ground. Norman said it was the most difficult instrument landing he had ever made. Good for him, I thought, not to mention me.

Norman was flying during a trip to hear another preacher. He virtually screwed the plane to the ground on the Snyder airport's windy runway. I looked behind me and Lanny Voss was white as the proverbial sheet.

The smell of jet fuel was almost overpowering on an Aeroflot flight from Simferopol, Ukraine to St. Petersburg, Russia, on a mission trip. A giddy attendant let his friends get a few puffs of oxygen to better keep from passing out.

On a flight back from the National Women's Basketball Hall of Fame in Knoxville, Tennessee, where his late father, Claude Hutcherson, had been inducted, Mike Hutcherson caused me a bit of alarm by going sound asleep. Thank goodness for autopilot.

My favorite story, though, is the time Mike flew Wayland President Roy McClung, Flying Queens coach Dean Weese, Carolyn, and me to Wichita Falls for a Pioneers playoff game.

When I awoke from a nap, Dean said we were setting down in Lubbock because the weather was bad, and we'd have to drive home. Turns out that Mike had turned the plane around and we were flying back to Wichita Falls.

We checked into a motel, not looking forward to spending the night in our skivvies. The clerk gave Dr. McClung the key to an occupied room. Fortunately, he came to no harm.

The skies weren't too friendly that night and the folks in the room might not have been either.

*　　*　　*

Paul Sadler

In the hot pursuit of trivial information

I've never been one much for board or parlor games—Monopoly the exception. But I love Trivial Pursuit.

That's because many friends have said, "Andrews, you have so much crap in your head, you're perfect for this game."

Walter Wright, choral director at Plainview High for the past 30 years, said he would use me as his "Life Line" if he ever was chosen to be on *Who Wants to be a Millionaire*. By the way, Walter did win a chifforobe on *The Price is Right* during a choir trip to California.

One Friday years ago, I went to my appointment with Dr. Stewart Webb, longtime optometrist whose office was in the Skaggs Building at the time. He had a globe in the waiting room, so I wiled away the time by looking at capital cities on the globe, noticing the capital of Morocco is Rabat.

That evening, Carolyn and I went to Walter and Sharon Wright's to play Trivial Pursuit, and I promise you this question came up: "What is the capital of Morocco?"

"Ruh-baht," I said slowly and distinctly.

Howls of disbelief erupted from the Wrights and several other couples. "How did you know that?" someone demanded.

"Until today at noon, I didn't."

I say that trivia is only as good as the questions to which you know the answers.

But, as stunned as the people at the aforementioned party were, so was I when I posed a question to Dr. Paul Sadler, Dean of the School of Religion and Philosophy at Wayland.

"Who stole home for Cincinnati in the World Series against the Yankees in 1961?"

I was certain that Paul—a big sports fan—would have no clue about such a random item.

He thought for a moment and then responded, "Elio Chacon."

I almost fell to the floor and assured him, "I am in the presence of trivia greatness."

*　　*　　*

The Classics Four: None can compare
(*I wrote this column in 2004*)

I felt a bit sad and a bit nostalgic last week when I came across a 1994 story announcing the death of humorist Lewis Grizzard.

Can it really be 10 years since the Atlanta—based columnist, author and stand-up comedian passed on?

I was also sad to thumb through the pages of *The Herald* last week and realize that not only is Grizzard (pronounced Gruh-zard) gone but also three other features I would put in the "classic" category—the

Calvin & Hobbes comic strip, Erma Bombeck's humor column and the Far Side comic.

I say "classic" because no one has been able to replace or match those features.

They would be in the Bob Hope-Katherine Hepburn-Babe Ruth-Albert Einstein category. Those four alone were worth the price of the paper.

And their absence from *The Herald* is through no wish of ours: Ms. Bombeck died two years after Grizzard and C&H creator Bill Watterson and Far Side genius Gary Larson decided to discontinue the daily grind but still offer plenty of their products via other venues.

We were among the first papers to buy the Grizzard's column. It ran for 14 years and I liked it because he was my age, from the South and I could relate to his life's experiences.

My favorite Grizzard column—and he could make anything funny— was about riding in a taxi with "an Egyptian AJ. Foyt" who drove fast and wild and yelled "Yakma doonga!" in response to every question Grizzard asked.

At the end of the ride, Grizzard handed the man a $10 bill and when he gave him back his change, Grizzard stuck the extra money in his pocket. The irritated taxi driver said in perfect English: "What, no tip?"

To which Grizzard replied tersely: "Yakma doonga!"

I bought the Calvin & Hobbes cartoon because I thought it would appeal to our younger readers, but it seemed to be a hit with everybody.

Calvin, the brash, wirehaired, modern-day Dennis the Menace, and his imaginary tiger friend launched off into many a wild adventure in their "transmogrifier"—otherwise, a simple cardboard box.

The Far Side took a weird look at the world, often through the eyes of animals or monsters. I always said, "There are people who understand the Far Side and those who *say* they understand the Far Side."

A couple of my favorites:

* Cows are STANDING in the pasture talking. As a vehicle approaches, one shouts, "Car!" and they all get down on all-fours and begin grazing. As soon as the car passes, they stand up and start talking again.
* A Neanderthal has thrown a spear at a mammoth, just missing his target. Several of his kind, hiding behind nearby rocks, yell in uinison, "Air spear! Air spear!" as fans would do on a missed shot in basketball.
* A fellow is walking down the street, whistling as he goes. From a side street, a truck approaches. A collision appears imminent. The caption reads: "Joe was walking down the street and was suddenly run over by the Old Age Truck."

Boy, do I relate to that.

Erma Bombeck, who could write very poignant, heartwarming or heart wrenching columns, was best known for her sassy, sometimes quirky humor.

* "Shopping is a woman thing. It's a contact sport like football. Women enjoy the scrimmage, the noisy crowds, the danger of being trampled to death, and the ecstasy of the purchase."
* "Never go to a doctor whose office plants have died."
* "Seize the moment. Remember all those women on the Titanic who waved off the dessert cart?"
* "Every day of his or her life a child is plotting an event that will age you 20 years in 20 seconds."
* "Education is so important when it comes to domesticity. I don't know why no one ever thought to paste a label on the toilet tissue spindle giving 1-2-3 directions for replacing the tissue on it. Then everyone in the house would know what Mama knows."

* "I'm trying very hard to understand this generation. They have adjusted the timetable for childbearing so that menopause and teaching a 16-year-old how to drive a car will occur in the same week."
* "Most children's first words are "Mama" or "Daddy." My kid's first words were, "Do I have to use my own money?"
* And my all-time favorite: "Relatives start to smell after two or three days"

Yep, the Classics Four.

*   *   *

Mr. Principal, can you please spank my child?

Ron Miller, who later became superintendent of Plainview schools, asked me to be Principal for a Day when he was holding that post at College Hill Elementary.

My job was to shadow Ron one morning and then have lunch.

All went routinely until a young woman showed up with her five-year-old daughter in tow, asking if Ron could spank her because she just wouldn't mind.

I don't know if Ron would have let me stay in his office while he applied board to butt, but I was glad to get a phone call about that time from The Herald.

Ron administered a couple of hearty swats, accompanied by howls from the youngster.

"Do you get this kind of request very often?" I asked.

"You'd be surprised," Ron replied.

I already was.

*   *   *

A clever but costly practical joke

I've never been one for practical jokes, but this is told as a true story.

In the early 1950s when the Korean War was on, Lloyd Woods (later to become mayor of Plainview) sent a couple of fake telegrams to insurance partner James Wallace Davenport.

The first said something like, "Capt. Davenport, you are hereby ordered to report for active duty to Camp Hood, Texas, on or about June 16, 1952."

The story goes that Davenport sold his car in preparation for moving. He received another telegram or two before the Western Union manager got nervous about possibly getting into trouble for his part in this charade.

When he walked into the insurance office and picked up the latest missive, James Wallace saw him and the light came on.

He jumped up and starting screaming obscenities at Lloyd, who ran out the door. James Wallace chased him up Austin and down Broadway, threatening bodily harm if he caught him.

Sometime later the two men were out on a business visit when a dog began chasing Woods. Davenport locked the car doors but Lloyd leaped on the hood, then on the roof, and jumped up and down until it caved in.

That's what I call an expensive practical joke.

*   *   *

NBC "Today Show" personality 'plugs' Plainview

NBC's "Today Show" hit the airwaves 62 years ago and longtime viewers may recall that Plainview received some publicity from that program thanks to a local connection.

Jack Lescoulie, a veteran show business personality, was a friend of Plainview native and NBC executive Jimmy Fletcher and got into the habit of including Plainview in his morning weather forecast.

Although he had sandy red hair, Plainview folks really didn't find that out for sure until he came to town since "Today" was aired in black and white during Lescoulie's tenure.

In April of 1961—just 11 months after nationally known radio commentator Paul Harvey was Commencement speaker at Wayland Baptist College—Lescoulie came to Plainview to speak at an all-sports banquet sponsored by the Kiwanis Club, dedicated the Babe Ruth Park (named in his honor) on the property now occupied by Wayland's J.V. Hilliard Field, rode in a downtown parade and received numerous accolades.

He was welcomed by banners that said "Plainview, Adopted Home of Jack Lescoulie" and was accompanied by Hots Michael, a piano player, mind reader and hog raiser (in his backyard) from Chicago; Col. Pat Young, a highly-decorated veteran who was chief Marine information officer in New York, and Fletcher.

Lescoulie started in show business at the age of 7 in 1924 with a song-and-dance routine with his sister. He later did animal sounds (such as elephants and parrots) and cartoon voices.

He served as a combat reporter during World War II and later started a popular early-morning radio program in New York with future TV game show host Gene Rayburn. He became a producer for CBS-TV and then joined Dave Garroway when "Today" debuted Jan. 14, 1952.

Lescoulie opened the first show with these words: "This is Today, January 14 on NBC. We are in touch with the world . . . we will keep you informed."

He did a lot of features on the show, including anything having to do with sports (he was a former sports broadcaster) and also the weather.

He briefly hosted "Tonight: America After Dark," in 1957, after Steve Allen left the "Tonight" show.

Lescoulie once said, "The closer you come to being yourself on the screen, the longer you last (because) on television there's always the risk of a quick shot in an off-guard moment, a chance insight; and if you're playing a part, you'll be exposed."

Dave Garroway was among half a dozen prominent well-wishers to send a congratulatory telegram to the toothy Lescoulie on his visit here. It said: "Dear Teeth, have a great time and add some love and peace (Garroway always signed off by saying "Peace") to our friends in Plainview."

The visiting entourage got boots and hats and a complete western outfit for Lescoulie's three children.

The four visitors wowed the audience by singing the Plainview High School song (to the easy tune of "O Christmas Tree"). They also told no off–color jokes because they reportedly spent the afternoon screening each other's stories.

On "Today," the following Monday, Garroway was absent and Lescoulie hosted the show, saying he had the "time of my life" over the weekend in Plainview," acknowledging Mayor M.B. Hood and all the courtesies paid him.

He had vowed he would come back but he eventually faded from the picture and died in 1987 at the age of 69.

*   *   *

Eddie Turner

I can't afford the prices they charge here

Eddie Turner, who got out of Wayland the year after I did, has managed the Wayland University Store for 40 years.

Blessed with a beautiful tenor voice, Eddie led music at First Baptist Church in his hometown of Hale Center for 38 years before retiring last year.

At our Ring Ceremony, he has been gracious to sing a wonderful song called "No Small Dreams," written by Wayland music professor Dr. Gary Belshaw as part of the Centennial celebration in 2008.

The title comes from a favorite saying of Dr. A. Hope Owen, president of Wayland from 1953-63. The first verse says:

> *Dream, dream no small dreams*
> *Pursue no trivial visions*
> *For they have no power*
> *To inspire the souls of men.*

Eddie is part of the "Old Men's Club" at Wayland that also includes Tom Hall, Paul Sadler, Danny Murphree, and me. We regularly eat lunch in the cafeteria and either try to solve or add to the world's problems.

Tom has good-naturedly, but with a sour expression, gotten on Eddie's case about one thing and another for years. He loves to recall the time Eddie was rummaging through his lap drawer and Tom asked, "What are you looking for?"

"I'm trying to find some breath mints," Eddie said, continuing his search.

"You've got all kinds of breath mints up at the counter," Tom reminded.

Without looking up, Eddie responded, "I can't afford the prices they charge in here."

Now that's an inspirational response.

*   *   *

Two unusual high school alma maters

Every time Plainview and Pampa met in football, you were always assured of hearing two familiar songs.

That's because the PHS Alma Mater was written back in the 1930s to the tune of "Maryland, My Maryland" or a more familiar title, "O, Christmas Tree" and Pampa's school song was to the tune of "Let Me Call You Sweetheart" – "Dear Old Pampa High School, we're in love with you."

In case you made it through Plainview High School without learning the song, or can't remember all the words, here it is:

> The name that thrills with every sound
> Is Plainview High, Our Plainview High
> We 'll shout its praises, round and round
> Plainview High, Our Plainview High

We'll fight for honors on the field
We'll force our strongest foes to yield
While 'blazoned on our warrior's shield
Is Plainview High, Our Plainview High

To thee we give our sacred trust
Plainview High, Our Plainview High
Our banner n'ere must touch the dust
Plainview High, Our Plainview High
With courage bold, we hoist to view
Our Scarlet Red and Navy Blue
To show the world we're proud of you
Plainview High, Our Plainview High

I was surprised a couple of years ago to hear the strains of Texas Tech's "The Matador Song" being played by the Dumas High School Band. Since Dumas is older than Texas Tech, I wondered if Tech stole its music from the Moore County school or that tune was actually written by someone else.

Nonetheless, partly because my daughter finished her secondary education at Texas Tech, I learned "The Matador Song" and love the last four lines:

Fearless champions ever be.
Stand on heights of victory.
Strive for honor evermore.
Long live the Matadors!

On the subject of songs, while I wrote a column years ago about the development of the Plainview High Alma Mater, I never found the origin of the fight song that goes:

Fight, Bulldogs, win the game
On to victory
Shouting with loyalty supreme
We'll flash the colors of our team
And we will fight
Fight, fight, fight

Fight, Bulldogs win the game
On to victory, on to fame
Make it clean, make it true
You can beat 'em if you do
So it's fight, fight, Bulldogs fight

Several years ago I was watching a Navy-Notre Dame game and heard the fight song tune in the background. . . never having heard it anywhere other than at a Plainview High game. But when I called the band departments of both universities and hummed the tune, persons answering the phone both said that song wasn't part of their repertoire.

Maybe a high school band happened to be on hand and playing the song that day. Or maybe my humming sounded like a combination of "O Christmas Tree" and "Let Me Call You Sweetheart."

*   *   *

Tom Baker...a true Optimist

I liked being a member of the Optimist Club

I was a member of the Noon Optimist Club for about 35 years, serving as president in 1978-79.

Unfortunately, the club disbanded in 2012 after serving this community for 65 years—most auspiciously as sponsor of the Summer Baseball Program for more than 40 seasons.

I always thought the Optimist Creed must have been written by a preacher who jotted down several good ideas for a sermon but couldn't settle on one:

Promise yourself. . .

* To be so strong that nothing can disturb your peace of mind.
* To talk health, happiness and prosperity to every person you meet.
* To make all your friends feel that there is something in them.
* To look at the sunny side of everything and make your optimism come true.

* To think only of the best, to work only for the best, and to expect only the best.
* To be just as enthusiastic about the success of others as you are about your own.
* To forget the mistakes of the past and press on to the greater achievements of the future.
* To wear a cheerful countenance at all times and give every living creature you meet a smile.
* To give so much time to the improvement of yourself that you have no time to criticize others.
* To be too large for worry, too noble for anger, too strong for fear, and too happy to permit the presence of trouble.

The late Manuel Ayers, who worked for Cloverlake Dairy and later was a Farm Bureau agent, convinced me to join the club, and nobody better embodied Optimism than the late Tom Baker, who also was an insurance man.

I enjoyed Optimist meetings each Tuesday at noon, regardless of whether we met at the Hilton Hotel, the Holiday Inn, Country Club, or the Cotton Patch while I was attending, eventually becoming the oldest active member of the club.

Some memorable events:

* The late Ken Haralson sat in his chair, wet from a glass of water poured in it, then jumped to his feet and slapped Roger Horan in the back of the head. I thought we were about to witness a big fight until I realized they were brothers-in-law and Roger loved playing jokes on Ken.
* A club member, apparently forgetting where he was, prayed: "Lord, thank you for letting us come together to study your Word." It would have been a lot more interesting and profitable than some of the programs we had.
* Another guy, who lived out of town but his business brought him to Plainview each week, was called on to bless the meal.

As we bowed our heads, he began, "I pledge allegiance to the flag . . ." I looked up and Tom Baker's mouth was wide open in astonishment.

*   Donnie Brumley secured the assistance of several other club members to "tag team" a prayer.

A couple of years before the club officially disbanded and turned the baseball program over to the YMCA, I wrote a letter to the national office, stating our intentions.

But when we had our meeting to take the official vote and I asked how many of the members intended to join the Kiwanis Club, which had planned to assume sponsorship of the baseball program, none of the 10 or 12 attending raised their hand, including me—nothing against the Kiwanians.

Discussion ensued and the consensus was "we can't let this club die."

Sadly, about all we did was just buy a little more time.

I always liked what someone said about the difference between a pessimist and an optimist: The pessimist says, "Man, it can't get any worse than this!" But the optimist says, "Oh, yes, it can!"

That's certainly looking at the sunny side of everything.

*   *   *

Close encounters with pachyderms

When I was member of the Noon Optimist Club, we sponsored the Carson & Barnes Circus, headquartered in Hugo, Oklahoma, on three different occasions.

As organizer of one of the visits, I was honored—and I use the term loosely—to ride an elephant at the front of the parade around the tent.

As the big fellow sauntered along, I held onto a rope for dear life, feeling for all the world as if I was about to slide right down its trunk.

I promised the Lord if he'd let me live, I'd never do that again. Same promise many years earlier while riding The Hammer at Joyland Park in Lubbock. Same promise made about five years later when Carolyn and I signed a waiver to ride in a Monte Carlo pace car at the Texas Motor Speedway during a newspaper convention, and the car was doing about 100 mph right along the wall.

The last time the circus came, the elephants were lumbering into the tent just as I was just leaving. I skinnied up as best I could and remained very still as eight or 10 pachyderms marched past.

I was quite grateful they had already done their "business" or chose not to do it as they passed me.

It would not have been a pretty sight.

*   *   *

Dance with the one who brungs you

Anita Mamy, a delightful young lady from the African nation of Guinea, worked in the Advancement Office my first couple of years at Wayland.

I tried to teach her several Texas expressions, including one by the late University of Texas football coach Darrell Royal who said, "Dance with the one who brung you."

I told Anita that meant in football that if the running game is working, stick with it. If the passing game is doing better, stay with that.

Several weeks later, she asked, "Danny, how long have you and Carolyn been married?"

I told her "40 years."

"It looks like you are going to stay with the one who *brungs* you."

The wording was off a bit; the analogy spot on.

*   *   *

No television: How about some Jerry Clower?

My kids claim they were culturally deprived, if not abused, when we went about five years without television after both of ours pooped out at the same time in the late 1980s.

I can't recall what we did to fill the time. Studied, read, maybe even talked to each other. I know anytime we went to someone else's house, the kids were mesmerized watching TV.

I think Carolyn contends I was too cheap to buy a new TV. At least I'm not accused of getting us into a "food cult," as my kids allege she did when organic and natural food was all the rage for the first time 30 years ago.

One thing my kids did was listen to Jerry Clower tapes. This outrageously funny man told true and not-so-true stories about growing up at Rt. 4, Liberty, Mississippi, attending East Fork Consolidated School District, and associating with the Ledbetters—Uncle Versie, Aunt Pet, Ardel, Burnel, Raynel, W. L., Lanel, Odell, Eudel, Marcel, Claude, Newgene, and Clovis.

Pat Marse and I picked up Jerry at the airport in Lubbock on one of his two trips to Plainview to do Chamber of Commerce banquets. I interviewed him in the car and thought, "It's hard to tell where the real Jerry Clower starts and ends since he's always 'on.'"

One night, attired in a red suit with ruffled white shirt and white patent leather boots, he stood on a table in Wayland's McClung Center to tell some of his stories.

As a youngster, he said he hated a staple of his diet, boiled okra. "You eat boiled okry?" he asked. "It'll rope up and slime up on ya. I eat so much boiled okry when I's a kid, I couldn't keep muh socks up."

One of my favorite Clower stories is about the farmer who stole a pair of mules during the Depression, changed their appearance, made a crop with those mules, and fed his family.

However, he was arrested and brought to trial in Liberty, Mississippi. The jury stayed out about 30 minutes and brought in a verdict: The man is innocent, and he can give the mules back.

"The judge thowd a fit. 'The very idea that a man can be found innocent and give the mules back! We got to have justice in this courtroom! You jurors get back in there and bring back a verdict commensurate with the crime!'"

This time the jury stayed out about 15 minutes. "Do you have a verdict?" the judge demanded.

"We have, your honor," the foreman said. "We find the man innocent, and he can *keep* the mules."

As Larry the Cable Guy says, "I don't care who you are, that's funny."

On TV or otherwise.

*   *   *

Sliding under the car, falling in the tub

I've never been accused of being well-coordinated, but some things that have happened to me just have to be ascribed to circumstances beyond my control.

Several years ago, I went to the home of my good friend Tom Baker (I happen to now live in the house he last occupied) to interview his brother-in-law, former PHS, Rice University, and pro football star Bill Howton.

Bill played for Green Bay, Cleveland, and for the first four Dallas Cowboy teams. He was until 1965 the all-time leading receiver in the NFL and was elected in 1958 as first president of the players union.

As I walked to the car on a snowy night, my feet went out from under me and I slid about halfway under the vehicle. Fortunately, Bill was there to help me out and up.

I was casually attired that evening. Not so several years later when I took a fellow, who came to church and alleged to be down and out and needing to get to San Angelo, to the bus station. I bought him a ticket and returned to my car. It had rained, and I slipped on some water and again unceremoniously slid under the car in my nice pinstriped suit.

My first thought was, "Lord, I'm trying to help somebody and here's where I wind up."

Sad thing is, the guy only lived a few blocks from the church and was a "professional bum."

Twenty-five years ago, I was in Beaumont and actually fell *out* of the shower, and a couple of years ago I was getting out of the shower in Denver when I lost my footing and fell backwards *into* same.

The loud "thud" caused my alumni assistant, Blake Durand, to holler, "Are you OK?"

I insisted I was. I feared he might go blind if he came in and saw an old naked man with his legs dangling over the side of the tub.

*   *   *

Tattoos: Two friends reveal their secrets

It's a personal opinion, but tattoos are one of the worst things to ever happen to the human race. However, I admit that when I was at *The Herald*, I thought if I ever got one, it would it would be in the shape of a newspaper and say: Born to Edit.

Several years ago, a friend who was prone to gossip—both spreading and receiving—called me and said, "Did you know Jim Ferrell has a tattoo?"

Now, I was quite close to the Chamber of Commerce manager, a rather conservative chap, and was certain that Jim Ferrell would not have a tattoo.

But, when I inquired as to the veracity of this information, Jim slowly rolled up his sleeve to show off a small but attractive battleship. Only a bit unusual, it struck me, since Jim was an Army man.

When I shared this story with another good friend, Gary Lloyd, telling him I just couldn't believe Jim had a battleship for a tattoo, Gary said, "Like this?" as he rolled up his T-shirt sleeve to reveal a similar but less attractive caricature.

A four-letter expletive issued forth from my mouth as I wondered, "What is this world coming to?"

Well, I knew, because both of them had motorcycles and do-rags. Just middle-aged crazy, that's all.

Jim has moved on to Lubbock where he plays golf eight days a week, and Gary lives in Prosper. I told Gary we quit having funerals in Plainview since he used to sing at about half of them.

One of those funerals would have been mine if my friends had kept up this outrageous behavior.

*   *   *

Karaoke: Nobody throws tomatoes or tortillas

I have never claimed to be a great singer, though I enjoy music of just about all stripes, heavy metal excluded.

Twenty years ago, Carolyn and I served as hosts for a *Herald*-sponsored cruise out of Los Angeles to Catalina Island to Ensenada, Mexico.

One afternoon they had a karaoke session (you sing to recorded music with the lyrics flashed on a screen in case you forget the words), and I decided I'd make my debut in front of total strangers.

Now, if you know anything about karaoke, you know that the folks who want to sing the most are usually the ones who sing the worst. Enough said.

I thumbed through a folder of possibilities and chose Bobby Darin's finger-snappin' 1958 hit, "Mack the Knife."

> *Oh, the shark, babe, has such teeth, dear*
> *And it shows them pearly white*
> *Just a jackknife has old MacHeath, babe?*
> *And he keeps it out of sight.*

I could hardly believe it when a newlywed guy behind me in line asked what I was going to sing and when I told him he said, "Aw, man, that's my favorite song. I was hoping to sing it."

"Go ahead," I said with as much grace as I could muster. I thought I might try Roger Miller's "King of the Road" but lost my courage.

Ten years later, Carolyn and I took a cruise to Alaska and I decided I was not going to miss the opportunity again to sing karaoke. So on consecutive nights I did "That's Life" by Frank Sinatra, "The Gambler" by Kenny Rogers, and "Little Red Riding Hood" by Dallas's own Sam the Sham and the Pharaohs . . . *Owwwoooo!*

Fast forward to 2011 when several of us on a pastor search committee for First Baptist Church went to lunch at Pico de Gallo in downtown San Antonio. Yes, folks were being urged to show their stuff.

When the keyboardist came to our table, my friends—knowing my natural shyness—urged me to sing. The musician suggested "Fly Me to the Moon" by Frank Sinatra, but I was not familiar with that tune. He turned a couple of pages and—if I'm lyin', I'm dyin'—said, "How about this one?"

It was "Mack the Knife." I struggled through it to polite applause.

At least no one threw tomatoes or tortillas.

*　　　*　　　*

Just call it "The Amazing Snake Story"

I don't recall ever publishing anything that got more laughs and response than "The Snake Story."

Arthur Miller, a Plainview High graduate who was a postal carrier in Petersburg for years, sent it to me, and I used it for a column. It obviously wasn't true but it was hilarious, and my dear friend John Anderson said he used it for years anytime he gave a speech.

Reportedly, some truckers saw the paper out at the Kettle Restaurant and were on their CB radios telling other truckers about it.

Here is a longer, more embellished version I found on the Internet.

A couple in Sweetwater, Texas, had a lot of potted plants and during a recent cold spell the wife was bringing them indoors to protect them from a possible freeze.

It turned out that a little green garden grass snake was hidden in one of the plants, and when it warmed up, it slithered out and the wife saw it go under the sofa. She let out a very loud scream.

The husband, who was taking a shower, ran naked out into the living room to see what the problem was. She told him there was a snake under the sofa. He got down on his hands and knees to look for it.

About that time, the family dog came and "cold nosed" him in the butt. He thought the snake had bitten him, so he fainted. His wife thought he had a heart attack, so she called an ambulance.

The attendants rushed in and loaded him on the stretcher and started carrying him out. About that time the snake came out from under the sofa and the Emergency Medical Technician saw it and dropped his end of the stretcher. That's when the man broke his leg, and why he's in the hospital.

The wife still had the problem of the snake in the house, so she called on a neighbor man. He volunteered to capture the snake, armed himself with a rolled-up newspaper, and began poking under the couch.

Soon he decided it was gone and told the woman. She sat down on the sofa in relief. But, in relaxing, her hand dangled between the cushions, where she felt the snake wiggling around. She screamed and fainted, and the snake rushed back under the sofa.

The neighbor man, seeing her lying there passed out, tried to use CPR to revive her. The neighbor's wife, who had just returned from shopping at the grocery store, saw her husband's mouth on the woman's mouth and slammed her husband in the back of the head with a bag of canned goods, knocking him out and cutting his scalp to a point where it needed stitches.

An ambulance was again called and it was determined that the injury required hospitalization. The noise woke the woman from her dead faint, and she saw her neighbor lying on the floor with his wife bending over him, so she assumed he had been bitten by the snake. She went to the kitchen, brought back a small bottle of whisky, and began pouring it down the man's throat.

By now the police had arrived. They saw the unconscious man, smelled the whisky, and assumed that a drunken fight had occurred. They were about to arrest them all, when the two women tried to explain how it all happened over a little green snake. They called an ambulance, which took away the neighbor and his sobbing wife.

Just then, the snake crawled out from under the couch. One of the policemen drew his gun and fired at it. He missed the snake, and hit the leg of the end table that was on one side of the sofa. The table fell over and the lamp on it shattered. As the bulb broke, it started a fire in the drapes.

The other policeman tried to beat out the flames and fell through the window into the yard on top of the family dog. The pooch was startled, jumped up and raced out into the street, where an oncoming car swerved to avoid it and smashed into the parked police car and set it on fire.

Meanwhile the burning drapes had spread to the walls and the entire house was blazing. Neighbors had called the fire department, and the arriving fire truck had started raising his ladder as they were halfway down the street. The rising ladder tore out the overhead wires and put out the electricity and disconnected the telephones in a 10-square city block area.

Time passed and both men were discharged from the hospital, the house was rebuilt, the police acquired a new car, and all was right with their world.

About a year later the Sweetwater couple was watching TV and the weatherman announced a cold snap. The husband asked his wife if she thought they should bring in their plants for the night.

She shot him!

*   *   *

Random thoughts: Sometimes my mind wanders

There's a scene in the Oscar-winning movie, "No Country for Old Men," where Tommy Lee Jones (Sheriff Ed Tom Bell) tells Carla Jean Moss a story about a guy suffering a freak injury while trying to shoot a trussed-up cow ready to be slaughtered.

When he finishes, Carla Jean asks, "Why are you telling me that?" and the sheriff says, "I don't know. My mind wanders."

Well, so does mine, and that's why I'm offering these random tidbits.

* One of my treasured possessions is a night shot of the Texas Capitol with the University of Texas tower, lit in orange, in the background. It was taken by Van Redin of Plainview and given to me by his grandfather, Alvin Redin. Van has taken photos for many movies and promises he'll introduce me some day to one of the all-time great actors, Robert Duvall. Van calls him "Bobby."

* I used to give former Plainview City Councilman John Bertsch, a native of Bismarck, North Dakota, a hard time about proposing that the city buy a snow plow. It wouldn't seem so funny back in February of 1956 when Plainview received 24 inches in 24 hours, a state record that stood for about 50 years.

* Seven former Wayland Flying Queens or Queen Bees and one former Pioneer started the women's basketball programs at and/or served as head coach at major colleges: Marsha Sharp (Texas Tech), Cherri Rapp (Texas A&M and North Texas), Linda Tucker (Rice), Valerie Goodwin (Oklahoma), Judy Bugher (Oklahoma State), Margie Hunt McDonald (Wyoming) and Carla Lowry (Sam Houston State). Bobby Jack Frye, who actually played for the Pioneers on a Flying Queens' scholarship, started the program at TCU and coached for several years. Wonder if any other university can match that achievement.

* I refereed several games for Wayland graduate Joe Lombard at Nazareth and Canyon. He has won 10 state championships at Canyon to go with six at Naz and his overall record is an amazing 1,192-113, which means he's going to beat you nine out of every 10 times you play. The Lombard family has the distinction of having three state championship coaches as Babs won at Hale Center in 1979 and Tate won at Wall last year while Dad was adding another to his list.

* Kenny Redin, who claims he and I called the first games Joe Lombard ever coached at Nazareth, has long contended that the use of eye black to reduce sun glare causes diarrhea. I have not been able to verify that.

* I hope Greg Feris, who recently retired after 24 years as athletics director at Wayland, let new AD Rick Cooper know I would hardly have any shirts were it not for those generously furnished by the athletic department. I also hope Greg told Rick that his wife, Janie, a former Flying Queen, needs to gush over any pictures I show of my grandchildren, as my dear sweet friend Glenda Feris did. Perhaps this comes under "and other duties as should be assigned."

* When a player showed Texas A&M basketball coach Shelby Metcalf his report card with 5 F's and a D, Metcalf surmised: "Looks like you're spending too much time on one subject."

* Wayland played the Aggies at College Station in 1975. The lead on my story said: "One of the more raucous yells in Texas A&M's 117-65 win over the Pioneers on Monday night was 'Beat the hell outta Wayland.' Truthfully, they did."

* The late Colin Coe, a first baseman for the Bulldogs my junior year who got dismissed from school for wearing an FFA jacket with the back cut out, had a zany sense of humor. With a guy on base, you could hear him saying in a gruff voice, "It is and they do," mimicking a commercial where two guys are on another planet and wondering if it's inhabited and if the residents like Oscar Mayer wieners. An "alien" pops up and says, "It is and they do."

* Former Oklahoma City and University of Texas basketball coach Abe Lemons said he didn't think coaching track was too hard: "Just tell 'em to keep to the left and get back as fast as you can."

* After a football game in Borger, Sutphen's Restaurant wasn't prepared to feed Plainview fans, just the team. Dee Martin, president of the Bulldog Booster Club, asked the manager, "Can't you just whip up some eggs for us?" Aw, y'all come on in.

* Plainview added a new sports program after losing to Stephenville, 9-6 in regionals in 1992. Future Baylor coach Art Briles' team attributed its strength at the line of scrimmage to a powerlifting program. The next year or so Plainview started powerlifting.

* When Plainview played Andrews in bi-district on a cold, snowy day in 1992, Damian Nails went over the 2,000-yard rushing mark for the season. I sent Tim Fox, a future Herald sports editor, to the field with my gloves to loan one of the officials. The guy lost them and sent me a replacement pair – not quite as nice as the originals.

* One night at Lubbock's Lowrey Field, lightning struck in a field across the highway from the stadium, causing a big fireball. That was just as the second half was about to get underway. One of the officials took off running for the field house, barely slowing to inform the referee of his intentions before racing up the steep ramp. Turns out he had almost been struck by lightning a year or so earlier in Odessa and was taking no chances. So, they finished the game one striped-shirt short.

* I calculated I have covered for the paper or broadcast in more than 100 venues through the years. I was dictating a story on the phone after the Queens won the regional tournament at North Texas State in 1978 and made up a score of another game until I could call and verify the real outcome. Another reporter overheard me and reported the bogus score. At that same tournament, Flying Queens Coach Dean Weese said

things didn't exactly get off to a rousing start. Denton is a long way from Missouri, North Carolina State and Ohio State – the other teams in the tournament – and everybody was on spring break. Dean said for the pre-game ceremonies, "There were about 15 people there and the national anthem record stuck."

* After Rod Ansley scored a PHS record 58 points in a basketball game against Hobbs as a sophomore in 1997, I spent a good portion of Saturday morning trying to verify that Rod had broken the previous mark of 50 as my friend Tom Baker said his brother-in-law Bill Howton had scored in the late1940s against Borger. The most I could ever find Bill scoring was 38. "Well, it seemed like 50, the basket was so big that night," said Bill. The previous record was 47 by Gil Wright in the early 1980s against Coronado.

* Willie Ansley, Rod's older brother and one of the most talented all-around three-sport athlete in PHS history, was the No. 1 draft choice of the Houston Astros in 1989 after leading the Bulldogs to the state quarterfinals. Willie hit a homer out of the Amarillo Sandies' park onto Bell Avenue. It bounced into the yard of some nearby apartments. Parks Supervisor Carl Holland, whose son, Petey, was on the team, measured the ball as stopping 596 feet from home plate. Several players from the Tascosa team, getting set to play the Dogs the next day and sitting on benches near third base, bowed as Willie rounded third.

* A Wayland assistant track coach wasn't very happy that his wife signed him up for a halftime contest that awarded a trip for two to Hawaii if someone hit three out of five free throws and then a half-court shot. Lo and behold, the reluctant coach did just that – and traded the trip to Hawaii for one to Florida where his family lived.

* In the early 1980s, women's basketball briefly had a 3-point shot if a player was intentionally fouled on a breakaway to the basket. I called such a foul in a tournament at the old Lubbock

Christian fieldhouse, a converted airplane hangar. I think there were only three fans in the cavernous gym and they gave me "what for," not being aware of the rule.

* A Plainview-Lubbock High game was a bit awkward for me years ago because I was doing the PA at Bulldog Stadium and the Westerners' middle linebacker seemed to be making all the tackles. His name was Danny Andrews.

* When Alesha Robertson-Ellis was in the eighth grade and already excelling in several sports, I told her, "One of these days, people are going to be saying, 'Didn't Alesha Robertson have some brothers who played at Plainview High?'" Stan and Matt Robertson were outstanding athletes but Alesha led the Lady Bulldogs to three straight state championships in 2001-2002-2003, was named all-state three times, All-American, and went on to star at Texas Tech. In her first year, she coached the Flying Queens to a spot in the national tournament and was named co-Coach of the Year in the Sooner Athletic Conference.

* Asked how she, at 5-7, did such a good job guarding the opponent's top player, usually several inches taller, and blocking out on rebounds, former Lady Bulldog Dana Reinart said, "I just use my God-given rearend."

* I broadcast a Wayland baseball game on the Internet without benefit of commercials. Communications guru Steve Long said almost with awe in his voice, "Did you know you talked for over 2 ½ hours tonight." All I could say was, "Thanks, but that's not a personal record."

* Wayland got clobbered 109-49 by Eastern New Mexico at Portales back in 1969. I was taking pictures and their mascot intentionally ran into me as hostile fans repeatedly yelled, "Sit down, bus driver!" at coach Bob Clindaniel. I would like to have banged that mascot over the head with my camera.

* It came as a considerable shock to Flying Queen Barbara McAninch when she picked up a bottle of what she thought

was water and squirted sticky "Tough-Skin" into her mouth at a game at the high school gym.

* One windy Fourth of July, Travis Hart and I took our kids to shoot fireworks near the Ollie Liner Center. I had this awful thought: "What if our firecrackers started a fire and burned the Ollie Liner Center down? The editor of the newspaper and the pastor of First Baptist Church would have to leave town."

* One Easter weekend, KVOP radio sponsored an Easter egg hunt at Regional Park. About a thousand candy eggs were strewn across an open space and youngsters lined up, then raced to gather as many as they could. A mother drove up with her two young sons and asked if this was where they were hunting for eggs. I told her the event had just ended. "My kids didn't get (a certain barnyard excrement)," she fumed. "Well, ma'am," I said, "that's not what they were hunting for."

* Wonder, in retrospect, if chasing the DDT-spraying machine on warm summer nights as a kid actually was good for my long-term health. Sure hasn't hurt my longterm memory.

Edwards Brothers Malloy
Thorofare, NJ USA
October 22, 2014